GEOFFREY HOSKING
GEORGE SCHÖPFLIN
editors

Myths and Nationhood

HURST & COMPANY, LONDON

*in assocation with the
School of Slavonic and East European Studies,
University of London*

Copyright © by C. Hurst & Co. (Publishers) Ltd., 1997
First published in the United Kingdom by
C. Hurst & Co. (Publishers) Ltd.,
38 King Street, London WC2E 8JZ
in association with the School of Slavonic and
East European Studies, University of London
All rights reserved.
Printed in England

ISBNs
1-85065-333-X (*cased*)
1-85065-334-8 (*paper*)

PREFACE

The stormy end of the twentieth century, both in Europe and elsewhere, has once again confirmed what the rest of the century demonstrated in ample measure: that the beliefs a people holds about its shared fate represent one of the fundamental driving forces of modern society. National myths are crucial to understanding the world we live in.

Yet strangely, although they are constantly being evoked, little concerted work has been done on the nature and functions of myths concerning nationhood. For that reason, during 1995–6 the History and Social Science Departments of the School of Slavonic and East European Studies jointly organized a seminar series to investigate the subject. The sessions were exceptionally well attended and the discussions they generated extremely stimulating and revealing. We soon found ourselves wandering far beyond Central and Eastern Europe, and accepted that as a positive advantage. We also found — contrary to what many of us had expected — that democratic 'civil' societies appeared to rely on myths just as much as authoritarian 'ethnic' ones.

In the mean time the School was moving towards the establishment of a Centre for the Study of Nationalism in Europe, and it was decided that its first venture should be the running of a two-day international conference on 'Myths and Nationhood'. This was held in October 1996, and the present volume makes available, in revised and updated form, the papers delivered then.

We are grateful to the Humanities Research Board of the British Academy for contributing financially towards the conference, and to the School of Slavonic and East European Studies for providing us with a forum and organizational back-up.

School of Slavonic and East GEOFFREY HOSKING
European Studies GEORGE SCHÖPFLIN
University of London
March 1997

CONTENTS

THE CONTRIBUTORS

BRUCE CAUTHEN, who is completing his doctorate at the London School of Economics, is a member of the Executive Committee of the Association for the Study of Ethnicity and Nationalism and an editor of *Nations and Nationalism*.

NORMAN DAVIES is Emeritus Professor of Polish History at the School of Slavonic and East European Studies, and his two studies of Polish history, *God's Playground* (2 vols, 1982) and *The Heart of Europe* (1984), have been internationally acclaimed. His most recent work, *Europe: A History*, was published in 1996.

MARY FULBROOK is Professor of German History at University College London. Her publications include *A Concise History of Germany* (1990), *The Divided Nation: Germany 1918–1990* (1991), *Anatomy of a Dictatorship: Inside the GDR, 1949–1989* (1995) and *The Two Germanies 1945–1990: Problems of Interpretation* (1992). She also edited *National Histories and European History* (1993) and *German History since 1800* (1997), and was joint editor, with David Cesarini, of *Citizenship, Nationality and Migration in Europe* (1996).

SUSAN-MARY GRANT is Lecturer in United States History at the University of Newcastle-upon-Tyne. Her doctorate, on the growth of nationalism in the north-eastern United States in the early to mid-19th century, will be published in 1998. She is currently writing books on the American Civil War and on the emancipation process between 1850 and 1880.

GEOFFREY HOSKING is Professor of Russian History and Deputy Director of the School of Slavonic and East European Studies. His research interests include nation-building and state-building in the Soviet Union. He is the author of *A History of the Soviet Union* (1992), *Beyond Socialist Realism* (1980) and *Russia: People and Empire, 1552–1917* (1997).

JOHN D. KLIER is Corob Professor of Modern Jewish History at University College London. His specialization is the history of the Jews in Eastern Europe, and he is the author of *Imperial Russia's Jewish Question, 1855–1881* (1995).

AGITA MISĀNE is a Research Associate at the Institute of Philosophy and Sociology of the Latvian Academy of Sciences, concerned with the phenomenology of religion, pre-Christian beliefs and traditional cultures in the north-east Baltic region. She has edited a collection of essays on sacrifice, *Upuris: Reliģiju zinātne. Filozoja. Kristīgā Prakse* (1995).

JOANNA OVERING, now a Professor at the School of Philosophical and Anthropological Studies at the University of St Andrews, was previously at the London School of Economics in the Department of Social Anthropology. Her research interests focus on the philosophy of power, equality and materiality expressed by the Piaroa, an indigenous people of the Venezuelan Amazon Territory.

AIJA PRIEDĪTE is a Research Associate at the Institute of Philosophy and Sociology of the Latvian Academy of Sciences, concerned with the history of ideas in Latvia, particularly the development of the identity discourse in Latvia in the late 19th and early 20th centuries. She has published many articles on the history of ideas, and since 1991 has lectured at the University of Riga.

SONJA PUNTSCHER RIEKMANN is a Senior Research Fellow in the Research Unit for Socio-Economics of the Austrian Academy of Sciences, and teaches at the University of Vienna. A former member of parliament, she is often invited to lecture on Europe in political fora. She is a board member of the European Foundation for the Improvement of Working and Living Conditions (Dublin), and has published widely on questions of European unification and international integration.

GEORGE SCHÖPFLIN lectures in politics at the School of Slavonic and East European Studies, and is a regular guest lecturer in Britain and abroad. He is the author of numerous articles on the politics of Central and Eastern Europe and the nature of ethnicity, and of the book *Politics in Eastern Europe 1945–1992* (1993).

ANTHONY SMITH is Professor of Studies in Nationalism in the European Institute at the London School of Economics. His books include *The Ethnic Origins of Nations* (1986), *National Identity* (1991) and *Nations and Nationalism in a Global Era* (1995); he has co-edited, with John Hutchinson, *Nationalism* (1994) and *Ethnicity* (1996). He is a founder and former President of the Association for the Study of Ethnicity and Nationalism, and chief editor of its journal *Nations and Nationalism*.

KIERAN WILLIAMS is Lecturer in Politics at the School of Slavonic and East European Studies. His research interests include coalition formation and termination, constitutionalism, executive power and security issues in East-Central Europe, and he is the author of *The Prague Spring and its Aftermath: Czechoslovak Politics 1968–70* (1997).

ANDREW WILSON is Lecturer in Ukrainian Studies at the School of Slavonic and East European Studies, and was a Senior Research Fellow at Sidney Sussex College, Cambridge. The author of *Ukrainian Nationalism in the 1990s: A Minority Faith* (1996), he is currently working on the role of historical myths in reshaping national identities in the former Soviet Union.

THE ROLE OF MYTH: AN ANTHROPOLOGICAL PERSPECTIVE, OR: 'THE REALITY OF THE REALLY MADE-UP'

Joanna Overing

As an anthropologist whose area speciality is the Amazon, my role here is obviously not to reflect upon the 'myths of nationhood' as they pertain to Eastern Europe, but rather to speak about anthropological approaches to mythology and recent directions within this area of study. Many scholars, in embarking upon a study of the role of myth in the creation of the present-day 'nation-states' of Eastern Europe, will be crossing disciplinary boundaries into an area of concern that is typically anthropological. My wish is to indicate the strengths or weaknesses of certain anthropological treatments of the relation of myth to social process and practice. I wish also to highlight some of the more perplexing issues inherent in the topic of myth itself, and our study of it.

The first relevant question in the study of myth is: how do we know that something falls within the genre of 'myth'? How do we decide to categorize this, but not that, as 'myth? Why, for instance, should we decide to use the term 'myth' and not 'history' in describing a particular piece of discourse? Whether the context is Amazonia or Eastern Europe, the boundaries between myth and history are not clear, and one reason for this is that the category of myth is not easily defined. We can perhaps say that the use of the term 'myth' is more a judgemental than a definitional or propositional procedure: its attribution requires a judgement having to do with standards of knowledge or its organization. There are many anthropological approaches to the understanding of myth, and closely related to any one of them, whether functionalist, structuralist or Marxist, are specific judgements about knowledge that are peculiar to the history of Western thought.

Myth and the Greeks

As Vernant tells us,[1] we have inherited our concept of myth from the Greeks, for whom 'myth' came to be viewed as a category of fictitious discourse. Within Greek philosophy, as it developed between the

---

1. J.-P. Vernant, *Myth and Society in Ancient Greece*, Cambridge, MA, 1990, p. 203.

fourth and eighth centuries BC, myth (*muthos*) became understood as a form of speech opposed to the reasoned discourse of *logos*. As such, myth became defined as discourse opposed both to truth (myth is fiction) and to the rational (myth is absurd). The historian Thucydides acclaimed both clarity and the presentation of facts as the markers of good history, and at the same time disdainfully rejected the fabulous in *muthos*.[2] Plato, in *The Sophist*, disparages his Heraclitean predecessors, criticizing them for beguiling childish minds with the dramatic events of mythical tales. The 'old wives' tales' of *muthos*, with its emphasis upon the marvellous, belonged to the poetic genres, and not to truthful discourse (*alethinos logos*).[3] Aristotle, in *Metaphysics*, condemns the mythology of Hesiod, saying that 'It is not worthwhile to consider seriously the subtleties of mythologists. Let us turn rather to those who reason by means of demonstration.'[4]

Earlier in Greek history, when the poetic discourse of *muthos* was highly valued within both community life and learned society, the opposition between *muthos* and *logos* was not made. Through mythic narrative the speaker could captivate and charm an audience by speaking of the 'fantastical' adventures and misadventures of supernatural beings belonging to a different time and mode of living than ordinary people. While mythic narrative had its capacity to scandalize reason, it was also through the narration of the dramatic antics of the gods that fundamental truths of existence could be expressed.[5] According to Vernant,[6] one fundamental characteristic of myth is its capacity to give pleasure and to involve the emotional participation of an audience. Good myths have entertainment value, and the magic of their poetry delights the audience.[7] This affective, performative aspect of myth is important to its power. Its dramatic appeal works not only to capture and impress an audience, but also to convince them.

Vernant argues[8] that the later privileging of *logos* over *muthos* was directly associated with an increasing emphasis on the written text as against the tradition of oral poetry, and also with the political process of democratizing speech. Discourse became 'common'. No longer the

---

2.   See Thucydides, II, 22, 4. See also the discussion of this text by Vernant, *Myth and Society in Ancient Greece*, pp. 208–9.
3.   Aristotle, *Metaphysics*, III, 1000a, 11–20. See Vernant, *Myth and Society in Ancient Greece*, p. 209.
4.   See *ibid.*, pp. 210–11.
5.   *Ibid.*, pp. 203, 220.
6.   *Ibid.*, pp. 206–7, 220.
7.   See also Overing on the performative value of an Amazonian mythic narration: J. Overing, 'There Is No End of Evil: The Guilty Innocents and their Fallible God' (hereafter 'There Is No End of Evil') in D. Parkin (ed.), *The Anthropology of Evil*, London, 1985.
8.   Vernant, *Myth and Society in Ancient Greece*, pp. 207–8.

exclusive privilege of those who possessed the gift of eloquence, it belonged equally to all members of the community. Thus *logos*, as text, was brought into the public square. The logic used in debate became one where each man could fight on equal terms through discussion and counter-argument. The rules for discourse were no longer a matter of overcoming an opponent through a pleasure-giving, spell-binding performance. Rather, the purpose of *logos* was to establish the truth based on a logical, critical and detached intelligence alone. Everything earlier attributed to speech as the power to impress and convince was reduced to *muthos*, 'the stuff of the fabulous, the marvellous'.[9]

The battle of Greek intellectuals to destroy the respectability of *muthos* in order to privilege the logic of *logos* in both intellectual and public discussion is a local history. It is also apparently a political, and not merely an intellectual, history. Nevertheless, it is a tradition that we have inherited, and all modern studies of myth must be framed within the context of this local debate carried out in Greece from the eighth through to the fourth century BC.[10] The battle was never entirely straightforward. Plato, for instance, did not totally deny the potency of mythology, and at times used myths to elaborate his own philosophical theories (as he did with the myth of Prometheus in *Protagoras*, and the myth of Er in the tenth book of *The Republic*). For Plato, those who were looking for the 'real truth', '*the really real*', were merely naive.

It is unsettling that similar arguments over the potency of the participatory versus the disengaged, the absurd versus the logical, the affective versus the intellectual, the contextual versus the universal, are continuing today. One reason for this is that it becomes difficult to reconcile our own great thirst for *the really real* with the fact that most of our existence is expressed through '*the really made-up*'. As the anthropologist Taussig asks,[11] 'why is it that what seems most important in life is made up and is neither more nor less "social construction"?' He continues: 'would that it would, would that it could, come clean, this true real. I so badly want [...] that complicity with the nature of nature. But the more I want it, the more I realise it's not for me. Nor for you either.' Thus he decides to consider the social power of make-believe, or the reality of the really made-up through which we all cannot help but live our lives. Taussig thereby takes a stance with regard to a crucial debate within anthropology over how to interpret people's insistence that gods, demons and spirits do exist.

---

9. *Ibid.*, p. 208.
10. See Vernant's discussion in *ibid.*, p. 203.
11. M. Taussig, *Mimesis and Alterity*, London, 1993, pp. xv–xix .

Myth, Anthropology, and the Study of Phantom Realities

On the whole, anthropology has inherited a view of myth that fits well with the view of the rationalists of fifth century BC classical Greece. The mythic is a world of illusions. Myths are the sort of story that old poets used to tell and that old women still tell their children: they are fictitious stories about the past. Thus myth is one of those phantom realities of other cultures that anthropologists study. Myths pertain to the domain of the phantasmogorical; they are narratives that express the fantasy origins of a people. They contrast with history, which details truthfully the real events of a people's past.

The evidence that the predominant view in anthropology has been that myth is wrong-headed and pertaining to the world of illusions is rather straightforward. In 1873, in his *Introduction to the Science of Religion*, Müller wrote that myths are products of some sort of disease of the language, and evidence of a dark shadow which language throws upon thought. A more generally held view in anthropology, as Vernant notes,[12] is that myth gives evidence to a barbarity which lies at the heart of culture from which all our science and much of our religion proceed. Lévi-Strauss, who writes so masterfully and elegantly on the structure of myth in his *Introduction to a Science of Mythology*,[13] notes that 'we have to resign ourselves to the fact that the myths tell us nothing instructive about the order of the world, the nature of reality, or the origin and destiny of mankind'.[14] While the scientist tells us of reality, the content of myths belongs to the domain of illusions. For the structuralist Lévi-Strauss, the value of myths is that they exemplify in their richness the universal analogical mind at work. The myth is an exemplar of the work of *unconscious* logical processes. However, the mediation of the great contradictions of life that myths express, those of life and death, health and disease, the social and the non-social, is all an illusion. So too are the events they unfold. I shall come back to structuralist methodology.

The anthropological dilemma is that we study phantom realities, other peoples' creations and constructions of reality. We look at their culture, their ritual, their myths. All are understood by us as belonging to the world of the imaginary. Like narrative, and as narrative, they are fictive. We know that rain is H_2O, or water, and not the urinating of the supreme deity; but then rain fertilizes crops, and the deity is the source

---

12. Vernant, *Myth and Society in Ancient Greece*, p. 227.
13. Claude Lévi-Strauss, *An Introduction to the Science of Mythology*, 4 vols, New York, 1969–81. He perceives his massive work as a mere 'introduction' because he considers the science of myths still to be in its infancy.
14. Claude Lévi-Strauss, *An Introduction to the Science of Mythology. Vol. 4: The Naked Man*, New York, 1981, p. 639.

of all creation in the world...[15] The paradox of our work is that a large part of our chore is to translate for our readers the world as the 'native' understands it. Like good Collingwood historians, our chore is to get into other people's heads in order to perceive the universe as they understand it. At the same time, we are also Western academic specialists, and thus what we translate is understood by us, and I suppose by our readers, to be imaginary. Our view conflicts with the one we study. Another people's interpretation is that they are presenting to us their own true postulates of reality (rain really is the supreme deity urinating). Myths, for instance, express what is 'natural' to this world; through a process of 'naturalization', they make self-evident the basic presuppositions and values of a people.[16] As Malinowski observed, for the people using mythology, their myth is 'a reality lived'[17]. The methodological problem we face is how to reconcile these two contradictory concerns, that of translating as *they* understand, and that of translating as *we* understand.

Let me tell you a story of my own. A relevant question to ask any reader is how they understood that sentence about my story? What is a 'story'? Should I tell of a made-up, fictive happening? Will my narrative concern a real event?

I was sitting with a Piaroa shaman and his son along a tributary of the Orinoco in the Venezuelan Amazon Territory. I wanted the shaman to tell me more of the episodes from Piaroa mythology that he had begun a day or so before. 'Please tell me another myth', I said. 'What is a myth?', they asked. This was early in my fieldwork, and I was using my bad Spanish with the son, whose Spanish was only slightly better than my own. I replied that a myth is a 'story'. 'What is a "story"?', they demanded. A 'story' 'tells of someone's adventures', and I tried to speak of plot. 'It is like the story of Wahari, your creator god, when he created people from the sacred Lake of Origin', I explained. Frustrated, I explained further that 'a story is made up, created. It is *fiction* like the movies in the frontier town, where you go to see Tarzan and Kung Fu films.' This piece of information surprised them, for they thought the films were documentaries of actual events. 'We have no such tales', they said firmly. It was a week or two before I succeeded in unruffling feathers sufficiently to get another mythic event told to me.

For the Piaroa, this people of the Venezuelan rain forest, what we call 'myths' belong to a genre of what they call 'old talk', or 'before

15. This is a piece of logic from the Piaroa, a people with whom I conducted research in the Amazon Territory of Venezuela.
16. See Roland Barthes's witty critique of the myths of French advertising, *Mythologies*, London, 1973. His argument is that these myths make natural the petit-bourgeois values of French culture.
17. B. Malinowski, *Myth in Primitive Psychology*, New York, 1926, p. 18.

talk', in contrast to the 'new talk' of today. 'Old talk' is *true* talk, and the richer the language of the myth-teller, the more complex the metaphoricity, the *truer* it is, and the more powerful. The Piaroa have a notion of metaphor akin to our own, which entails the creating of a fiction by drawing together two separate domains. They consider the use of such metaphor in everyday punning and word-play to be 'false', 'not true', while the contrary is the case for the use of metaphor in mythic narrative. The telling of a myth is intended to display one's knowledge of cosmology, and of the cosmogonic events of creation-time history. In the telling of myths, a shaman displays his knowledge of ontological matters, and also his power in dealing with them.[18] This was a sharp lesson for this anthropologist; I had indeed offended![19]

On Anthropological Approaches to Myth

During the nineteenth century, the anthropological study of myth was framed by the powerful paradigm of evolutionism, which became increasingly the characteristic marker of all social theory of the period. Embedded in most nineteenth-century social thought was the naive positivist belief in the inevitable development of stages in progress through which people moved, from the darkness of superstition to the light of reason. Myth was defined as a savage mode of thought, a primitive reminder of a past the West had overcome. In the twentieth century, with a reappraisal of the excesses of evolutionary generalizing, myth was no longer denounced as an absurd and logical scandal. Instead, its mysteries and richness became a challenge for science to unravel.[20] In accord with the emerging stress within anthropology upon the 'psychic unity of the human mind', the intellectual capacity of the 'primitive' was no longer thought at fault. Indeed it became the anthropological programme to make this point very clear.

While the general stress within anthropology has been that 'natives' are rational, the puzzle nevertheless remains of how to interpret the strange statements they make, the beliefs they espouse. Are their

18. See J. Overing, '"Today I Shall Call Him 'Mummy'": Multiple Worlds and Classificatory Confusion' (hereafter 'Today I Shall Call Him "Mummy"') in *idem* (ed.), *Reason and Morality*, London and New York, 1985, and 'The Shaman as a Maker of Worlds: Nelson Goodman in the Amazon' in *MAN*, New Series, 25, 1990, pp. 601–19, on the Piaroa use of metaphor.

19. As anthropologists are increasingly working with literate peoples aware of Western values, they find they must tread carefully with their use of words. Wendy Doniger O'Flaherty, in the preface to her *Other Peoples' Myths*, New York, 1988, notes that the very use of the term 'myth' had offended in her earlier translation of Hindu myths (*Hindu Myths*, Harmondsworth, 1975).

20. See also the discussion of this transformation in Vernant, *Myth and Society in Ancient Greece*, p. 235.

propositions about the world wrong, though their capacity for reason sound? Or are these propositions rationally serving other social or psychological purposes that make their fit with the conditions for truth in the world irrelevant? The specific questions raised, and the solutions given concerning the rationality of mythic discourse, have been in large part determined by the particular approach of the investigator. In their treatment of myth, anthropologists have nevertheless continued to view mythology as fictive, as comprised of fabulous, untrue stories about unreal gods and culture heroes that erroneously explain a people's past to them. The rationalist distinction of fifth-century BC Greek philosophy between *logos* and *muthos* is still prevalent in considerations of myth. The tenacity of this view has had a profound effect on most anthropological treatments of myth. I shall mention a few examples.

A usual way of categorizing modern anthropological approaches of myth is to distinguish between functionalist, symbolist and structural modes of analysis. To a certain extent, their boundaries are blurred, and we find structuralists today labelling themselves as 'symbolists'. I shall distinguish instead two broad schools of thought: those, on the one hand, forthcoming from Durkheim, and, on the other, those attached to the structuralism of Lévi-Strauss. This distinction is not wholly satisfactory because of the influence of Durkheim upon the work of Lévi-Strauss. It nevertheless pays tribute to the two powerful thinkers most responsible for the two profound revolutions in the development of modern anthropology, that is, functionalism in its various colours, and formal structural analysis.

British anthropology has been profoundly affected by Durkheimian thinking about the role of myth in society. In this view, the stress is placed upon the value of myths to society. The function of myth is not to deliver 'metaphysical truth', because its content is irrational and untrue. Its efficacy is that it provides a necessary sticking plaster for the social structure. It serves as a symbolic statement about the social order, and as such it reinforces social cohesion and functional unity by presenting and justifying the traditional order. Mythic discourse reminds a community of its own identity through the public process of specifying and defining for that community its distinctive social norms. Whether or not people believe in the irrational content of myth is irrelevant, for the symbols of myth have metaphoric value and serve a crucial social function in maintaining the given social order. In his discussion of the role of myth, Malinowski emphasizes its pragmatic value in enforcing belief: 'Every belief engenders its mythology.'[21] The narratives of myth have the function of legitimating the social structure, and so myths come into play when the social or moral rule

21. B. Malinowski, *Magic, Science and Religion*, Garden City, NY, 1954, p. 84.

demands justification and sanctity. Malinowski stresses the social power of myth, and the potency of its use in matters of political concern that have to do with the legitimation of the inequities of privilege and status.[22]

The strength of the functionalist framing of myth is that it contextualizes myth within the daily social and political life of the community. Thus myth is seen as one aspect of a wider social arena. The functionalists also insist, however, that the meaning of myth is located only in the arena of pragmatic sociocultural interaction. Malinowski is very firm about the metaphysical paucity of myth. In his words, 'myth is not a savage speculation about origins of things born out of philosophic interest'.[23] In other words the 'savage's' interests are not philosophical, but psychological. Myth, in its role of legitimating the tradition of the group, fulfils the affective need of knowing the efficacy and correctness of the group's own way of doing things. In stressing the practical social use of myth, the functionalists have been able to ignore the problem of knowledge and belief, and the 'illogical', 'contradictory' material faithfully transcribed, but often hidden in their fieldnotes. Although the social use of myth is given full attention in British anthropology, the value of its contents tends to be denied or ignored.

The other solution to the problem of strange statements has been to place them within the category of metaphor, and thus view them as having symbolic, but no literal, value. Anthropologists tend to label statements as metaphorical when they are obscure, ambiguous, and perhaps outrageous to our ear: 'my brother is a parrot', for example, or 'when I die I shall become a cannibal god'. By resorting to metaphor, we can say that 'natives' do not really mean the crazy things they say: because they are as rational as we are, they must be speaking metaphorically. It is easier for us to accept the poet than to accept a person who claims to believe what is mad and irrational according to our own empirically based truth conditions and formal rules of logic. As I have argued elsewhere,[24] it is our own metaphysical prejudices which prevent us from learning enough about the worlds and cultures of others to disclose the sensibility of their mythic narratives. The discussion of the obfuscating and reductive role that the notion of metaphor has played in anthropological analyses of myth is relevant to both functionalist and structuralist approaches. The emphasis that Lévi-Strauss places upon the importance of metaphoric thought to mythic construction is absolutely crucial to his structural methodology.

22. *Ibid.*
23. *Ibid.*, p. 83.
24. Overing, 'Today I Shall Call Him "Mummy"'.

Lévi-Strauss took the lead after the Second World War in the theoretical reflection of problems of myth through the exploration and analysis of a vast body of American Indian mythology, which resulted in the four volumes of his *Introduction to a Science of Mythology*. His aim was to disclose myth's own specific features by treating the vast corpus of myths as an objective world that could be studied as itself. In developing his methodology, he drew upon structural linguistics, which stresses the greater importance of the rules governing language and its formal order over the particular utterances or speech of individuals. The allure of structural linguistics was that its methodology was acclaimed as the most 'scientific', the most akin to the natural sciences, of all the social sciences. Lévi-Strauss distinguished for myth, as the linguists did for language, its surface and underlying structures; and he also privileged the latter, as again did the linguists. For Lévi-Strauss, the myth's meaning dwells on its unconscious level, derived from analogical operations of the mind. The rich and strange metaphors of myth should be seen as forthcoming from a system of analogic classification and, as such, are illustrations of a universal and rational way of thinking, albeit an unconscious one, in which humans as intellectual beings always engage. The meaning of myth is not then to be found on the surface level of speech and performance, but in the system of relationships among the myth's elements that together form a synchronic system.

For Lévi-Strauss the surface level of myth, the level of narrative, provides in itself little of value, for it has no meaning. Meaning for him rests on the level of the unconscious. Metaphor is to be read as an unconscious, analogical process of classification. Thus a statement such as 'the tapir is a grandfather of my people' is not to be read as a literal statement, but analogically, as a statement of classification, to be compared to and integrated with other such statements. By arguing that the meaning of myth lies only on the unconscious level of its underlying structure, Lévi-Strauss was able to evade the issue of the fabulous in myth, and the problem of belief and knowledge. He scrupulously studied the contents of myth, only to deny their relevance. In contrast to the functionalist approach, the major problem in structural analysis is that myth becomes decontextualized from everyday life. The performative aspect of myth is neglected, as too are its aspects that pertain to the social, the political and the philosophical.

There is an increasing interest within anthropology in rectifying the deletions and excesses of high functionalism and structuralism. The trend is to stress, as Malinowski once did, the importance of understanding culture, including its myths, from the indigenous point of view. We wish to understand the context of the *use* of myths in everyday life, their performative value as entertainment, as pedagogy, cure and explanation. We are asking about the role of myths in the framing of much of daily practice, and the relation of the poetics of myth to indigenous understanding of the everyday. In other words, the emphasis is now on the conscious use of myths through which basic (conscious) postulates of reality are also expressed, and as such made constitutive of everyday practice. In agreement with Taussig, we are looking at *the reality of the really made-up*. It has become, for instance, steadily more obvious to Amazonian specialists that we can understand the everyday behaviour of Amazonian peoples only by also understanding how *they* understand and use the mythic.

Mythology as History, or: Is There Such a Thing as an Indigenous Metaphysics and History?

Marshall Sahlins, in discussing the 'heroic history' of Polynesians, argues for its specific historicity.[25] He notes that it is specific in part because it is formulated through a cosmology that is peculiar to Polynesian culture. It is through Polynesian mythology that an outsider can gain access to this cosmology, for myth is the genre through which the indigenous cosmology is unfolded. It is through myth that postulates about the universe are expressed and explained. The mythic cycles deal with basic metaphysical questions about the history and development of the kinds of things or beings there are in the world, and also their modes of being and relationships. Polynesian historicity is made further specific by being attached to a social theory that is distinctive to the Polynesian way of life. Hence, Sahlins demonstrates that, for Polynesians, both mythology and social theory can be constitutive of a particular mode of historicity. A similar case can be made for the Piaroa of the Venezuelan Amazon Territory in their 'fallible gods history'. That their gods are fallible, rather than heroic, fits well with the more egalitarian ethos of Amazonia when compared with the notion of hierarchy which is part and parcel of Polynesian social theory.

Sahlins's discussion of Polynesian historicity is, in the most positive sense, a radical one, for he blurs the boundaries that we assume separate myth and history. He takes the relativist stance of Vernant, who argues that different types of cultural order have their own historical practice.[26] There are strong prejudices within anthropology that can make it difficult for us to recognize both the historicity of myth and the social theory and practice constitutive of it. For example, our assumption has been that myth is to be contrasted with history. History in our world-view tells of true events that take a linear and progressive course, whereas the events of mythology are but phantom

25.   M. Sahlins in *Islands of History*, London, 1985.
26.   See J-P. Vernant, *The Origins of Greek Thought*, Ithaca, NY, 1982.

realities which are assumed to have little relevance to any *real* world of action and experience. Thus our own notions of reality have tended to provide the yardstick by which to measure the contents of myth, and it is for this reason that so much of the general discussion about myth has revolved around issues that would otherwise be inexplicable. Mythic events have been counterpoised not only to history, but also to modern scientific findings about physical properties of the universe. The confusion arises from the contrasting of theories of existence that are, by and large, *social* theories of existence, and theories about the physical universe that are *asocial* in both scope and intent. It is not in the least surprising that the mythic event, when stripped of its social, moral and historical significance, is found to be lacking. But I dare say that it is not paucity that is the 'problem' with myth, but excess.

As discussed above, a prejudice against the narratives of myth is especially evident in the writings of Lévi-Strauss. Although he sees a continuity in the two endeavours of history and mythology, he should not be understood as also saying that the content of mythology should be taken seriously, either by us *or* by the indigenous peoples. In fact he professes no great confidence in Western historiography, and he stresses its inevitable creation of fictions.[27] However, if (Western) historiography comes out badly in Lévi-Strauss's scheme of things, he is even more unflattering about the possible merits of mythology. As already mentioned, he argues that myths can tell us nothing about the nature of reality. The dilemma might be rephrased to question just what it is, precisely, that we wish to include in the real world. For Lévi-Strauss, however, who is more certain about such matters, the real world is that which is disclosed through scientific endeavour. For him, the events unfolded in mythology are, with respect to this scientifically exposed real world, irrational and false, and thus comparable 'only to minor, lesser history: that of the dimmest chroniclers'.[28]

The history that Lévi-Strauss has judged as minimal knowledge, the Piaroa and the Polynesians would interpret as replete with knowledge. We return to the question of how we can handle such strong contradictions in judgements between the Western investigator and the indigenous peoples. To what extent and in what ways can we take the Piaroa seriously in their conclusions about the validity of their own knowledge system? Basically, Lévi-Strauss suggests that, with respect to mythology at least, we should not take the indigenous judgement at all seriously. His argument is based on the assumption that mythology has no relevance to that reality which is known and charted by the natural sciences and by our philosophers of science. Yet there is little reason why we should expect it to do so, since we could not but agree

27. C. Lévi-Strauss, *The Savage Mind*, Chicago, IL, 1966, pp. 242-3.
28. *Ibid.*

that in indigenous metaphysics many of the basic propositions about modes of being in the world are at variance with many of those that modern biologists and physicists would assume.

From the scientist's point of view, indigenous postulates about reality would be phantasmogorical. For instance, the Piaroa proposition that animals live as humans beneath the earth in their primordial homes would probably jar the scientific sensibility, as would the idea that their powerful shamans can walk in the 'before time' of the mythic past, or that monstrous spirit ogres dressed in *conquistador* armour were created in mythic time to guard today the resources of the jungle. These postulates about reality are not commensurable with the scientific theories of the real. Be that as it may, the implication of Lévi-Strauss's statements about the nature of reality is that it is singular: there is only one reality, and it is science alone that can unfold it. Because the world as presented through the mythic cycles is fantastic by the canons of that reality, indigenous peoples in their mythology have got it wrong. Since many of their reality postulates are unfolded through the exegesis of myth, the implication is, then, that one cannot properly speak of an indigenous metaphysics.

The Truth of Myths

There are two basic rules for mythic interpretation that I wish to stress, namely the recognition that (1) myths express and deal with a people's *reality postulates* about the world, and (2) mythic truths pertain more to a *moral universe of meaning* than to a 'natural' one (in the sense of the physical unitary world of scientists). For those educated within a Western tradition, myth is a strange place indeed to discover 'truth'. An Amazonian mythic universe appears as a nonsensical anti-world, the world as it today is not, where identity is fragile and ephemeral, causality perverse, time erased or distorted. Nevertheless, even the most absurd of happenings has a moral and ontological implication for what it means to be a human being alive today on this earth.

My favourite example of an absurd myth, which at the same time expresses a powerful moral message relevant to the accomplishment of a viable human existence, is a vignette from the Piaroa mythic cycle. It is about the day the people 'lost' their blue crystal anuses and genitals. This momentous event occurred when their creator god and his brother-in-law began to *quarrel* over the former's continuing incest with his sister, who was married to the brother-in-law. It was the quarrel that was the significant causal event, and not the incest *per se*. A few comments on the Piaroa mythic cycle are in order to aid a successful 'reading' of this particular narrative: poisonous relations between creator gods always serve as a marker of moral note; the creator gods often exchanged anuses and eyes in the creation of a being; and, finally, blue was specifically the sign of ignorance, or a demonstration of a 'lack of thoughts'. According to shamanic exegesis, the Piaroa loss of their colourful anatomical parts enabled them thereafter to order their own sexual actions through their thoughts, the master of which resides in the eye, rather than through their anus, the centre of the senses. This seemingly whimsical story of a 'ridiculous' happening is about the Piaroa acquisition of *social consciousness*. It is when they received knowledge of the poisonous implications of incest — the quarrel — that they acquired an ever-present consciousness of the social other. The shiny blue anus became transformed into the knowledgeable eye, which became the dwelling of a person's 'master of thoughts'. The image is one of defecation, a matter of the 'life of the senses', being replaced with social knowledge, a matter of the 'life of thoughts'. Because sexuality became a business of the intellect, carnal desire could be made moderate as it was mastered by thought. This is a myth that resonates deeply with Piaroa values of social living. They are a people who place extraordinary stress upon the importance of personal moderation in daily life, and for them the personal mastery of their life of desires is a prerequisite for the achievement of a successful social existence.

The Piaroa live within an evaluative universe, which contrasts with the unitary, objective universe of the Western scientist. All postulates about reality in an evaluative universe, including those about physical reality, are tied explicitly to a moral universe. For example, for the Piaroa personal malevolence is ultimately the cause of all deaths. It is normal among the tropical forest peoples of the Amazon for postulates about physical reality to be constitutive of other postulates which are social, moral and political in scope. This is in contrast to normal modern Western scientists who understand the facts with which they deal as autonomous from value. Scientists at work ostensibly ignore factors that are social, political and moral in sense, while the indigenous postulates cannot be so decontextualized. This is why a main concern in anthropology is the power of the actors' thinking as social and moral beings, and not as physicists.

The fact that indigenous postulates about reality are (consciously) not decontextualized from social, political and moral concerns, and thus from everyday practice, is not a trivial matter. A Piaroa theorist making a statement about physical reality is not making the same sort of statement as a Western scientist would make. For instance, a Piaroa shaman explained to me that a curiously eroded, steep-sided mountain not too distant from his home was a transformation of the Piaroa creator god's original tree of life, the fruit of which had been filled with the disease of paranoia. The metamorphosis from tree to mountain at the end of mythic time served to neutralize some of the dangers of paranoia by containing their force from the original tree of life within the mountain's solid mass. In contrast, the geologist, to explain the origin of this Guianese sandstone formation, would write of ancient desert conditions and the effect of wind storms. While the statements of explanation certainly vary, it cannot be determined that one is right and the other wrong (better or worse) according to the same *standards of judgement*. The two statements, that of the shaman and that of the physicist, are incommensurable in the sense that one cannot be reduced to the other and thereby judged by the same set of standards. This is Nelson Goodman's point when he contrasts what he argues to be the equally rigorous, but different, standards of judgement appropriate to the arts with those appropriate to scientific endeavour.[29]

To recognize the incommensurability of standards of judgement is not the same thing as saying that it is impossible for the scientist and the Piaroa specialist to understand each other. The geologist is interested in providing a natural explanation for physical phenomena, while the indigenous specialist of myth is not. Their *intent* is therefore different. The shaman's statements, which are contextualized within the framework of the practical business of healing and protecting, must also coincide with the processes of an evaluative cosmos and its history. When the shaman must cure a case of paranoia, the complex, historical origins of this disease in mythic time are of greater concern to him than the physicality of mountainness. Thus, in his telling of the mythic event, an important reason for the tree of life to be transformed into a mountain was because its malignant powers were driving too many of the inhabitants of mythic time crazy with the disease of paranoia. Natural origins were not the shaman's concern, while moral and social ones were. In Piaroa historicity the historical process always incorporates mythic events. Mythic time in Piaroa historicity is not time that is past (done and over with); it is in a sense omnipresent, having continual effect upon the present. Also, because the gods and other beings of mythic time have, eternally, the agency to act upon present-day time, the effect of mythic time upon the present is as unpredictable as the specific intentionalities of the particular mythical agents. Thus Piaroa historicity cannot assume a bedrock of lineal happenings.

A critique of the postulates about reality associated with this particular example of Amazonian historicity from the point of view of a Kantian universe, one obeying universal and natural law, would be, if not politically absurd, then certainly logically inappropriate. As MacIntyre has argued, the superiority of the Newtonian universe belongs to a specific history that is typified by a particular set of

---

29. See N. Goodman, *Ways of Worldmaking*, Brighton, 1978.

problem-solving interests.[30] These interests are largely not those of Amazonian peoples, who have a history separate from the Newtonian one. It is partly because the interests of the Newtonian physicist and the Amazonian specialist of mythology are different that their focus upon the content of their universes differ. In the former the universe is filled with matter, while in the latter it is comprised of agency, often personalized in intent and action. In the Piaroa case, the reality of humans as social, moral beings is constitutive of the shaman's postulates about reality. To judge him wrong on his statements about physical reality would be to strip such postulates of their social, moral and political value, but to do so would be nonsensical, since that is what they are saliently about. Thus we cannot judge the shamanic specialist of myths wrong in his postulates about the world without *at the same time* judging him wrong in his theories about the reality of humans as social, moral beings. Any such judgement would, then, be an evaluative, and not an objective, one.

The fact is that local metaphysical postulates about reality (for example, that sorcerers exist, as do gods; that time does not flow only in a linear fashion) should not be interpreted in the same light and in accordance with the same standards as those of physics. Since they are incommensurable, have distinct concerns, and belong to separate histories, they require different standards of judgement. We could at the same time happily argue that one set of postulates is just as true of reality as the other. However, the expertise associated with each set deals in the main with differing aspects of reality. The one, as Horton has cogently argued for 'tribal' Africa,[31] is focused upon the contextualized reality of the human world of interpersonal relationships, while the concern of the other is a physical reality totally decontextualized from the personal, as well as a good many other aspects of being human. Finally, as Weber noted long ago, any attempt to reduce the rationality of the unitary objective view to the evaluative — and vice versa — can only result in a mutuality of judgement, that of madness.

Myth and the Expression of Identity and Difference

In this last section I would like to comment on an aspect of mythic commentary of particular importance in this volume, and that is the

---

30. See A. MacIntyre, *After Virtue: A Study in Moral Theory*, London, 1985, pp. 267–9.

31. R. Horton, 'Material-Object Language and Theoretical Language: Towards a Strawsonian Sociology of Thought' in S.C. Brown (ed.), *Philosophical Disputes in the Social Sciences*, Brighton, 1979. See also Overing, 'There Is No End of Evil', and *idem*, 'O mito como história: um problema de tempo, realidade e outras questões' in *Mana*, 1, 1996, 1.

stress in myth upon modes of power. Since myth concerns the adventures and battles of heroes or gods constructing the universe in which we live, it inevitably deals with the mighty forces of creation and destruction which have allowed for our particular humanity, and those of our enemies, of whom we must beware. Often tales of great moral complexity, these mythic episodes that deal with the multiple faces of power endow a people with their images of selfhood by stating sets of identity criteria for a people and a community. The myth about the Piaroa acquisition of social consciousness given above is a good example of such a myth, for it states the socially dangerous side of sensual might, and discloses the socially superior nature of considered thought, the sign *par excellence* of Piaroa identity. Thus we find that myths of identity are equally myths of alterity, or significant otherness, for to state identity is also to speak of difference.

The images of identity and alterity that play such an important role in myth have obvious political as well as social implications. Myths are usually expressive of specific political visions that distinguish the relative worth of an array of modes of power. In these schemes the appropriateness or monstrosity of specific modes can usually be clearly spelled out. I have compared certain Western and Amazonian myths of alterity,[32] and the contrast is highly interesting. The Western examples are the European myths of the Amazonian peoples used during the conquest of the Americas, while the indigenous myths are those the Piaroa tell of their European other, the white man. Myths of alterity are not usually subtle, for they dwell upon the exaggerated excesses of the despised and threatening other. While both sets of myths make clear the monstrosity of their respective other, they are basically incommensurable systems of alterity.[33] Both portray the bestial, violent and cannibalistic Wild Man, along with his cohort, the sexually profligate Wild Woman. But there the similarity ends. The salient difference between the two is that the Eurocentric discourse, born within a hegemonic and totalizing rhetoric of hierarchy, was highly exclusive in its view of humanity. In contrast, the Amazonian discourse on alterity, more inclusive in its classification of humanity, can best be understood as proceeding from a rhetoric of equality.

In the Amazonian example, the boundary between self and other is not so clear-cut as in the European case. The critical distinction within the Piaroa scheme of alterity is between the might and force of a 'life of the senses' and the potency of their own valued 'life of thoughts'

32. J. Overing, 'Who is the Mightiest of Them All? Jaguar and Conquistador in Piaroa Images of Alterity and Identity' in A. James Arnold (ed.), *Monsters, Tricksters, and Sacred Cows: Animal Tales and American Identities*, Charlottesville, VA and London, 1996.

33. See also P. Mason, *Deconstructing America: Representations of the Other*, London, 1990.

which allows them to live a proper social existence. Although the Piaroa privilege their 'life of thoughts', they also recognize the fact that they too live a 'life of the senses'. Thus in their imagery of alterity no absolute boundary between self and other is drawn. While the root metaphor for alterity in Piaroa discourse is that of 'the cannibal other', such an image can hardly preclude, in any absolute manner, the Piaroa themselves. As eaters of animal flesh, they too are predators of the jungle. In the highly egalitarian Piaroa ontology of existence, predators are the prey of their own prey. Their myths of alterity become a means through which the ambiguity of the human condition can be understood. They do so by playing upon the complexity of what it means to be human and alive, providing a means for the examination of all aspects of being human in their most extreme and exaggerated expression. Each aspect is capable of a positive and destructive turn. The Piaroa stress is on the human predicament itself, and thus on the absurdities and evil, as well as the positive strengths, of human power.

In the European imagery, however, the emphasis was on inversion,[34] and on the right of Europeans as superior beings to subjugate the inferior other. In this vision, all evil and danger was assumed to come from without, and not from within. The Western discourse also stressed the impotence of the other, and thus it tended to inferiorize absolutely the indigenous other by making its excessiveness a mark of lack of power. Sexual and culinary excess is a key operator in both the Amazonian and the Western version,[35] and we can fruitfully ask why sexual and culinary perversity is such a good way of considering difference. While for the indigenous discourse sexual excess speaks of a superfluity of power, in the logic of conquest it becomes the sign of degeneracy, and thereby impotence. The Piaroa do not totally denigrate 'the power of might', for they find that the force of the white man's rifle is useful, especially in the hands of their Master of the Jungle in his protection of their own jungle space. In other words, they do not categorize the power of the other as absolutely inferior, no matter how distasteful its excessiveness might be for interior social matters. What is inappropriate for everyday life can be exceedingly useful for external political matters.

Myths pertaining to a people's understanding of power and its moral worth cannot be detached from that people's knowledge and creation of a history of power. By the seventeenth century, in Enlightenment versions of the history of power, it was understood that human beings had the right of sovereignty over the earth's resources. Power over

34. See R. Corbey and J. Leerssen (eds), *Alterity, Identity, Image: Selves and Others in Society and Scholarship*, Amsterdam and Atlanta, GA, 1991, for insightful discussions of the various symbolic possibilities of expressing otherness.
35. P. Mason, 'Continental Incontinence: Horror Vacui and the Colonial Supplement' in *ibid.*, pp. 152–90.

nature, over the inanimate and the wild, was established as a natural right of humankind. The majority of such histories told of the progress of humankind in its quest for primacy over nature. They began with primordial humankind living in a state of ignorant unity with nature, and concluded usually with humankind's rational domination of it. In myths of the right to domination, human beings alone were given the gift of reason. It became therefore their obligation to control nature, all those things of the wild.

In the Piaroa history of power, humankind did not win the right to take possession of the earth's resources. They did not obtain the power or right to dominate nature and the wild. In their view such a right would be much too dangerous, for it was the increase in the capacity to use the earth's resources during mythic time that led to the unbridled passions of avarice, vanity, arrogance and pride. In Piaroa ontology there is no 'nature', no inanimate or value-free universe which human beings can dominate. The notion of 'nature' belongs to the Western paradigm of power, and not to the Amazonian one. In Piaroa theory there is no 'natural' order of subjugation between themselves and any other agency in the universe. While the Piaroa cannot through domination appropriate for themselves the power of others, they also do not see themselves as dominated by any other agency in the universe. There can be no victors and vanquished in any absolute sense. The best that human beings can do is to achieve equal relations in their often dangerous dealings with beings of other spaces and times.

The power of mythic schemes of alterity should not be underestimated, for people and nations act in accordance with such myths. This is one reason that I find it unhelpful to speak of 'the mythic' as an illusory and irrational way of thinking. To categorize it as such does not reduce its strength in the ordering of people's actions, whether of the everyday or on a grander scale. It demeans the other, even when they are our own historical selves. It also reflects a deep naivety about the relation between action and the reality of 'the really made-up' of which such action is constitutive.

THE FUNCTIONS OF MYTH AND A TAXONOMY OF MYTHS

George Schöpflin

This analysis begins from the proposition that there are certain aspects of our world that cannot be encompassed by conventional rationality. Various processes, ideas, values, mechanisms and so on remain hidden from customary modes of scrutiny and yet have significant implications for the way in which individuals and collectivities live. As Mary Douglas puts it: 'A good part of the human predicament is always to be unaware of the mind's own generative powers and to be limited by concepts of the mind's own fashioning.'[1]

The difficulty is that, at some level, Enlightenment rationality presupposes that all actions can be understood by the cognitive instruments that its practitioners fashioned.[2] The problem, however, was and is that personal idiosyncrasy is imported into this process by selection. No one can have total knowledge, hence selection is inevitable, but the criteria of selection are immediately open to question. Myth, and the analysis of myth, is one of the ways of looking at the criteria of selection, at the covert part of thinking and the biases, slants and prejudices that are, as will be argued, a necessary part of the way in which collectivities define their universe.

Myth is one of the ways in which collectivities — in this context, more especially nations — establish and determine the foundations of their own being, their own systems of morality and values. In this sense, therefore, myth is a set of beliefs, usually put forth as a narrative, held by a community about itself. Centrally, myth is about perceptions rather than historically validated truths (in so far as these exist at all), about the ways in which communities regard certain propositions as normal and natural and others as perverse and alien. Myth creates an intellectual and cognitive monopoly in that it seeks to establish the sole way of ordering the world and defining world-views. For the community to exist as a community, this monopoly is vital, and the individual members of that community must broadly accept the myth. Note here that myth is not identical with falsehood or deception. Members of a community may be aware that the myth they accept is not strictly accurate, but, because myth is not history, this does not

---

1. Mary Douglas, *Implicit Meanings*, London, 1975, p. xiv.
2. Ernest Gellner, *Plough, Sword and Book: The Structure of Human History*, London, 1988.

matter. It is the content of the myth that is important, not its accuracy as a historical account.

Myth, therefore, is one of a number of crucial instruments in cultural reproduction.[3] It acts as a means of standardization and of storage of information.[4] It provides the means for the members of a community to recognize that, broadly, they share a mindset, they are in much the same thought-world. Through myth, boundaries are established within the community and also with respect to other communities. Those who do not share in the myth are by definition excluded. All communities recognize a boundary of this kind. Myth is, then, a key element in the creation of closures and in the constitution of collectivities. At the heart of this argument is the proposition that myth is vital in the establishment of coherence, in the making of thought-worlds that appear clear and logical, in the maintenance of discourses and generally in making cosmos out of chaos.[5]

It is important at this juncture to define the relationship between myth and ritual and myth and symbol. In simple terms, myth is the narrative, the set of ideas, whereas ritual is the acting out, the articulation of myth; symbols are the building blocks of myth and the acceptance or veneration of symbols is a significant aspect of ritual. A ritual generally observes the procedures with which a symbol is invested, which a symbol compels. Thus myths are encoded in rituals, liturgies and symbols, and reference to a symbol can be quite sufficient to recall the myth for members of the community without need to return to the ritual.

It follows that what is not symbolized is either very difficult to communicate or cannot be communicated at all, because it is not a part of the fund of knowledge of the community. The language of symbols, rituals, myths and so on is, consequently, a part of the web of communication shared by any community and is, incidentally, more significant than language itself. Members of a community of shared symbols can continue to recognize one another and maintain communication even after they have abandoned their language (in the philological sense). The relationship between grammatical language and symbolic language is a continuous one; each can sustain the other. In cases where a particular community shares its language with another, the symbolic differentiation can be vital in marking out the distinction. Thus the web of symbols carrying myth shapes and reshapes language, and it includes the techniques by which comprehension is sustained — the methods of standardization through

3.   Pierre Bourdieu, *The Field of Cultural Production*, Cambridge, 1993.
4.   Norbert Elias, *The Symbol Theory*, London, 1991.
5.   The reference is to Mircea Eliade, *The Myth of the Eternal Return: Cosmos and History*, London, 1991.

which the functions, processes and exchanges in the community are understood.[6]

Acceptance of and participation in ritual, one of the instruments of standardization, is vital, if not indeed obligatory, if the system is to be sustained, but belief in the ritual and the set of explanations attached to the ritual are less important.[7] Indeed, the belief may be vague, ill-defined and shadowy, understood in different ways by those who come into contact with it. In this sense, ritual is more a stylized statement of belief than a fully-fledged internalization of what the ritual supposedly expresses. But this does not imply that participation is purely formal. Ritual is important, even when the participants interpret the rites differently, because it is an emotional participation, an involvement at the non-conscious level, the terms of which condition the nature of beliefs and establish the parameters of the credible.[8]

Ritual is the means of establishing patterns of social dependence, of ensuring that the participants recognize one another and that they are in a mutual interdependence, so that sharing in the ritual is the moment of anchoring the institutions concerned; the specific rationalization of the ritual is entirely secondary.[9] So, what is crucial here is that ritual persists even while the nature of the belief (and thus of the actual content of myth) shifts, and ritual ensures that the myth persists too, though fairly clearly in a continuously altered form.

The outcome of participation in ritual and, therefore, of accepting that one's relationship to the community is structured by myth, is the strengthening of both the collectivity and the individual's role in it. The individual is linked by this action to all others who do likewise, and, centrally, precisely because ritual does not impose uniformity of belief, each participant can retain his or her individuality, personal orientations and values — within the parameters acceptable to the community. It is in this sense that ritual produces bonds of solidarity without demanding uniformity of belief. People can act together without consensus. Myth as the content of ritual, then, is an essential aspect of community maintenance. Thus consistency is created through communication and action, even while the participants have different beliefs and, indeed, conflicting beliefs.[10] In the political realm, this is significant because it creates potential means of allegiance on the basis of social identification. Social in this context clearly includes ethnicity and nationhood.

6. Elias, *The Symbol Theory*.
7. David I. Kertzer, *Ritual, Politics and Power*, New Haven, CT, 1988.
8. Ernest Gellner, *Anthropology and Politics: Revolutions in the Sacred Grove*, Oxford, 1995.
9. Kertzer, *Ritual, Politics and Power*.
10. *Ibid.*, p. 8.

Here again the notion of standardization is useful. Language in the broad sense, including both symbolic and grammatical codes, exposes a community to a particular experience, to particular ways of constructing the world. Those who control the standardization process derive power from doing so, so that the question of who is able to control the myths of the collectivity is an important one. Those who can invoke myth and establish resonance can mobilize people, exclude others, screen out certain memories, establish solidarity or, indeed, reinforce the hierarchy of status and values.

So far it has been tacitly assumed in this analysis that all communities share roughly the same level of density and intensity of myths. This is not necessarily the case. Evidently some communities will have evolved a much more complex, much richer set of myths than others. This allows the community in question to withstand much greater stress and turbulence (political, economic, social, and so on) than those with only a relatively poor set of myths. Thus it is difficult to integrate a rural population when the integrating community has no strong myths of urban experience. When two such communities are engaged in a contest, the weaker one may find that some of its members shift their allegiance, that is, assimilate.

(a) Myth can, therefore, be seen as having a variety of roles, functions and purposes. It is an instrument of self-definition, in that those who accept the beliefs encoded in myth also accept membership and the rules that go with membership, above all the particular world-view that the myth reflects. Myth attributes special qualities to the group, extends its distinctiveness and creates a boundary. It gives content, at the same time, to the self-apperception of the community.

(b) Equally, myth can be an instrument of identity transfer.[11] It enables a new identity to be superimposed on an older one, so that the collectivity sustains itself by creating an identity homogeneous enough to let it live with, say, major social upheaval. Modernization, the shift of the peasantry from the countryside to the towns, is an illustration of this. By the same token, through myth the assimilation of ethnically different groups is accelerated, as the myth-poor community accepts that upward social mobility demands the abandonment of its culture, language and myth-world in exchange for something superior, for a better world. Essentially, this was the aim of Communism in Central and Eastern Europe.

(c) Another aspect of myth relates to communication. As already argued, solidarity is established, through myth and ritual, without consensus, but this does little to resolve the basic ambiguity that is present in all exchanges and communications. This dilemma is all the more acute when the society in question is moving towards greater

11.   John Armstrong, *Nations before Nationalism*, Chapel Hill, NC, 1982, p. 130.

diversity of individuals and experiences, especially the influx of outsiders, with whom the original members lack secure modes of communication. Thought, emotions and grammatical language can never be congruent, hence myth is a means of transcending this gap by establishing an illusion of community.[12] Cognitive processes cannot grasp the entirety of reality, so that, in order to construct some kind of meaningful collective existence, aspects of experience have to be represented in a mythical and symbolic fashion. From this perspective, symbolic forms are not the imitations but the organs of reality — the agency by which anything real becomes an object for intellectual apprehension and thus made visible to the community. Thus myth is a kind of simplified representation, an ordering of the world in such as way as to make sense of it for collectivities and thus make it binding on them.[13]

(d) Yet again, myth is also a way of delimiting the cognitive field and thus simplifying complexity. The standardization of cognitions generates coherence and makes a collective response possible. There is a danger when the coherence so created is not congruent with reality, when the perceptions of a community are at variance with the logic of other processes, such as technological change. The loss of reality-congruent knowledge is likely to be highly damaging.

In these conditions, standardization can be imposed on the community to resist the external influence that is seen as dangerous — despite the gap, possibly a growing gap, between the empirical data and the way in which they are interpreted. Awareness of the gap triggers negative reactions because this amounts to an acknowledgement of the community's inability to influence events[14] and can result in a serious crisis of meanings, a loss of coherence, a cognitive anarchy when the community feels its own existence to be in danger. In these circumstances, until coherence is restored, perhaps by the redefinition of myths, the members of the community may well indulge in highly destructive behaviour and be at the mercy of political charlatanry. The Serbs of Bosnia are a case in point. Communities will go to great lengths to prevent these gaps from becoming exposed.

On the other hand, a negative outcome is not the only option; when using myth, a standardization is imposed in order to cope with the crisis of reality-incongruent knowledge. Myth can be employed as a device for weathering a crisis, for securing the cohesiveness of the community while measures are taken to effect the metamorphoses needed to deal with structural changes in question. It can be argued, for instance, that the strong emphasis on tradition in Britain during the

12. Ernst Cassirer, *Language and Myth*, New York, 1946, p. 5.
13. *Ibid.*, p. 9.
14. Elias, *The Symbol Theory*, p. 72.

1950s and 1960s was a way of dealing with the shock of winning a war and losing the peace. Eventually, the tradition-permeated discourses gave way to others more in tune with then current realities.

(e) In politics, the role of myth is central, though it is hardly ever articulated in this way; indeed, practitioners will actively resist any suggestion that in 'modern', 'rational' politics, myth and ritual have any role all.[15] In a broader analysis, it will be clear that myth is, in fact, a significant factor in conditioning the limits of the possible, in establishing the cognitive field and in underpinning the rule-boundedness which makes politics work. Through myth, as already argued, communication within the community is intensified, making it far simpler to transmit the messages from the ruler to the ruled and enhancing the solidarity, and thus the trust, between the two parties. The way in which Slobodan Milošević used the various myths of the Serbian past in the late 1980s to amass power was a classic illustration of a successful instance of this. In neighbouring Hungary, József Antall was able to mobilize only a part of Hungarian opinion by his reliance on myth (such as that of there being '15 million Hungarians'); he had obviously picked the wrong myth.

In socially and particularly in ethnically divided societies, the use of myths almost invariably enhances the division, unless there are myths that unite the groups across the divide. It is possible to conceptualize myths of citizenship that transcend ethnicity — the Swiss identity is an excellent example — but these are rare. It is far easier to use ethnicity as the identifier and to exclude ethnic aliens, or indeed use them as the negative 'other', the object against which mobilization is needed. The outcome of this state of affairs is that myths of collective existence within the ethnic group are emphasized and a harder boundary is drawn against outsiders.

This process is usually dynamic and to some extent imitative. If one group feels that it has to rely more and more heavily on myths of collective existence, its demonized other — its *Doppelgänger* — will generally do likewise. Thus once the Romanian state relaunched its commitment to the myth of Daco-Roman continuity in the 1970s,[16] a section of the Hungarian minority began to use a myth of Sumerian descent as a counter. A process of this kind tends to be dynamic, polarizing and, once launched, hard to break. On both sides of the divide, mythopoeia is the order of the day and symbolic politics then permeates political discourse. The consequence is that communication across the boundary becomes extremely difficult, given that mythicized

---

15. Simon Jenkins in *The Times, passim,* is an excellent example of intellectual resistance of this kind.
16. Katherine Verdery, *National Ideology under Socialism: Identity and Cultural Politics in Ceausescu's Romania,* Berkeley, CA, 1991.

language is devised for intra-community communication, not across boundaries. In trans-boundary communication, myths distort perspectives and confuse participants, because their role is to strengthen collective solidarity and not to clarify exchanges with another community.

(f) Myth is equally a way of offering explanations for the fate of a community, for accounting for failure, for the negative outcomes of particular strategies. It can be used to make sense of otherwise inexplicable phenomena — to be precise, phenomena which are inexplicable at the collective level. Myth can be used to solidify the group in adversity by attributing cause, an explanation that satisfies the community or, for that matter, individual members of the community, by offering an answer that can be probed no further. At the simplest level, this may be of the kind 'the flood was caused because the river god was angry' or, at a more sophisticated level, 'our misfortunes are caused by evil aliens beyond our control'. Argumentation of this kind is the first step towards the construction of conspiracy theories.

The difficulty with processes of this kind is similar to those already examined — at what point does the reference to myth, the deployment of myth, reach the stage where it is an instrument for the rejection of responsibility, for the refusal to admit error, for the unwillingness to acknowledge that a particular event or set of events is likely to cause a breach in the community's hard-won coherence? As long as political élites or leaders seek to address their constituencies, they will invariably refer to myth, but there are many situations where the society in question lacks the cognitive instruments to see the message that is hidden behind the myth and will accept the causation that it is being offered as proper explanation for its fate. The use of xenophobic narratives and scapegoating is an easy next step.

(g) This immediately raises the question of exactly who does control myth and which myths they appropriate. The evident answer is the political and intellectual élites in the community, those who are able to gain the ear of society, those who control the language of public communication — politicians, the monarch, the bureaucracy, perhaps the priesthood, writers and so on. Usually such communication is the work of a series of cross-cutting élites, rather than a single one. The impact of the electronic media should be noted in this context, because television not only reaches a very large number of people and thus penetrates into areas of society not easily reached otherwise, but also because the visual image is excellent at creating a sense of mythic reality and verisimilitude which are then very hard to check against other experiences.

For a myth to be effective in organizing and mobilizing opinion, it must, however, resonate. A myth that fails to elicit a response is either alien to the community, or inappropriate at the time when it is used, or, conceivably, evokes a response only in a small number of those addressed. This proposition is significant because of the popularity of analyses that stress the 'invented' and 'imagined' nature of national sentiment.[17] It seems that there are clear and unavoidable limits to invention and imagination and these are set by resonance. This is significant because it underpins the proposition that myth cannot be constructed purely out of false material; it has to have some relationship with the memory of the collectivity that has fashioned it. There has to be some factor, some event, some incident in the collective memory to which the myth makes an appeal; it is only at that point that the reinterpretation can vary radically from a closer, historical assessment. It is hard to see how the Czechs or Slovaks, say, could define their mythopoeias by inventing a strong seafaring tradition.

In this connection, myth plays a role in the maintenance of memory; the range of forgetting, which part of memory is made salient, how it is understood and how the resonance itself is to be controlled — these are all a part of regulation by myth. The exclusion of certain events from public consciousness, the consequent refusal to acknowledge that these events took place, making memory morally suspect, can all be derived from myth. The difference between mythic exclusion and Orwellian totalitarian thought-control is that myth is harder to engineer from above, it must go with the grain of the collectivity's memories and start from a position that seems 'normal' and 'natural'.[18]

(h) The cognitive delimiting created by myth can have a very negative result in blocking rational enquiry and the understanding of change. By using myth to elicit a largely emotional response, political leaders can seek to block reform or soften the impact of a change in circumstances, as discussed above. But there is a stage beyond this, where a political élite deploys myth in order to preserve its power by erecting barriers to comprehension, by stressing myth to ensure that its actions cannot be challenged because the means of making that challenge are not there. The very language of contest is made to seem unavailable as words acquire the very particular, constricted meanings with which myth invests them, and the range of understanding is greatly narrowed.

This process will frequently go together with the construction of mythic enemies who are attempting to destroy the collectivity in a

---

17. Eric Hobsbawm and Terence Ranger (eds), *The Invention of Tradition,* Cambridge, 1983, and Benedict Anderson, *Imagined Communities,* second edition, London, 1991.
18. On Orwellian dystopias, see Erika Gottlieb, *The Orwell Conundrum,* Ottawa, 1992.

demonic conspiracy. In a worst-case scenario, a mechanism of this kind can end up as a self-fulfilling prophecy. The danger against which the myth is used does not actually exist, but it is painted in order to deflect attention from something else. But, after repeated reference to the danger, those stigmatized as hostile begin to accept the demonic role assigned to them and behave in accordance with it. The relationship between Serbs and Croats and between Serbs and Muslims in the first half of the 1990s conforms fairly closely to this model. Of course, this pattern of abuse of myth cannot last for ever, reality will break through, but the way in which it breaks through and how it is then decoded will certainly be conditioned by the mythicized experience.

(i) Myth may be in the political realm and, particularly where nationhood is involved, is intimately bound to culture. Culture embodies a variety of myths — this is what makes cultural determinism so dubious a predictor — giving a collectivity a choice of which myth to resort to in different circumstances. Culture may be defined as a system of collectively held notions, beliefs, premises, ideas, dispositions and understandings, to which myth gives a structure. This system is not locked in people's heads, but is embodied in shared myths and symbols which are the main vehicles through which people communicate their world-view, value orientations and ethos to others.[19]

Politics is not, as a rule, studied as part of a cultural system. Often it is conceptualized as governed by strictly rational and transparent considerations of a purely utilitarian kind, in which costs and benefits are the classical model. Politics is examined as 'give and take', in which people follow their interests as consumers of benefits, rights, duties, privileges; that is, politics is about interest groups, economic forces and power relations. However, what the analysis of myth suggests is that politics is an aspect of the overall cultural system. Every political action is embedded in a wider cultural context. Cultural presuppositions and values may not be seen as narrowly political — influencing political action — and symbolic action is not perceived as a central means of interaction between political élites and public opinion, yet they do have this role. In this sense, myth creates a field in which interests are conveyed in a symbolic fashion or with considerable symbolic baggage.[20]

Mythic and symbolic discourses can thus be employed to assert legitimacy and strengthen authority. They mobilize emotions and enthusiasm. They are a primary means by which people make sense of the political process, which is understood in a symbolic form.

---

19. Ladislav Holy, *The Little Czech Nation and the Great Czech Nation: National Identity and the Post-communist Social Transformation*, Cambridge, 1996.
20. *Ibid.*

Attitudes are, therefore, shaped more by symbolic forms than by utilitarian calculation. The potency of symbols in the political process derives from the fact that they are vehicles for conceptualization.

At the same time, the shared cultural notions underlying and giving meaning to events are invoked in symbolic form, and likewise in specific discourses, as either explicit or implicit assumptions which underlie their logic or are their explicit subject. Discourse in this sense is socially constituted communication which leads to the production of texts and narratives which can embody and locate myth. Myth as time-honoured tradition and deep-rooted cultural notion is reproduced and thus perpetually re-created in the present. These discourses are the locus of a 'management of meanings' by which culture is generated and maintained, transmitted and received, applied, exhibited, remembered, scrutinized and experimented with. Each culture constructs its discourses in opposition to another and this allows the culture to see itself as enduring, as unique, as a bearer of moral worth.[21] The element of comparison is vital here. Collectivities will monitor themselves against others, so that ethnicity is neither exclusively internally generated nor solely defined by its external boundaries. It is a perpetual interaction between the two. Further, it is an ongoing process, a continuous re-creation in contemporary discourses, a work in progress without final form, though the participants will see it as stable and possibly static.

Myths: A Taxonomy

A great variety of myths can be identified. Indeed, there is no limit to myth, that is its great Protean strength. However, a number of fairly standard myths can be found, notably in Central and Eastern Europe, and what follows is an account of some of these. There is no attempt to be exhaustive and, it should be stressed, the categories are not exclusive. Several myths can overlap, feed on one another or contradict each other. Myths may need to be relatively coherent internally, but a culture with a repertoire of many myths can live comfortably with a considerable diversity of mythopoeias.

(a) *Myths of territory* are fairly common. These claim that there is a particular territory where the nation first discovered itself or assumed the form that it aspires to, or expressed itself in its finest form in and through that territory. Often, this was a land where its purity was safeguarded, where its virtues were best preserved before contact with aliens. Thus myths of territory can tie up with myths of a 'Golden Age', like the legendary Tir nan Og of Celtic mythology, a land of

---

21. Donald Horowitz, *Ethnic Groups in Conflict*, Berkeley, CA, 1985.

harmony and plenty. These myths are extended to the current political limits of the state. In essence, these myths are bound up with the sacralization of territory, a particularly powerful imperative whereby a community will defend its frontiers to the last and is incapable of seeing it as 'real estate', as a possible bargaining counter. This makes secession or cession one of the hardest of political actions because territory is sacred space, where the existence of the community is preserved from pollution and thus its means of cultural reproduction is kept safe from outsiders.

Everything that symbolizes that territory — flags, maps, anniversaries — serves to reinforce the myth and to exclude alternative rationalities, such as financial calculation. This has extensive implications for political action and behaviour. It suggests that states, when faced with what looks like a territorial claim, even when it is not argued in territorial terms, will readily reinterpret it that way, with the result that political negotiation becomes virtually impossible. The major reorderings of state frontiers in Europe are almost always associated with a major upheaval, such as defeat in war or the collapse of Communism, and new frontiers are either imposed from above (generating new myths) or affect territories that already have a separate existence, so that the loss can be integrated into a new myth structure. The separation of Norway from Sweden or Slovakia from the Czech Republic illustrates the latter proposition; the disintegration of Austria-Hungary is an example of the former.

(a) *Myths of redemption and suffering* claim that the nation, by reason of its particularly sorrowful history, is undergoing or has undergone a process of expiating its sins and will be redeemed or, indeed, may itself redeem the world. The prevalence of this myth, which is very common in Central and Eastern Europe, can be explained by the legacy of Christianity in conjunction with a sense of geographical, political and cultural marginalization with respect to Europe. Because most, if not all, of these cultures regarded themselves as on the edge of Europe,[22] a sense coupled with an experience of loss of power to external conquerors, these myths have had an explanatory function for survival and purposiveness. Indeed, in their form of being the 'last bastion of Europe' against the Barbarian hordes of the East, they are linked to *antemurale* myths,[23] that the nation in question bled to near extinction precisely so that Europe could flourish.

These myths, therefore, should be understood as myths of powerlessness and compensation for that powerlessness. They make a virtue of fatalism and passivity, claim a special moral superiority for having suffered — this is a key aspect of Christian doctrine in any case

22. Czeslaw Milosz, *The Witness of Poetry*, Cambridge, MA, 1983.
23. Armstrong, *Nations Before Nationalism.*

— and thereby demand recognition for certain claims in the present. These myths have implications for the way in which the individual's role is understood with respect to the community, in that it weakens individual responsibility by suggesting that history or malign forces have caused the suffering, that it was 'the will of God'. In effect, this myth is saying something significant about the way in which cause and effect are decoded and about how much control the individual or society has and may have over power.

There are countless examples of this type of myth. The Serbian myth of Kosovo essentially begins with the redemptive element, in that the defeat of Kosovo Polje is explained by the choice of heavenly glory over earthly power. Self-evidently, this is an *ex post facto* rationalization of the military defeat of the Serbian forces by the Ottoman armies in 1389 and the subsequent conquest of Serbia. In the Serbian case, the myth gains added strength by incorporating a directly divine moment in the narrative figure of the two falcons which are sent by God as a messenger to the Serbian leader. In the modern context, this myth has very powerful implications for Serbian–Albanian relations and, for that matter, for the way in which Serbs perceive their relations with the rest of the world. At the mythic level, the Albanians are reconfigured as Turks, the ancient enemy, who are polluting the sacred land of Serbian suffering. This myth clearly made it easier to give credence to the concept of a suffering Serbia in Yugoslavia, an idea that began to gain ground in the 1960s, and to legitimate the demand for Serbian separatism well before the collapse of the state.

The Romanian myth of the magical lamb, the *miorița*, is an analogue, as are its functions. Here the story is that of the magical lamb that warns its owner that his fellow shepherds are planning to kill him, but instead of taking action, the shepherd contemplates the beauties of nature and accepts the inevitable.[24] The moral is clear. There is nothing to be done, power will always be exercised without the individual having much control over it and it is morally superior to accept it. This proposition then legitimates inaction and passivity, acceptance of hierarchy, authoritarianism, the irrationality of power and distrust of others.

(c) Closely related to the above are *myths of unjust treatment*, in which history is a malign actor that has singled out the community for special, negative treatment, for disfavour. The group has suffered, but that is its fate. Here the motif of helplessness tends to be strong.

The use of the mythic narrative of the deportations of Latvians by the Soviet authorities after the Second World War is one illustration. In this case the function of the myth seems to be that the Latvians

---

24. Michael Shafir, *Political Culture, Intellectual Dissent and Intellectual Consent: The Case of Rumania*, Jerusalem, 1978.

underwent terrible suffering, that their Calvary could only make sense if in some way it could be seen as having a collective purpose — they were, after all, deported because they were Latvians — and that their suffering was, on the one hand, not in vain because eventually Latvia regained its independence, but, on the other, fruitless because the land that they regained was not the one that they had left in that it was now heavily populated by others, the very Russians who had caused their suffering.

Implicit in this myth, as well as in those of redemption, is that the world, in this instance Europe, owes those who have suffered a special debt, that the victims of the suffering are helpless because they suffered for the wider world and the wider world should recognize this, thereby legitimating the group's very special moral worth.

The growing use of 'holocaust' to describe any particularly terrible collective experience should also be seen in this context. This pattern appears to be on the increase in the United States, where it is becoming a way of legitimating one's collective ethnic claims to recognition in the cultural contest of American life. Used first, evidently, by Jews, the idea was then taken up by Blacks, significantly so in the term 'the Time on the Cross', and more recently an attempt was made to redefine the Irish famine as 'holocaust'. It is as if an ethnic community in the US can only claim fully-fledged legitimacy in the world of ethnic competition if it can argue that it has undergone some special redemptive experience that gives it the necessary moral worth in the eyes of society. It is noteworthy that this appropriation of the word 'holocaust' has led some Jewish commentators to drop it and to use the word 'Shoah' (desolation), in order, presumably, to make distinct the nature of the mass murder of Jews in Europe. It is an open question what will be the response to this bid, which has affinities with a myth of election.

(d) *Myths of election* and civilizing mission are, again, fairly common in the region. These state that the nation in question has been entrusted, by God or by History, to perform some special mission, some particular function, because it is endowed with unique virtues. The Christian origins of this are very evident. In the modern world, the religious motif has been transmuted into something secular, like the particular virtue of civility or literacy or capacity for modernity or simply being more 'European' than anyone else. This myth then legitimates an assumption of moral and cultural superiority to all competitors and rivals and requires them to recognize one's unique moral worth.

The Czechs claim this uniqueness in terms of democracy, that they are simply by virtue of being Czech capable of being democratic, indeed more democratic than all others. The Hungarians sustained their multinational state before 1918 by claiming that their civilizing mission over the non-Magyar minorities legitimated their policies of assimilation, and this is a motif that still surfaces occasionally in their dealings with Slovakia and Romania. The Poles claim to be European by a set of criteria abstracted from a mythic definition of Europe to which the Poles conform by virtue of their Polishness.[25] This, on the basis of the myth, entitles them to the special favour of Europe, whether by means of early integration into the European Union or NATO or simply being accepted as a European state like any Western state. Sometimes this myth can be closely linked to a myth of civic virtue, of being exempt from ethnic intolerance and discrimination against others. Traces of this can be found among the Czechs and, for that matter, among the French.

(e) *Myths of military valour* are tied to the foregoing, but have a few features all of their own. These myths give saliency to the special regard in which a collectivity holds itself because it has performed deeds of military valour. This valour can be attributed either to an aristocracy or to the people. In some instances, the myth is tied closely to the idea of insurrection or revolution: the group finds the truest expression of its essence by rising against intolerable tyranny. This is potentially a homogenizing myth, in which taking part in the collective diminishes the role of the individual but enhances the group because of the very particular demands and qualities of group violence. These myths can be used to legitimate force as an instrument of change, to characterize a particular regime as tyrannical and, therefore, to justify mass violence against it, to downgrade incremental change as useless ('cowardly') and to deride compromise and negotiation as something that the community despises ('dishonourable').

This myth is clearly present throughout the Balkans, but also in Hungarian and Polish mythopoeias; the post-war Lithuanian guerrilla war against the Soviet authorities should likewise find a place in this category. The myth obviously sustained and fuelled armed resistance by giving it the force of precedent, by screening out suggestions for negotiation and by emphasizing collective heroism. It is noteworthy that, since the collapse of Communism, these myths have tended to play a rather restricted role, as the post-Communist states continue with their experiment in democracy, which places violence beyond the boundaries of the legitimate.

(f) Linked to revolutions are *myths of rebirth and renewal*. These are ultimately related to the Christian themes of rebirth (palingenesis) and the Second Coming (Parousia), but are also present in ancient mythical motifs like the phoenix, which, though adopted by early Christianity, had classical and pre-classical antecedents. Here the idea is that the present is tainted and must be cleansed, and through that purgation a

---

25. Witold Wirpsza, *Pole, wer bist du?*, Lucerne, 1971.

better world can be created. The direction looks both forward and backwards, in that the past is unacceptable and, therefore, the group must distance itself from it, but at the same time there is hope for a better world if the renewal takes place. It is significant that both concepts are present. If a group has committed some particular act of violence towards another group, such as ethnic cleansing or its analogue, the purge of class enemies — and these portentous words have gained wide currency — then, by claiming that a renewal or rebirth has taken place, the perpetrators can argue that they have shed their sins. To be fully effective, though, the victims must in some symbolic way accept this and, ideally, be included in the cleansing ritual.

Equally, as far as the future is concerned, rebirth can create a sense of a clean slate, a new start, in which the awfulness of the past can be forgotten. At the end of the day, this is a way of legitimating change, of understanding far-reaching transformation, of creating mythic order in the chaos of a major political shift.

Examples of myths of renewal are widespread in contemporary Europe. Arguably, 1945 and the end of the Second World War have some of these functions, containing the proposition that, in the new post-war world, only democracy would rule — a demand of particular weight with respect to Germany and Italy. It was present explicitly during the Solidarity period in Poland, which was actually termed *odnowa*, renewal. The slogan of a New World Order propagated during the early 1990s should also be noted here, even if it had next to no resonance.

Last in this section, mention should be made here of the closely related *myths of foundation*. Every group, every political system, virtually every area of human endeavour has to make a start and seeks to mark that by some special act which is accorded mythic qualities. In this connection, one is dealing with a moment of novation which is not necessarily as drastic and radical as a revolution, but which, it is felt by the participants, deserves special note in order to point to the future. The implicit, sometimes explicit, message is that afterwards everything will be different ('better') and that the newly founded system has dispensed with whatever made the old reprehensible.

Some general elections have this function, such as the 1945 election in the United Kingdom. A new constitution obviously acts as a marker of this kind; both the German Basic Law and the fifth French constitution do this. It is, in fact, noteworthy that the French state is customarily referred to as the Fifth Republic, thereby symbolically delimiting it from its predecessors, but equally claiming the continuity of republican virtue that is at the heart of French politics, the legacy of the French Revolution. And all the first post-Communist general elections functioned in a similar way, to mark the end of Communism and create something new, different and superior — democracy.

(g) Every ethnic collectivity will have one or possibly more than one *myth of ethnogenesis and antiquity*. Myths of this kind fairly obviously answer the question of where we are from in our collective existence. However, these myths can become more than just self-legitimation when used to try to establish primacy over all other ethnic groups in a given territory. The argument is that, because one group was there first, it has a superior right to that territory over all others, meaning that, say, the rights of citizenship must take second place to those of ethnicity and that those who have primacy also have the right to define (and maybe circumscribe) the rights of citizenship. Reference has already been made to the Romanian–Hungarian mythic dispute over Transylvania, and the use of the Daco-Roman continuity myth and that of a Sumerian descent to counter this, respectively.

(h) *Myths of kinship and shared descent* are linked to the idea of the organic nature of the ethnic group, to the concept of the nation as family and thus to the exclusion of ethnic aliens. The myth implies that there is certain genetic transmission of the specificity of the group from which others are automatically excluded. In some circumstances, this is transmuted into racism and myths of racial superiority and inferiority. Among the functions of this myth is to impose a well-defined set of moral propositions on a group, usually a group speaking the same language, that is in the process of being welded into a nation. The model of the family, customarily the patriarchal family, is employed to make sense of the very different wider world of modernity for those who make the symbolic journey from country to town and discover that an entirely new set of cognitions is necessary in the new environment and that they may encounter ethnic aliens. The proposition that they and the fellow members of their language community share special characteristics because they are biologically related can provide the coherence that conditions demand.

However, it should be noted that myths of shared descent are not employed in anything like an equal fashion and that some groups, those which have launched a strategy of assimilation, cannot logically use them. Here the assimilands must accept the cultural codes of the group into which they are assimilating, but kinship will be loosely defined. Thus, in Europe, Austrians, Germans, Hungarians, French and others have been assimilating nations and, while they may have myths of kinship (in French colonies, for example, African children were taught that their ancestors were the Gauls), these cannot be insisted on with any vehemence. By contrast, where a group may feel itself at risk with respect to its future, possibly because it feels itself 'swamped' by aliens, it may emphasize or re-emphasize its ethnic purity by referring to racial or genetic uniqueness. The concept of 'purity of blood' (*limpieza de sangre*) in Spanish myths is a good illustration, in that it served to protect a self-image after the *reconquista*, that the Moors and Jews of reconquered Andalucia had disappeared, leaving only pure Spaniards. There are analogous, though less explicit, elements in both Romanian and Serbian patterns of exclusion.[26]

As will be seen from the taxonomy, myths may be closely interconnected; methodologically, they are sometimes difficult to delineate from one another and they may both overlap and be contradictory. But this last factor is immaterial. Precisely because the function of the myth — one of its functions — is to construct coherence, different myths receive emphasis at different times to cope with different challenges. Their underlying function is the same, though: to ensure that the integrity of the group is safeguarded, that cultural reproduction is not prejudiced, and that the collective world made simple by myth remains, so that individuals may construct their identities as individuals and simultaneously as members of a community.

26.   Milorad Pavić, *The Dictionary of the Khazars*, London, 1989.

THE 'GOLDEN AGE' AND NATIONAL RENEWAL

Anthony Smith

People often remark on the Janus-nature of the nation, at once visionary and nostalgic, backward-looking, yet oriented to the future. Some have seen this as the key to nationalism's success. But they view this duality in essentially instrumental terms: the return to the communal past is necessary if the masses are to be mobilized. For Kedourie,[1] the appeal to the past is part and parcel of the leaders' demagoguery, playing on the atavistic emotions of the masses. For Tom Nairn,[2] élites in the periphery, realizing their helplessness in the face of the onslaught of uneven capitalism, have to appeal to the sentiments and cultures of the masses. For Hobsbawm,[3] the élites must fabricate a sense of community for the newly enfranchized and mobilized masses, while for Benedict Anderson[4] they must create an imagined political community among people who will never see each other through the representations and narratives of the printed word.

In each case the élites are pictured as seeking to control the masses through a project of social engineering. This they do by creating a cultural artefact, the nation, in order to prevent social breakdown and channel social change and political mobilization. The concept of a nation, however, cannot be sustained without a suitable past and a believable future, and this requires a community's history and destiny to be formed out of whole cloth. In order to create a convincing representation of the 'nation', a worthy and distinctive past must be rediscovered and appropriated. Only then can the nation aspire to a glorious destiny for which its citizens may be expected to make some sacrifices.

1. Elie Kedourie, *Nationalism*, London, 1960, introduction.
2. Tom Nairn, *The Break-up of Modern Britain: Crisis and Neo-nationalism*, London, 1977, chapter 2.
3. Eric Hobsbawm and Terence Ranger (eds), *The Invention of Tradition*, Cambridge, 1983, chapter 7.
4. Benedict Anderson, *Imagined Communities: Reflections on the Origins and Spread of Nationalism*, London, 1983 (hereafter *Imagined Communities*), chapters 2–3.

A 'Usable Past'?

From the standpoint of 'modernists' and instrumentalists, the communal past forms a repository or quarry from which materials may be selected in the construction and invention of nations. The assumption here is that nations need *usable pasts*, their uses being largely determined by the needs and preoccupations of present-day élites. Curiously, this is an assumption shared by many nationalists in their drive to create nations.[5]

There are a number of dimensions of a usable past. The first is that history serves the interests of élites who use selected aspects of the past to manipulate mass emotions. To generate but also control mass mobilization, élites invent traditions and tailor national myths and symbols for mass consumption. A Saddam Hussein pictures himself as a latter-day Assyrian monarch, the former Shah holds court at Persepolis on the 2,500th anniversary of the Achaemenid kings, while Tilak invokes the cult of Kali to stir up the Bengali masses against partition.[6]

Second, the communal past can be treated as the legitimizer of unpalatable social change. When the nationalist regimes of new states need to force through unpopular measures and radical policies, it is often necessary to appeal to precedent and the traditions of 'our forefathers' in order to smooth their passage. Again, the example of Tilak and his use of the Bhagavad-Gita is a case in point: Krishna's advice to the hero, Arjuna, on the need for courage in battle was used to inspire collective resistance to the British.[7]

Third, the communal past can provide a series of *exempla virtutis* to inspire public emulation, indeed a public morality. This was the aim of the French *patriots* in the Revolution, when they appealed to the civic virtue and heroism of Brutus, Scipio and Cincinnatus; or the American patriots who saw Washington as a latter-day example of classical virtue.[8]

---

5.   Nkrumah, for example, annexed the ancient empire of Ghana some three hundred miles away for this purpose, and Ataturk proposed the Sun Language theory to explain the origins of the Turks. On this general issue, see Elisabeth Tonkin, Maryon McDonald and Malcolm Chapman (eds), *History and Ethnicity*, ASA Monographs 27, London, 1989, introduction.

6.   Hobsbawm and Ranger (eds), *The Invention of Tradition*, chapter 1; but see also Paul Brass, *Ethnicity and Nationalism*, London, 1991, chapters 1–2.

7.   See Mary Matossian, 'Ideologies of "Delayed Industrialisation": Some Tensions and Ambiguities' in J.H. Kautsky (ed.), *Political Change in Underdeveloped Countries*, New York, 1962; M. Adenwalla, 'Hindu Concepts and the *Gita* in Early Indian Thought' in R.A. Sakai (ed.), *Studies on Asia*, Lincoln, 1961.

8.   Robert Rosenblum, *Transformations in Late Eighteenth Century Art*, Princeton, NJ, 1967, chapter 2.

Fourth, where territory is contested, the communal past may be used to provide prior title for one or other ethnic community or nation. Here, different but parallel communal pasts are usually invoked, as has been the case with Tamils and Sinhalese, and with Israelis and Palestinians, each national community selecting different periods and aspects which undergird its claim.[9]

Finally, the communal past is malleable. It represents, in the instrumentalist view, a construct of present generations, to serve their needs and interests, with each generation tending to change 'its' past in line with its perspective, providing new selections of, and interpretations for, what it considers significant. Thus different generations have reinterpreted the Swiss foundation myth, the Oath of the Rütli (1291),[10] for their own ends; successive generations of Afrikaners have reinterpreted the message of the battle of Blood River (1838);[11] and a modern generation of Israelis have found in the siege of Masada (73 AD)[12] a new significance unknown to older generations.

The past may have many uses, but it also has drawbacks in the formation of nations. It is often an ethnic past, when what is required is a more unifying civic nationalism which will draw in other *ethnies* who have no connection with the communal past of the dominant *ethnie*. It is therefore likely to prove divisive. Moreover, the malleability of the past, while helpful for such ethnic incorporation, may engender successive revisions and contestations, which have an unsettling effect on 'national identity'. Alternatively, a particular official version of the communal past can become a fixation and evoke nostalgia for the 'good old days' at a time of rapid change; and it may be simply irrelevant to the needs of the present, a utopian diversion from the real tasks ahead.[13]

All this may well be true in particular cases, but none of these considerations go to the heart of the matter. The question we have to consider is why so many people so often turn back to the collective past and seek in it something that appears to be missing in the present and which they think will assist them in shaping the future. We have

9. See K.M. de Silva, *A History of Sri Lanka*, London, Berkeley and Los Angeles, 1981; Sylvia Haim (ed.), *Arab Nationalism, An Anthology*, Berkeley and Los Angeles, CA, 1962.

10. Georg Kreis, *Der Mythos von 1291: Zur Enstehung des schweizerischen Nationalfeiertags*, Basel, 1991.

11. Leonard Thompson, *The Political Mythology of Apartheid*, New Haven, CT and London, 1985.

12. Barry Schwarz, Y. Zerubavel and B.M. Barnett, 'The Recovery of Masada: A Study in Collective Memory' in *The Sociological Quarterly*, 27, 1986, 2, pp. 147–64.

13. See Yael Zerubavel, 'The Multivocality of National Myth: Memory and Counter-memories of Masada' (hereafter 'The Multivocality of National Myth') in *Israel Affairs*, 1, 1995, 3, pp. 110–28.

to ask why it is that cultural collectivities so often define themselves in terms of a distinctive past and seek in that past a guide to their destiny. And we need to understand why a heroic past proves so often to be a 'usable past' and vice versa, and why it helps to shape the future even as it is shaped by the present. This applies with special force to the concept of the nation. If we succeed in answering these questions, we may go a long way to explaining the enormous appeal and durability of nations and nationalism.

The hypothesis that I want to consider is that the collective appropriation of antiquity, and especially of shared memories of the 'Golden Age', contributes significantly to the formation of nations. The greater, the more glorious that antiquity appears, the easier it becomes to mobilize people around a common culture, to unify the various groups of which they are composed and to identify a shared national identity.

The Appropriation of 'Antiquity'

The concept of 'antiquity' in which the ideal of the 'Golden Age' is embedded and which forms the object of nationalist rediscovery and reappropriation, is multi-faceted and subject to continual reinterpretation.

Its primary referent for early modern European intellectuals was classical antiquity, the civilization of Greece seen at first mainly through the lens of philosophy and imperial Rome, and from the eighteenth century, more directly, from a study of Homer and Athenian art and literature. In this context, the battle of the ancients and moderns and, later, Winckelmann's essays on Greek art set the tone for later interpretations, not just of Greek civilization, but of the whole notion of a 'Golden Age' and its links with the possibility of, and need for, a 'classical revival'. The 'Golden Age' of Periclean Athens had, by the beginning of the nineteenth century, become the standard and model for subsequent ideals of the golden age in other periods and civilizations.[14]

With the burgeoning of Romanticism, a second, broader concept of antiquity emerged. Now it embraced not just classical Greece and Rome, but the whole ancient world: ancient Egypt and Mesopotamia, Persia and Anatolia. This new concept went hand in hand with the amazing archaeological discoveries of the nineteenth century in Assyria and Sumeria, Achaemenid Iran and Hittite Anatolia, and fed the

---

14. On the classical revival in general, see Hugh Honour, *Neo-Classicism*, Harmondsworth, 1968. For the acceptance and application to nineteenth-century French and English society of the classical Greek canon, see Athena Leoussi, 'The Social Significance of Visual Images of Greeks in English and French Art, 1833–80', unpublished PhD thesis, University of London, 1992.

Romantic quest for an idealized distant past of humanity and a growing interest in archaeological verisimilitude of the 'first civilizations'. It also reflected an increasing differentiation of antiquity as a separate epoch from more recent, medieval histories.[15]

By the early twentieth century, the net of 'antiquity' had been extended to all pre-medieval civilizations: Shang China, the Indus Valley civilization of Harappa and Mohenjo-daro, Minoan Crete and, later, Han China, the kingdom of Axum, even the Maya of Yucatan. Each of these civilizations could then be fitted into the familiar tripartite periodization of evolutionary social theory (ancient/medieval/modern) and thereby reflect the upward march of humanity towards the apex of civilization, the modern West.[16]

By the mid-twentieth century, the evolutionist account was seriously undermined, and with it the tripartite historical progression. This allowed a much wider and more flexible range of pre-modern civilizations to be included under the rubric of 'antiquity': the Incas and Aztecs, Oyo and Benin, Ghana and Songhai, the Caliphates, Muscovy, Sung China, the Shogunates of Japan, as well as Western feudal states. Once again, this selection reflected a Western bias, but this time with only two stages — 'before and after (European colonialism)'.[17]

Now, at each stage, the number and types of 'Golden Ages' increased, and with them the range and meanings of the concept. From being at the outset an epoch of moral virtue and literary and artistic creativity, as in Periclean Athens or Republican Rome, the idea of the 'Golden Age' was extended to cover every kind of collective achievement from religious zeal to military expansion and economic success. From an age of virtue it became a moment of 'glory'. At the same time, it retained its original ideas of purity, authenticity and normative distinctiveness. In Herderian fashion, it defined the 'true character' of a people, or even humanity, what it would and should be if only the people had been 'true to themselves' and had been left alone.[18]

Of course, the ideal of a 'Golden Age' is not a creation of the nationalists and the Romantics. It can be found among several peoples in the ancient world. The Sumerians of the late third millennium under the Third Dynasty of Ur harked back to an idealized Sumer of the pre-

15. Sabatino Moscati, *The Face of the Ancient Orient*, New York, 1962; Glyn Daniel, *The First Civilisations*, Harmondsworth, 1971.
16. On evolutionism and its models of the development of civilization, see Shmuel Eisenstadt (ed.), *Readings in Social Evolution and Development*, Oxford and London, 1970; for a critique, see Robert Nisbet, *Social Change and History*, Oxford, London and New York, 1969.
17. See *ibid*.
18. See Isaiah Berlin, *Vico and Herder*, London, 1976.

Akkadian Early Dynastic era.[19] The Egyptians of the Saite and Ptolemaic periods looked back to earlier periods and dynasties. Hesiod wrote of a golden age of the human race, while ancient Greeks of the classical era idealized the heroes of their Homeric epics,[20] and the Romans looked back to the moral virtues of a Cincinnatus and Scaevola,[21] or located a mythical golden age among the Hyperboreans at the northernmost rim of the world.[22]

We find a similar nostalgia for golden ages of heroism and chivalry among the Welsh and Anglo-Normans for the age of Arthur,[23] among later Frenchmen for the era of Charlemagne, among Arabs of the later Sultanates for the Age of the Companions or the Caliphates, and Persians of the Samanid and Seljuk eras for the age of the Sassanids and their legendary battles with the land of Tur'an.[24] Above all, there is the attempt to link present dynasties and peoples with illustrious ancient pedigrees stretching back to Aeneas or Noah.[25]

As modernization invaded different parts of the globe, the number and range of rediscovered golden ages multiplied. This was partly the result of the sheer spread of social change, which disrupted so much of traditional routines and mores, and partly the result of the scientific discoveries and reconstructions of past epochs through disciplines like history, archaeology, philology and anthropology. But perhaps the most important spur to the proliferation of 'Golden Ages' was the nationalist intellectuals' drive to rediscover the past of every ethnic community for which they wished to secure political recognition. For nationalists, 'antiquity' became almost synonymous with ethnic liberation and efflorescence. Even civic nationalists had to hold up to their countrymen and women a shining exemplar of communal life in the distant past, preferably in the same area, but certainly linked by cultural affinity if not direct ethnic descent. Soon, however, it was not enough to look back to ancient Sparta and Republican Rome, in the manner of the French *patriots* of the Revolution; the true golden age had to be located in the pasts of the ethnic community or nation and it had to be a heroic age which could dignify the nation-to-be.[26]

19. George Roux, *Ancient Iraq*, Harmondsworth, 1964, chapter 10.
20. B.G. Trigger, B.J. Kemp, D. O'Connor and A.B. Lloyd, *Ancient Egypt: A Social History*, Cambridge, 1983, part 3.
21. Pierre Grimal, *Hellenism and the Rise of Rome*, London, 1968, pp. 211–41.
22. Stuart Piggott, *The Druids*, London, 1985, chapter 4.
23. J. Alcock, *Arthur's Britain*, Harmondsworth, 1973.
24. Richard Frye, *The Heritage of Persia*, New York, 1966, chapter 6.
25. John Armstrong, *Nations before Nationalism*, Chapel Hill, NC, 1982, chapters 2–3; Susan Reynolds, 'Medieval *origines Gentium* and the Community of the Realm' in *History*, 68, 1983, pp. 375–90.
26. See Robert Herbert, *David, Voltaire, Brutus and the French Revolution*, London, 1972. This development can be traced in European painting and sculpture from the late eighteenth to the early twentieth centuries, as well as in some Latin

Types of 'Golden Age'

Typically, we find more than one type of 'Golden Age' being reappropriated by the nationalist intellectuals of particular communities. These ages may be economic, an era of flourishing cities and great wealth and fertility — the Indus-valley civilization of Harappa and Mohenjo-daro, the city-states of Sumer, the Minoan palace-cities of ancient Crete or the civilization of Teotihuacan in Mexico — a kind of Rousseauan dream of natural efflorescence before the corruptions introduced by modern civilization. Alternatively, they may be political, ages of rapid military expansion and imperial grandeur, such as we find under the late Assyrian monarchs from Tiglath-Piliser III to Asshurbanipal, or the Persian empire of the Achaemenids ruling from Susa and Persepolis, or the great age of Augustus and imperial Rome. More often still, the golden age is religious. It is an age of holiness and purity, manifest in the excavations and monuments associated with ancient texts and rites and temples, whether among the Maya of Yucatan, or the early Christian Irish monasteries, the age of Solomon and the Temple in Jerusalem, the Indian temples at Benares and other holy sites or the Armenian or Russian churches and monasteries of the early medieval era — each of them associated with sacred texts. Finally, there is the golden age of intellect and beauty, in which philosophical, literary and artistic creativity was particularly concentrated: the Periclean age in ancient Athens, the Arab Caliphates from Baghdad to Cordoba, post-Vedic India's city-states, the China of Confucius and the late Chou dynasty. Though these kinds of golden age frequently overlap with each other, they present a standard of heroism, glory and creativity which subsequent ages failed to match, but which can spur modern generations to emulation.

Both the range and interpretations of 'Golden Ages', as seen through the lens of modern nationalisms, are illustrated by examples from communities as far apart as Mexico, Ireland and India. In the Irish case, two such golden ages achieved widespread popular support in the nineteenth century. One was Christian and Catholic, and centred on the activities of St Patrick and the subsequent age of monastic

American art in the twentieth century. In the early stages, Greco-Roman models and themes predominated; later subjects and modes of portrayal drawn from medieval and pre-colonial histories and sources prevailed, as the spirit of historical verisimilitude and archaeological drama became widespread. See Rosenblum, *Transformations in Late Eighteenth Century Art*, chapter 1; *French Painting, 1775–1830: The Age of Revolution*, comp. Detroit Institute of Arts, Detroit, 1975; Dawn Ades (ed.), *Art in Latin America: The Modern Era, 1820–1980*, London, 1989 (hereafter *Art in Latin America*); A.D. Smith, 'Art and Nationalism in Europe' in J.C.H. Blom *et al.* (eds), *De onmacht van hetgrote: Cultuur in Europa*, Amsterdam, 1993, pp. 64–80.

Christianity, exemplified in the characteristic round towers and crosses of the Irish countryside, studied by the archaeologist George Petrie. This was an age that combined saintly conduct and holiness with scholastic learning, as Irish missionaries and monks travelled throughout the Western world to instruct and convert the heathen, and hold up a beacon of learning in the era of barbarian kingdoms.[27]

The other golden age was pagan, the earlier centuries of the High Kings of Tara and the heroes of the Ulster cycle of epics, an era of warrior bands and companies of bards, which had been rediscovered by O'Grady and Lady Gregory and popularized by Yeats. The heroes of this era — Cuchulain, Fin MacCool and Oisin — championed an aristocratic warrior order which appealed to intellectuals in search of strength and nobility in an era of oppression and rural strife in the aftermath of the Great Potato Famine. Both of these golden ages served to remind Irishmen and women of a great, if distant, past before their island fell under British domination, and thereby instilled a measure of pride at a time of renewed nationalist activity in the 1880s and 1890s.[28]

Mexico presented a different, but equally complex, cultural ground. There had been an early 'Aztecist' rediscovery by some Creole intellectuals, notably Clavijero, in the late eighteenth century, but it was not until the late nineteenth and early twentieth century that a more systematic rediscovery and appropriation of the pre-Colombian pasts of MesoAmerica began. Again, a number of possible 'Golden Ages' presented themselves. One was the wealth and scale of the central plateau city of Teotihuacan from the third to seventh centuries AD, with its huge temples and buildings, excavated and popularized by Manuel Gamio, who thereby demonstrated the vibrant life and strength of pre-Colombian 'Indian' civilization. From this point, a panorama of MesoAmerican civilizations was opened up, stretching from the Olmecs of the pre-Christian era to the Toltecs and Aztecs of the tenth to fifteenth centuries AD.[29]

27. See Jean Sheehy, *The Rediscovery of Ireland's Past*, London, 1980; Liam de Paor, 'The Christian Connection' in L. Smith (ed.), *The Making of Britain: The Dark Ages*, London, 1984.
28. Nora Chadwick, *The Celts*, Harmondsworth, 1970, pp. 100–9; F.S. Lyons, *Culture and Anarchy in Ireland, 1890–1930*, London, 1979, chapter 3; John Hutchinson, *The Dynamics of Cultural Nationalism: The Gaelic Revival and the Creation of the Irish Nation State*, London, 1987, chapters 2–4.
29. James Phelan, 'Neo-Aztecism in the Eighteenth Century and the Genesis of Mexican Nationalism' in Stanley Diamond (ed.), *Culture in History: Essays in Honour of Paul Radid*, New York, 1960, pp. 760–70; D.A. Brading, *The Origins of Mexican Nationalism*, Cambridge, 1985; Enrique Florescano, 'The Creation of the *Museo Nacional de Antropologia* of Mexico and its Scientific, Educational and Political Purposes' in Elisabeth Boone (ed.), *Collecting the Pre-Colombian Past*, Washington, DC, 1993.

Yet it was the Aztec city-state civilization of the central Mexican plateau, rather than the more distant Maya civilization of Yucatan, that was favoured by the Revolutionary governments after 1917. The reason was largely political. A new political order required a myth of the golden age that would help to weld an ethnically disparate nation together, by suggesting it was reviving its age of native independence and past political grandeur. Under President Obregon and his Minister of Education, Vasconcelos, the artistic movement of muralism was encouraged by public commissions to portray an idealized version of the glorious Aztec past and its tragic fate. The murals of Orozco, Diego Rivera and Siqueiros portrayed a heroic vision of the Aztec political golden age that underpinned the official cultural nationalism of the post-Revolutionary Mexican state with its use of Aztec symbolism and its ideal of racial mixing or *mestizaje* in mass civic education. But, despite the undoubted artistic flowering, the official cultural project and its muralist expression had only limited success. The modern Mexican state had inherited from the former Spanish provincial territory too many indigenous *ethnies* with their own languages and myths of origin for the Nahuatl Aztec-Spanish political mythology to take root outside the central plateau — quite apart from the modern distaste for aspects of the Aztec past.[30]

In modern Egypt, too, a similar duality of golden ages emerged in the late nineteenth century. With the rediscovery by Western archaeologists of the Pharaonic past, an Egyptian Pharaonic identity could be counterposed to the more traditional Arab-Islamic identity. By the turn of the century, there was an attempt to reform and liberalize the traditional Islamic identification under the auspices of Muhammad Abduh, which opened the way for a more secular liberal politics under Lufti al-Sayyid. At the same time, there was also an influential movement of retraditionalization through a return to a purer Islam (*salafiyya*), preached by Rashid Rida, which sought to re-link Egypt and the Egyptians to a wider Arab world.[31]

The problem of such Islamic Arabism, in the eyes of its critics, was that it tended to ignore the special needs of Egypt and the Egyptians. This was a theme stressed by Mustafa Kamil in his attacks on British hegemony, and later by Muhammad Heikal in his attempts to locate Egyptian identity in a special land with a millennial Pharaonic history. There was the additional problem of the Christian Copts who claimed

30. Jean Franco, *The Modern Culture of Latin America*, Harmondsworth, 1970; Ades (ed.), *Art in Latin America*, chapter 7; Natividad Gutierrez, 'The Culture of the Nation: The Ethnic Past and Official Nationalism in Twentieth-Century Mexico', unpublished PhD thesis, University of London, 1995 (hereafter 'The Culture of the Nation').

31. Nadav Safran, *Egypt in Search of Political Community: An Analysis of the Intellectual and Political Evolution of Egypt, 1804–1952*, Cambridge, MA, 1961.

to be the true Egyptians through lineal descent. Moreover, Islamic Arabism tended to assume a radical *discontinuity* not only between pre-Islamic and Islamic Egypt, but between the inhabitants of Egypt during each epoch. This seemed implausible in a population inhabiting a compact territory with its own very distinctive habitat and civilization. Pharaonism, *per contra*, represented a movement that stressed the clear links between modern Egypt and its ancient past, so visible to its present-day inhabitants through its extant monuments, and it therefore sought to explain the distinctive character and needs of Egypt and Egyptians by reference to its unique and formative early civilization. This in turn helped to elevate Egypt and its inhabitants in both psychological and political terms at a time of foreign occupation. Unlike the Islamic golden age of the Mamluks, the Pharaonic 'Golden Age' was decisively indigenous and political in character. It was an age of native imperial grandeur, and thus seemed more appropriate for an ideology of national liberation from an alien imperial power — until a new enemy, Zionism, reactivated the religious identity of Egypt and its Arab golden ages.[32]

A similar contrast between a more secular, political and a strongly religious identity and antiquity surfaced in Iran in the later twentieth century under the Pahlavis. The late Shah favoured a return to the golden age of the Persian Achaemenids with its imperial grandeur, as it fitted well with his own imperial dreams of an efficient, highly modernized and Westernized Iran. In this spirit, he convened in 1975 an imperial spectacle at the palace of Darius and Xerxes in Persepolis to mark the 2,500th anniversary of the Achaemenids, celebrating a pagan, pre-Islamic and secular era of imperial power and monumental art, brought to light by Western archaeology and scholarship. But the Shah's programme and his historical model failed to command any following among the ordinary people, let alone the bazaar merchants and clergy. They looked with more favour to the golden age of early Islam, and especially to the martyrdom of Hussein, the son of Ali, at Karbala in 680 AD and to his successors, the Imams. The Shiite version of Islam which became dominant in Iran since the Safavids in the sixteenth century, and which was further strengthened by Khomeini's return and the clergy's hegemony, has at present ousted the secularizing Achaemenid mythology and replaced it with a

---

32. James Jankowski, 'Nationalism in Twentieth-Century Egypt' in *Middle East Review*, 12, 1979, pp. 37–48; Simon Shamir (ed.), *Self-Views in Historical Perspective in Egypt and Israel*, Tel-Aviv, 1981, pp. 39–49; Israel Gershoni and James Jankowski, *Egypt, Islam and the Arabs: The Search for Nationhood, 1900–1930*, New York and Oxford, 1987, chapters 6–8.

revolutionary Islamic myth with its own sacred memories of an age of
religious fervour and martyrdom.[33]

Even greater possibilities were afforded to Russian nationalists by
the vicissitudes of Russian ethno-history. What they tended to share,
notably the Slavophiles, was an idealization of 'Old Russia' before the
Westernization introduced by the Petrine reforms. That 'Old Russia'
could stand for the early Romanov period in the seventeenth century, or
for the apogee of Muscovite glory under Tsars Ivan the Great and Ivan
the Terrible, or for the earlier resistance to the Tartar yoke and Teutonic
Knights from Alexander Nevsky to Ivan III, or even for Kievan Rus´
from the tenth to twelfth centuries. Alternatively, there were the golden
ages of pure religion, notably the monastic epoch of the fourteenth
century. In each case, 'holy Mother Russia' was opposed in power and
value to its enemies, from the Cumans and Tartars to the modern West
of capitalism and Nazism — even Stalin invoked the Church and
Russian national symbolism in the dark days of the Great Patriotic
War, and supported Eisenstein's epic films about Alexander Nevsky
and Ivan the Terrible.[34]

For Russian nationalists, pre-Petrine Muscovy especially held up a
model of purity, devotion and popular faith, for which they pined as
the antidote to the class conflict and individualism of the West. From
Dostoevsky and Mussorgsky's *Boris Godunov* and *Khovanshchina* to
the historical painters Vrubel´ and Vasnetsov and Stravinsky's *Rite of
Spring* — based on Roerich's archaeology of ancient Russian tribal
rites — a critique of Western values was mounted in the name of an
idealized Russian past which, by cutting itself off and standing apart
from the world, based state power on indigenous Christian faith, or
even subordinated power to the pagan religion of the people and hailed
backwardness as evidence of purity and superior faith.[35]

The same subordination of power to faith can be found among some
Indian nationalists, for whom the post-Vedic era of classical city-states
marked the apogee of Hindu Indian civilization even more than the later
Gupta empire, exactly because it saw the creation of so many Hindu
religious texts like the Upanishads and epics like the Mahabharata,

33. See Richard Cottam, *Nationalism in Iran*, Pittsburgh, PA, 1979, chapters 2–3, 6, 8;
     Nikki Keddie, *Roots of Revolution: An Interpretive History of Modern Iran*, New
     Haven, CT and London, 1981.
34. Baron Meyendorff and Norman Baynes, 'The Byzantine Inheritance in Russia'
     in Norman Baynes and H.St.L.B. Moss (eds), *Byzantium: An Introduction to East
     Roman Civilisation*, Oxford, London and New York, 1969; Michael Cherniavsky,
     'Russia' in Orest Ranum (ed.), *National Consciousness, History and Political
     Culture*, Baltimore, MD and London, 1975; Richard Pipes, *Russia under the Old
     Regime*, Harmondsworth, 1977, chapter 9.
35. Edward C. Thaden, *Conservative Nationalism in Nineteenth Century Russia*,
     Seattle, WA, 1964; Camilla Gray, *The Russian Experiment in Art, 1863–1922*,
     London, 1971, chapters 1–2.

along with the formation of new Indian religions like Buddhism and Jainism. This was the era that fired the imaginations of men like Pal, Banerjera and Aurobindo, a predominantly intellectual and religious golden age that could be counterposed both to Christianity and to the secular values of the West. The claim that 'India' had as great a civilization, and a philosophical and religious one at that, as any European 'nation', was an essential component of an increasingly Hindu Indian nationalism. The fact that this was essentially a North Indian golden age, and excluded Muslims and Sikhs and their golden ages, only served to strengthen the exclusive and hegemonic tendencies in Indian nationalism.[36]

If religious creativity was the criterion of Hindu Indian nationalist appropriation of the past, politics and statehood became the standard for Zionist ideals of Jewish history and destiny. From the early days of the Berlin and Galician *Haskalah*, the Davidic and Maccabean kingdoms became the guiding star of political Zionism. In terms of territorial extent, military prowess and political power, the United Monarchy and the Hasmonean kingdom suggested former eras of unifying sovereignty and secular splendour that were designed to console a politically powerless and scattered people — a choice that was soon reinforced by the growing conflict with the Palestinians and the surrounding Arab states, and by the terrible experience of the Holocaust. The spectacular discoveries of Solomonic constructions at Hatsor, Megiddo and Gezer, as well as Yadin's excavations at Masada and Nachal Hever, attested to the apparent desire of the Israelites at the time of Solomon to maintain a strong state, and of the Jews in the period from the Zealots to Bar-Kochba to strive again for their independence from Rome.[37]

It was only to be expected of a people whose religion had played so important a role in its formation and development that this exclusively secular political model would not go unchallenged. For religious Jews, including religious Zionists, other periods of Israelite and Jewish history, especially the Mosaic era and the age of the Second Temple and the Sanhedrin, the age of the rabbis which saw the creation of the Mishnah and Talmud, possessed far greater significance. In a sense, they adhered to the traditional conception of Jewry in the diaspora, except that they too located the golden age, not in Mesopotamia or Spain or Poland, but in ancient Palestine. But this choice also brought

---

36. B.T. McCulley, *English Education and the Origins of Indian Nationalism*, Gloucester, MA, 1966; Elie Kedourie (ed.), *Nationalism in Asia and Africa*, London, 1971, introduction; Mark Juergensmeyer, *The New Cold War? Religious Nationalism Confronts the Secular State*, Berkeley, CA, 1993, part 2.

37. Michael Meyer, *The Origins of the Modern Jew: Jewish Identity and European Culture in Germany, 1749–1824*, Detroit, MI, 1967; Yigael Yadin, *Masada*, London, 1966, and *idem, Bar-Kochba*, London, 1971; see Doron Mendels, *The Rise and Fall of Jewish Nationalism*, New York, 1992.

the deep tensions in Jewish ethno-history to the fore. These were not simply the opposition between the religious and the secular, of kings versus sages, so familiar in modern Israeli politics. The deeper tension that Zionism exposed was over the value to be placed on the Palestinian as opposed to the diaspora periods of Jewish history — a tension that the growing Israeli reappraisal of the Holocaust and the millennial history of Jewish persecution heightened, bringing in its wake a new appreciation of the high points of diaspora existence — economic, intellectual and religious.[38]

Similar combinations of themes — virtue, holiness, heroism, power, wealth and creativity — can be found among other peoples in all parts of the world. They have played an important role in cementing ethnic communities in the past and continue to do so in current debates about national identity, providing touchstones and inspiration even for more sceptical modern generations in moments of crisis and rapid change.

Functions of the 'Golden Age'

These examples suggest not only the range of models and historical periods selected for idealization, but also the ways in which politics and religion are frequently fused to generate powerful concepts of an ethnic past that can fire the imaginations of the members of a community.

These concepts serve a number of functions for both individuals and communities in a nationalist epoch. The first is to satisfy the quest for *authenticity*. For nationalists themselves, this has become a *leitmotif* of their struggle. They seek to 'realize themselves' in and through the nation-to-be, believing that the nation has always been there, concealed under the debris of the ages, waiting to be 'reborn' through the rediscovery of the 'authentic self'. The interesting thing is that many people, who are not part of the nationalist élite or movement, have engaged in their own quests for 'authentic identity' and have come to embrace the need for authenticity in their own lives and as part of a wider community that needs to be purified of external accretions.[39]

---

38. Dan Segre, *A Crisis of Identity: Israel and Zionism*, London, 1980; Yechiam Weitz, 'Political Dimensions of Holocaust Memory in Israel' in *Israel Affairs*, 1, 1995, 3, pp. 129–45.
39. The concept of authenticity is often closely linked to metaphors of rebirth and awakening, of the kind discussed by Raymond Pearson ('Fact, Fantasy, Fraud: Perceptions and Projections of National Revival' in *Ethnic Studies*, 10, 1993, 1–3, pp. 43–64). But it is also possible to strip the quest for authenticity of its evolutionary moorings, if the 'true self' following its own inner dictates is seen as having been always 'there' beneath any historical accretions, and hence sometimes clear and visible, at other times concealed and indistinct.

In this context, an 'authentic identity' can have two meanings. The first is that of origin: 'who we are' is determined by 'whence we came', a myth of origins and descent — from Philip of Macedon, Oguz Khan, Hengist and Horsa. The second is that of difference: 'who we are' is determined by our relations with the 'outsider', the other who is marked off from 'us' by not sharing in our distinctive character, our individuality. Memories of one or more golden ages play an important part here, for they hold up the values and heroes that we admire and revere — which others cannot and do not, because they have different values and heroes.

In this sense, the model of a golden age is used to establish and delineate the nature of the 'true self', the authentic being, of the collectivity. This is essential to an evolutionary perspective that sees nations as developing from small, original and pure beginnings in some distant time to a first pristine flowering in the golden age, followed by decline and ossification — until it experiences a second birth at the hands of the nationalists. The very distance of that pristine epoch lends to the community and its history an aura of mystery and an immemorial quality; conversely, the immemorial existence of the nation is a guarantee of its authentic nature, its original, unmixed and uncontaminated personality.[40]

The return in time is accompanied by a return in space, back to the 'homeland'. This is the second function of memories of the golden age: to locate and *re-root* the community in its own historic and fertile space. Like the community itself, the golden age (or ages) possesses a definite historical location and clear geographical dimensions in the land of the ancestors. The land is an arena or stage for the enactment of the heroic deeds and the contemplation of eternal verities which are among the main achievements of the heroes and sages of the golden age. It is also a landscape and soil that influences the character of that age, not only by giving birth to its heroes and sages, but also by forming and moulding the community of which they are members. Hence the need, in the eyes of nationalists, to re-root the community in its own terrain and liberate the land of the fathers and mothers, so that it may once again give birth to heroes and sages and create the conditions for a new collective efflorescence. Only by re-rooting itself in a free homeland can a people rediscover its 'true self', its ethno-

---

40. A.D. Smith, 'National Identity and Myths of Ethnic Descent' in *Research in Social Movements, Conflict and Change*, 7, 1984, pp. 95–130, and *idem*, 'Gastronomy or Geology? The Role of Nationalism in the Reconstruction of Nations' (hereafter 'Gastronomy or Geology?') in *Nations and Nationalism*, 1, 1995, 1, pp. 3–23; Pearson, 'Fact, Fantasy, Fraud'.

historical character, in habitual contact with its sacred places and poetic landscapes.[41]

Another important function of memories of the golden age is to establish a sense of *continuity* between the generations. The return to a golden age suggests that, despite the ravages of time and the vicissitudes of social change, we are descendants of the heroes and sages of that great age. This is achieved through the periodization of ethnohistory. The flux of ceaseless change is thereby rendered manageable through an intellectual framework which gives the people's history coherence and design, by relating earlier to later stages of their past. In this way, the nation is depicted as an outgrowth of earlier periods of the community's history, establishing itself as its lineal descendant through linkages of name, place, language and symbol, and in the stratification or layering of collective experiences, with lower 'layers' setting limits to higher ones, despite some breaks in experience. On this view, we can only grasp the 'meaning' of later periods of a particular community's history by studying the earlier, heroic periods. By establishing genealogical descent as well as cultural affinity with the heroic age(s), later generations realize their own genuine heroic individuality. Hence the task of nationalists is essentially one of political archaeology: to rediscover and reconstruct the life of each period of the community's history, to establish the linkages and layerings between each period, and hence to demonstrate the continuity of 'the nation', which is assumed to persist as a discrete, slowly changing identity of collective values, myths, symbols and memories, as, for example, many English people tacitly assume continuity through descent from their 'true ancestors', the Anglo-Saxons.[42]

A fourth function of memories of a golden age is to remind the members of a community of their past greatness and hence their inner worth. The quest for collective *dignity* has become a key element in national struggles everywhere, and the memory of a golden age affords a standard of comparison and evaluation in relation to both the past of the community and the histories of its neighbours. An appeal to the golden age elevates the inner, or 'true', essence of the community *vis-à-vis* both outsiders and the present degradations of the community. This is the point at which memories of the golden age are linked to

41. A.D. Smith, 'States and Homelands: the Social and Geopolitical Implications of National Territory' in *Millennium, Journal of International Studies*, 10, 1981, 3, pp. 187–202.
42. Hugh McDougall, *Racial Myth in English History: Trojans, Teutons and Anglo-Saxons*, Montreal and Hanover, NH, 1982; Lesley Johnson, 'Imagining Communities', paper for the conference 'Imagining Communities: Medieval and Modern', convened by the Centre for Medieval Studies, University of Leeds, 1992; Smith, 'Gastronomy or Geology?'.

myths of ethnic election: the chosen are worthy, their inner dignity contrasts sharply with their outward shame and humiliation.[43]

Memories of a golden age also proclaim an imminent status reversal: though at present 'we' are oppressed, shortly we shall be restored to our former glory. Thus contemporary Mongols, in their new-found freedom, can worship openly once again the figure of Genghis Khan in their aspiration to reclaim the power and glory that once was theirs, but has been lost for so many centuries to others. Memories of the golden age proclaim the hope of restoration of the community to its former high estate and true mission, thereby revealing the community's true worth and its ancient and noble pedigree. In their several ways, the discoveries at Great Zimbabwe, Teotihuacan, Masada and Vergina revealed to each community and to the world what nobility they once possessed and what they were capable of becoming if only they were free to follow their inner rhythms. Similarly, the compilation of Karelian ballads by Elias Lönnrot and his edition of the *Kalevala* restored to a small, neglected and politically submerged people a dignity and nobility that made the Finns, in their own eyes, the possessors of a history and an epic comparable to the Iliad, Ossian, the Nibelunglied and the Bible.[44]

Finally, the memories of a golden age mirror and point towards a glorious *destiny*, stemming from the true nature revealed in and by that golden past. In nationalist metaphor, its noble past prepares a community for its ordained destiny, and provides it with a hidden direction and goal beneath the obscuring present. In more concrete terms, each generation's understanding of the communal past and particularly of its golden age(s) helps to shape the future of that community. The selected elements of the heroic era in each generation's understanding will guide the community towards its goal and be recreated in its visionary future. So 'we shall be renewed as in the days of old', and 'be as we once were', in spirit.

In returning to the golden age of the Ramayana, Hindu Indian nationalists do not seek to resurrect it, but to recover the qualities of its heroes so as to recreate in modern terms the glory of the Indian past. Arab invocations of the Age of the Companions imply no return to the seventh century, rather the quest for inspiration and guidance from a pure and holy past for the creation of a united Arab nation. The ideal of St Joan which enthralled so many nineteenth-century French

---

43. See A.D. Smith, 'Chosen Peoples: Why Ethnic Groups Survive' in *Ethnic and Racial Studies*, 15, 1992, 3, pp. 436–56; Donald Akenson, *God's Peoples*, Ithaca, NY, 1992.

44. *Kalevala: The Land of Heroes*, introd. Michael Branch, trans. W.F. Kirby, London and New Hampshire, 1985, introduction; Lauri Honko, 'The *Kalevala* Process' in *Books from Finland*, 19, 1985, 1, pp. 16–23; E.R. Chamberlin, *Preserving the Past*, London, 1979.

nationalists did not entail a return to a golden age of royal faith of the fifteenth century, but a desire to liberate modern France from its corruptions, divisions and defeatism by ridding it of its external and internal enemies and providing inspiration and an emblem for a people that had lost its way. So the vision of the desired future transmutes the meaning of memories of the golden age in each generation, adapting them to present conditions (though within strict limits), and thereby enabling them to galvanize the community for collective action to achieve a better future. Equally, the memories of a golden age hold the key to unlocking the secrets of a community's destiny, providing a rough-and-ready compass for the journey, as well as a 'map' and a 'morality' for the road, one which will enable the members to return to their core ethnic values and realize their 'inner being'. In this way, they may be able to secure the only immortality which now has any meaning, the favourable judgement of their posterity.[45]

Nations Without a 'Golden Age'?

If the possession and recovery of one or more 'golden ages' contributes so much to the formation of nations, what of communities that appear to lack a glorious past, or indeed any past to speak of? Our hypothesis about the functions of the golden ages may hold for communities endowed with a rich and well-documented ethno-history, but it seems irrelevant to peoples with 'impoverished' or poorly documented ethno-histories, or for that matter to more recent immigrant states which are in the process of creating nations. We are back, it seems, with another version of Hegel's theory of 'historyless peoples'.

Let me start with the 'historically impoverished peoples'. Such 'impoverishment' is, of course, a relative matter and one that new historical, philological and archaeological discoveries can easily alter. I am thinking, for example, of the late eighteenth-century Romanian Uniate intellectuals' rediscovery of their 'Dacian' past[46] or the nineteenth-century rediscovery of Benin and Oyo,[47] as well as the Finnish case mentioned above. There are also, however, peoples whose ethno-histories have been submerged in those of more powerful or better-known neighbours. The Slovaks provide an example of a people whose intellectuals had actively to rediscover ancient heroes and a former Moravian kingdom in the ninth century, one that was separate

---

45. See Anderson, *Imagined Communities*, chapter 1; A.D. Smith, *The Ethnic Origins of Nations*, Oxford, 1986, chapter 8.
46. R.R. Florescu, 'The Uniate Church: Catalyst of Rumanian Nationalism', *Slavonic and East European Review*, 45, 1967, pp. 324–42.
47. John Peel, 'The Cultural Work of Yoruba Ethno-genesis' in Tonkin *et al.*, *History and Ethnicity*, pp. 198–215.

from the better-known Bohemian kingdom and heroes of the neighbouring Czechs.[48] Another example is afforded by the Ukrainians, whose distant illustrious past was incorporated in that of their Great Russian neighbours, who also claimed ethnic and cultural descent from Kievan Rus´ from the tenth to twelfth centuries.[49] In these cases, scholarship and nationalist fervour did succeed in supplying both peoples with an ethno-history of their own, including a golden age.

There are other cases, however, where records are more meagre and where history has been largely oral. Ghana provides an example of a state composed of several *ethnies*, including some with well-known ethno-histories like the Ashante, but which as a 'nation-to-be' could not boast a past that included most of the population. Its leaders, especially Nkrumah, had therefore to annex an ancient African history, that of the empire of Ghana, some 300 miles away, and regard it as its own, so as to confer on the population of the newly independent state a sense of dignity and enable its leaders to mobilize the people on the basis of a vision of former greatness.[50] Similarly, the ruins of Great Zimbabwe have been seen by some African nationalists as evidence of the former greatness of the indigenous people of the area, even though little is known about these mysterious ruins. Likewise, in Australia, sites like Ayers Rock have become increasingly national symbols of an 'Aborigine nation' that clearly did not exist prior to the coming of the Whites and probably not till well into this century.

So pressing, however, is the need for an ethnic 'golden age' in the construction of nations that states and populations that lack their own epochs of former glory may well annex the golden ages of other related communities or of lands with which they have historic connections. This has occurred among Blacks in the United States, who have looked to 'Ethiopia' as the great independent kingdom of Africa able to boast several ages of virtue and glory.[51] Alternatively, small communities have identified with the golden ages of a wider cultural-ancestral community, as occurred among some Turkic-speaking *ethnies* who

48.   See Roger Portal, *The Slavs: A Cultural Historical Survey of the Slavonic Peoples*, trans. Patrick Evans, London, 1969; David Paul, 'Slovak Nationalism and the Hungarian State, 1870–1910' in Paul Brass (ed.), *Ethnic Groups and the State*, London, 1985; Robert Pynsent, *Questions of Identity: Czech and Slovak Ideas of Nationality and Personality*, London, 1994.
49.   David Saunders, 'What Makes a Nation a Nation?: Ukrainians Since 1600' in *Ethnic Studies*, 10, 1993, 1, pp. 101–24.
50.   See Denis Austin, *Politics in Ghana, 1946–60*, London, 1964; Robert Rotberg, *The Rise of Nationalism in Central Africa*, Cambridge, MA, 1965; *idem*, 'African Nationalism: Concept or Confusion?' in *Journal of Modern African Studies*, 1967, 4, pp. 33–46; Chamberlin, *Preserving the Past*; Ali Mazrui, 'African Archives and Oral Tradition' in *The Courier*, February 1985, pp. 13–15.
51.   Theodore Draper, *The Rediscovery of Black Nationalism*, London, 1970.

identified with their forbears in Central Asia.[52] This may explain the attraction of 'Pan' nationalisms for those ethnic communities which lack their own well-documented and distinctive ethno-histories.[53] The heroic ages of large groups of peoples — Slavs, Turks, Arabs — can be appropriated, as were the empires of Ghana and Songhai by African nationalisms.

What of that other category of nations apparently without history, the new immigrant national state? In Australia and New Zealand, Canada, the West Indies, the United States and Argentina, the indigenous populations were either penned in or decimated or exterminated. Among those where some members survived the massacres and diseases brought by the Europeans, we are witnessing now the birth or revival of a pan-indigenous sentiment and network, together with claims to lands appropriated and cultures denigrated by the colonialists. Among Mohawks, Cree, American Indians, Aborigines and others, there are incipient movements for land rights and a return to the inspiration of a hidden and despised past, which may yet serve to unite and mobilize the often fragmented ethnic communities into a political nation.[54]

In fact, they may also be competing with the white colonists who may possess their own golden ages, be it those of the Pilgrim and later Founding Fathers of the White Americans, or the War of Independence fought by the Creoles of Argentina in 1810, the memories of the first settlements in Australia in 1788 and of the ANZAC expedition and sacrifice in 1916, or of the Battle of Quebec in 1759 and the 1867 Act of Confederation in British Canada (contested, of course, by the Quebecois with their own golden age). In these cases, the golden age is not only recent; as Benjamin West remarked of Wolfe's sacrifice on the Heights of Quebec, the classical *exemplum virtutis* was enacted in 'modern dress', and so was 'movable' and relative to the needs and preoccupations of the present generation. At the same time, even relatively recent immigrant national states appear to require some kind of memory of a golden age and heroic past if they are to weld together into a single cohesive nation so many immigrant part-*ethnies*. In fact, golden ages are not necessarily distant and venerable. They are constantly being created out of the crises and achievements of successive generations of a community, but once they are recognized

52. David Kushner, *The Rise of Turkish Nationalism*, London, 1976.
53. Hans Kohn, *Pan-Slavism*, second edition, New York, 1960; Immanuel Geiss, *The Pan-African Movement*, London, 1974; Jacob Landau, *Pan-Turkism in Turkey*, London, 1981.
54. F. Svensson, 'The Final Crisis of Tribalism: Comparative Ethnic Policy on the American and Russian Frontiers' in *Ethnic and Racial Studies*, 1, 1978, 1, pp. 100–23.

by later generations as heroic, they become an object of reverence and a standard for emulation.[55]

The attempt to use memories of a relatively recent golden age to create nationwide loyalties in immigrant national states is not without problems. For one thing, important groups of new immigrants may not accept these memories, or be indifferent or hostile to them — as is often the case with indigenous peoples in these states. They are, after all, the memories of the dominant *ethnie*. Thus Hispanics in the United States may reject the Founding, let alone the Pilgrim Fathers; Aborigines will be indifferent to ANZAC Day; and Indians in Trinidad will have their own memories of a golden past. In the more liberal democracies, this may prompt a move to celebrate ethnic diversity through policies of 'multiculturalism'. But this may in turn provoke a backlash from the radical Right of the dominant *ethnie*. Moreover, unless it is verifiably remarkable, a recent golden age rarely carries the resonance and potency of a well-documented and well-rehearsed antiquity. It may confer a measure of dignity but doubts about its authenticity are liable to creep in. This in turn may erode any sense of continuity and hence its usefulness as a guide to communal destiny.[56]

Authenticity, Inspiration and Reinterpretation

These considerations raise some more general issues about the uses of the ethnic past, and suggest that some pasts are more 'usable' than others — not in the crude rationalistic sense of manipulation of mass emotions by élites for their own ends, or of social engineering of myths, symbols and memories to create new traditions, but in helping

---

55. For West's remark, see *American Art, 1750–1800: Towards Independence,* comp. Victoria and Albert Museum, London, 1976, pp. 82–6. On the mingling of puritan millennialism and nationalism in the United States, see E.L. Tuveson, *Redeemer Nation: The Idea of America's Millennial Role,* Chicago, IL and London, 1968, and Conor Cruise O'Brien, *God Land: Reflections on Religion and Nationalism,* Cambridge, MA, 1988. For Australian nationalism and the ANZAC Day and monument, see Bruce Kapferer, *Legends of Peoples, Myths of States: Violence, Intolerance and Political Culture in Sri Lanka and Australia,* Washington, DC and London, 1988.

56. The problem with multiculturalism in this context is not just dominant ethnic resentment, but how to ensure cohesion and mobilization and even self-sacrifice among ethnically heterogeneous populations whose separate ethnic components are encouraged to celebrate their diverse origins and their distinct cultures and golden ages. For the Australian example, see Stephen Castles, Bill Cope, Mary Kalantzis and Michael Morissey, *Mistaken Identity: Multiculturalism and the Demise of Nationalism in Australia,* Sydney, 1988. For a brief discussion of the model of a 'plural' nation, see A.D. Smith, *Nations and Nationalism in a Global Era,* Cambridge, 1995 (hereafter *Nations and Nationalism*), chapter 4.

to form nations through such processes as *vernacular mobilization* and *cultural politicization.*[57]

Can we spell out in more detail the elements that go into the making of a past that can help to form nations? There are, I think, three elements that are essential for this purpose: authenticity, inspiration and the capacity for reinterpretation.

The phrase 'an authentic past' has several meanings. It can refer to the reappropriation of a communal possession, to the representativeness of shared cultural elements, to their indigenous and original qualities, and to their correspondence with 'objective' truth. An ethnic past can, and should be, authentic in all these ways if it is to serve the formation of nations. A 'usable past' and a model 'Golden Age' is not a form of invented tradition, nor is it made up of 'shreds and patches', nor again is it merely an imagined community. It refers to definite historical periods with their own dimensions and properties. At the same time, such a past is not any past, however well documented. It must be demonstrably 'our' past, or at least 'ours' by extension, and so capable of being connected and made relevant to the present of the people concerned. An ethnic past must also express the distinctive spirit of a period and community; and it must be created from within, not imported and imposed from without. Finally, the better documented and more securely dated and attested the golden age, the more it can bear the weight of emotion placed upon it, and withstand processes of demythologization.[58]

The second element in a nationally 'usable' ethnic past is its potential for inspiration. Again, there are several aspects. Not only must it be able to boast a 'Golden Age' for this purpose, one which is well attested; the heroic epoch must be able to kindle the imagination, not just of a few romantic intellectuals, but of large numbers of the population. It must have 'mythic' quality, that is, it must contain a widely believed tale or tales of a heroic or sacred past that can serve present needs and purposes, as the Homeric poems so clearly served the

57. See A.D. Smith, *National Identity*, Harmondsworth, 1991, chapter 3.
58. *Ibid.*, chapter 8; Smith, *Nations and Nationalism*, chapter 3. The term 'authenticity' is used in several ways. It can mean what the proposer chooses to regard as genuinely his, her or theirs; so, for example, 'authentic music' means 'my' music. Or it can mean that which inheres in the spirit of an age or community and expresses their spirit in pure form. Here 'authentic music' means 'representative of place or period' played on 'authentic instruments'. Authenticity can also refer to original as opposed to derivative, and indigenous as opposed to alien, cultural elements; in this sense 'authentic music' is the true expression of its creator and has no forerunners or models from which to borrow. Finally, it can mean that which is 'true' in the sense of valid; here music is 'authentic' if it is what its composer actually wrote, note for note, without any subsequent addition or embellishment. See Berlin, *Vico and Herder*, for Herder's understanding of 'authentic' culture and experience.

needs and purposes of an early aristocratic era in the Greek city-states, or as the heroic tales of Aeneas and Romulus served the needs of the senatorial oligarchy and imperial family in late republican and early imperial Rome.[59]

In the era of modern nations, the tales of a heroic past must have a much wider resonance. They must be applicable to all the citizens of the nation and must strike a chord in the hearts of the common people as well as the élites. To play its part in the formation of the nation, the golden age must be able to act as a model and guide to its destiny, demonstrating the capacity of the nation in the past to create a culture worthy of emulation, and highlighting the qualities — personal, political, intellectual and social — that can inspire national renewal and spur public emulation. This is undoubtedly what occurred at the onset of romantic neo-classicism in late eighteenth-century Europe and America, when the Greek and Roman past and its heroes were held up for public admiration and emulation in the French and American revolutions and thereafter in many lands. Soon the heroes and golden ages of peoples and cultures far removed from Europe were being extolled as guides and models in the creation of the new nations of Latin America, Asia and sub-Saharan Africa. In Africa, the quest for authentic pasts that could inspire the common people would evoke those qualities and dimensions that had in the past helped to create heroic cultures and great civilizations, as the researches of Edward Blyden and Cheikh Anta Diop sought to demonstrate.[60]

And third, the ethnic past and its golden ages must be capable of reinterpretation. These are, after all, periods of the community's history that have been selected and reassessed in the light of: a) present social and political needs — here the present shapes the past; b) the special qualities of that past, by tradition and common consent, and preferably also by modern scholarship — here the past shapes the future; c) its transmission in records and/or through oral memories.

Thus the golden age of Periclean Athens was disinterred by Greek intellectuals and professionals in the eighteenth century, and became influential among state élites after the Greeks won their independence. Clearly, the present needs and preoccupations of Greek élites led them to select and reinterpret this ancient epoch as a model for the future. But equally, the quite distinctive qualities of the past, according to older traditions as well as modern scholarship, helped to shape the future course of the Greek state — in mass education, in law, in

---

59. Henry Tudor, *Political Myth*, London, 1972; G.S. Kirk, *Myth: Its Meanings and Functions in Ancient and Other Cultures*, Cambridge, 1973; Sebastian Garman, 'Foundation Myths and Political Identity: Ancient Rome and Saxon England Compared', unpublished PhD thesis, University of London, 1992.
60. See Robert July, *The Origins of Modern African Thought*, London, 1968; H.S. Wilson (ed.), *The Origins of West African Nationalism*, London, 1969.

language, even in the economy, to the detriment perhaps of Greek modernization, yet to the advantage and power of Greek national pride and cohesion. At the same time, the hold of this seminal epoch on the modern Greek consciousness was increased by its transmission in records that are also sometimes masterpieces of art.[61]

Conversely, the return to the Davidic and Hasmonean kingdoms by modern Jews was partly shaped by the powerlessness of Jewish communities in the diaspora, a condition that was deepened by the experience of the Holocaust. But the choice of these models of ancient valour and power also helped to shape the destiny of an embattled modern Israel. The archaeological excavations at Megiddo, Hatzor, Nachal Hever and Masada simply reinforced the popular sense of authentic heroism and military exploits.[62]

The attempt by post-revolutionary regimes in Mexico to reassess the role of the pre-Colombian past and to establish the 'Aztec model' as canonical for *mexicanidad* is a further example of this two-way process. On the one hand, the needs of revolutionaries reacting to the Iberian positivism of the Diaz regime led to a revaluation of the heroic Aztec past. On the other hand, that past helped to shape the policies of post-revolutionary governments in mass education and culture in favour of the 'fusion of races'. Again, the Aztec past was partly chosen because, of all the pre-Colombian cultures, the Aztec was the best-known and attested, as well as being the most central. The fact that state cultural nationalism has so far failed to inspire the indigenous groups does not mean that for the *mestizo* majority, it has not served its purpose. [63]

These examples reveal that the selected golden age sets up the parameters which help to delineate present action and future goals. This is because it answers to the quests for authenticity, rootedness, continuity, dignity and destiny that I enumerated earlier. These quests determine which golden age is likely to be selected in any one generation. This is not just a question of competition for power between élites with different visions; rather, the relationship of these élites to 'the people' whom nationalism vests with power and authority, determines which of several golden ages will be chosen as a guide to national destiny. And where 'the people' are divided into rival *ethnies*, it is likely that the golden ages of the dominant community

61. A. Pepelassis, 'The Image of the Past and Economic Backwardness' *in Human Organisation*, 17, 1958, pp. 19–27; John Campbell and Philip Sherrard, *Modern Greece*, London, 1968; Paschalis Kitromilides, '"Imagined Communities" and the Origins of the National Question in the Balkans' in *European History Quarterly*, 19, 1989, 2, pp. 149–92.
62. Amos Elon, *The Israelis: Founders and Sons*, London, 1972; Zerubavel, 'The Multivocality of National Myth', pp. 110–28.
63. See D.A. Brading, *The Origins of Mexican Nationalism*, Cambridge, 1985; Ades (ed.), *Art in Latin America*; Gutierrez, 'The Culture of the Nation'.

will triumph. As the majority of the population emerge into the political arena, the type of golden age selected, or the type of reinterpretation accorded to it, will gradually change — often from dynastic to more communal golden ages. Hence the growing cult of St Joan in France, interpreted as a popular heroine of French religious nationalism, and the failure of the Achaemenid dynastic golden age sponsored by the Shah to strike a chord in the hearts of the Iranian masses. Lacking roots among 'the people', the age of Darius and Xerxes appeared to be inauthentic and remote, unable to inspire the people.[64]

Conclusion

The return to a golden age is an important, and probably an essential, component of nationalism. Its role is to re-establish roots and continuity, as well as authenticity and dignity, among a population that is being formed into a nation, and thereby to act as a guide and model for national destiny. An ethnic past is usable if it can be claimed as 'authentic' on several levels, if it can inspire the mass of the population and if it is relatively well attested. Equally important for a usable ethnic past is that it live in popular memory, that it can be recovered through artefacts, records and oral transmission, and that it can then be transmitted through a system of popular, public education as well as in the mass media.

Also important is the verifiability of the selected golden age. Nationalist fabrications may succeed for a moment, but their inevitable exposure is likely to divert energy and induce cyncism and apathy for the national cause. To inspire wonder and emulation, the golden age must be well attested and historically verifiable. Pure 'invention of tradition' is ineffective.

The memory of a golden age plays a vital part, then, in mobilizing, unifying and directing the energies of 'the people' to meet the challenges of nation-formation through a myth of national history and destiny. By serving as a model and guide to that destiny, ethnic antiquity, and especially the golden age, becomes a source of continual inspiration, establishing the authenticity and continuity of the community's culture and conferring dignity on nations-to-be and well-established nations alike.

64. See Marina Warner, *Joan of Arc*, Harmondsworth, 1983, chapter 13; Richard Cottam, *Nationalism in Iran*, Pittsburgh, PA, 1979, chapters 10–13.

THE MYTH OF EUROPEAN UNITY

Sonja Puntscher Riekmann

The main European myth today is the myth of Europe's unity. For many centuries it has been a dream rather than a myth, a dream of a few individuals, poets, philosophers and political thinkers whose vision was about a unified, and therefore peaceful, community. Needless to say that, dream reappeared every time Europe, or parts of it, underwent one of its numerous wars fought in the name of expansion or consolidation of territorial power, or in the name of religious supremacy and thus of cultural hegemony. Even the *cuius regio eius religio* compromise of 1555 did not bring peace to Europe because all religious controversies were, of course, deeply intermingled with political power games. Peace has only ever stemmed from political will and the attainment of an equilibrium of powers, never from unity. The 'Hundred Years' Peace' between 1814 and 1914 was the result of what was called the European Concert in which Britain, Russia, France and Austria were the major players, while Germany and Italy were still striving for national unity. The birth of the German nation generated a new and powerful European player and altered the whole power game on the continent. The Concert came to an end, and two disastrous wars followed. But the Second World War was a war different in character to many others which had taken place in Europe. It was the result of a totalitarian regime whose aim was to found an empire meant to last a thousand years: the Third Reich was the vision of a European empire under the rule of a self-styled superior race. Everything which could possibly undermine the stability of this empire had to be eradicated: the Jews, the Gypsies, the Communists, the disabled, homosexuals, and so on. To serve the cause of total stability — the key note of Nazi policy — the complete destabilization of the old order appeared to be a necessary evil.

On the ruins of this policy a new idea surfaced: the idea of a community of states giving up some of their sovereignty in specific economic fields. 'Pooling sovereignty'[1] has become a new term in international relations. But the founding fathers had more in mind than the supranational administration of coal and steel. Their aim was indeed a European community, if not the United States of Europe as

---

1. Robert O. Keohane and Stanley Hoffmann, 'Conclusions: Community Politics and Institutional Change' in William Wallace (ed.), *The Dynamics of European Integration*, London and New York, 1990, pp. 276–300.

envisaged by Winston Churchill in his famous speech in Zurich in 1947. But what were the real conditions for such a unity? If I dare to say none, it is because in the late 1940s concrete political interests were largely focused on the reconstruction of national economies ruined by the war, on the containment of the Soviet Union and Communism, and last but not least on the integration of an emasculated Germany in a new continental order. The new order was meant to make the economic reconstruction, and even the rearming, of Germany possible, while rendering a renaissance of its political hegemony impossible. But those who wanted more started to think about the bases on which to build European unity. This was an opportune moment for myth construction. By this, I do not mean to say that myths are the result of a voluntary act of a defined actor, although we could identify such actors. The claim is rather that, beyond the pragmatic project of constructing the ever closer union of six (and later more) nation-states on economic integration, the need for creating a founding myth was felt at least by some European intellectuals who began narrating the history of Europe as it had never been told before. The focus of this new narrative was no longer the perennial story of nation- and empire-building, of wars and domination, but one of a common destiny founded upon a common European culture. And this narrative, for the first time in European history, met a real political interest. It was Robert Schuman, one of the founding fathers of the European Community of Coal and Steel, who in 1963 emphatically wrote: 'Before becoming a military alliance or an economic entity, Europe has to be a cultural community in the highest sense of the word.'[2] The real story, though, up to this very day, is not one about Europe as a cultural entity, but as an economic one. This fact has important implications, as we shall see, for the narrative of European unity as a cultural entity.

This is the general framework in which the construction of Europe's unity as a myth is taking place. I will now analyse the details of this process by investigating first the special nature of myths that are supposed to lay the foundations of a political entity; second, the attempts to reconstruct European history as a common destiny; and third, the dialectical relationship between economic dynamics and myth construction in the Union.

1. The Rationality of Myth

A myth is a story told and retold by the members of a community about its inner and outer conflicts and conflict resolutions. It is a true

2.   Robert Schuman, *Pour l'Europe*, Paris, 1963, p. 35.

story in so far as it recalls events which have in one way or another shaped the community and its social order through the emergence and consolidation of beliefs and norms. At the same time, a myth transcends the truth of the events: a myth is not historiography. A myth is a particular form of rationalizing a conflict, but it is not a scientific one.

The myth of Oedipus, for example, tells the story of a young man being inescapably dragged into incest and patricide, while he thinks of avoiding his fate by flight. Doing so, he loses the only real chance he has: that is to discover the truth by asking those, whom he believes are his parents, whether what the oracle had told him is true. Oedipus' tragedy lies in becoming a perpetrator without knowledge, but at the same time avoiding the knowledge which is offered to him by a series of telling hints during the journey to Thebes. One lesson of the myth is that Oedipus could have known, if he had wanted to. The myth thus shows that silence is an irrational form of behaviour. Indeed, at the end of Sophocles' version of the myth, Oedipus challenges the system of common beliefs in affirming his individual guilt, saying: I, not the gods, have committed the crimes. The Greek myth of Oedipus is not just an early version of Freudian psychology as a modern science looking for the innermost instincts of human beings, but the story of an individual *and* a political conflict in that it questions the system of norms and disciplines of a given community.

Myths are stories about the quest for origins, writes Mircea Eliade. 'How have things begun?' seems to be one main question of all myths. Where is the last non-transcendable point at which everything started? Where can we let a genealogy begin? How and by whom have things been named? As we seldom know how and when and why things have begun, we have to invent a story about origins which makes sense to everybody. Through this we create a feeling of community. This is true of the sacred text of the Bible and probably of all religious texts. This is true of the grand narratives by which Homer explained the creation of the Greek world, and this is true of Virgil's *Aeneid*. Narrating the story of Aeneas, who flees from a blazing Troy, travels through the Mediterranean world, and lands in Italy where he founds the city of Rome, Virgil links the origin of the Roman Empire to the same historical event and place which was crucial for Greek history. Yet simultaneously, Virgil transcends the grandeur of the Greeks by choosing one of their enemies as the founding father of Rome. Thus the Trojan war becomes the non-transcendable point, the point of creation, at which the genealogy of the Roman Empire has to begin.

The quest of origin has also become an 'idée fixe'[3] of modern European intellectuals engaged in the narrative of a European myth. Suddenly it seems to be important to discuss the origin of the name of Europe. Is this continent really named after the princess Europa, who was abducted by Zeus and transformed into a bull, or is it named after the Semitic word *ereb*, meaning dusk or Occident? 'All confidence in the world begins with names, about which a story can be told', writes Hans Blumenberg in *Die Arbeit am Mythos*.[4] In *The Meaning of Europe*, Denis de Rougemont tells us his version of the story about the name of Europe: 'The Europe of the legend begins with a leap towards the West, the sea, and adventure. The myth of the abduction of a Tyrian princess by the high God of the Greeks [...] is a paraphrase of history; our Europe did indeed come from the near East.'[5] But de Rougemont also insists on the importance of the sequel to the myth of the abduction of Europa, the daughter of King Agenor, because this king:

ordered his five sons to set out in quest of their abducted sister, and each one sailed in a different direction. One of them founded Carthage, whilst others discovered the coasts of the continent from Spain to the Caucasus. Finally Cadmus, the most famous of them, went off first to Rhodes and then to Thrace and, in despair of finding his lost sister [...] went to the Delphic oracle and enquired 'Where is Europa?' 'You will not find her', replied Pythia. 'Your task is to follow a cow, driving her on before you without respite until she falls exhausted. On that spot, build a city.' Cadmus founded Thebes.[6]

And, in his *Vingt-huit siècles d'Europe*, de Rougemont takes up the Cadmus myth again, stating that, 'We shall only find Europe in making it, as the myth of Cadmus teaches us.'[7]

Now that the great European adventure leading to the conquest of almost the whole world has been completed — de Rougemont is writing his book in a period when the decolonization process is widely concluded — Europe has to 'return to itself' and to define a new project in order to regain a role in the international arena. For this aim Europe has to unite, but the unity has to be founded on the idea of a community which, in spite of the real history of divisions, is said to exist from time immemorial: 'A united Europe is [...] an ideal which has been accepted for thousands of years by the best spirits of Europe,

3. Mircea Eliade, *Die Sehnsucht nach dem Ursprung*, Frankfurt am Main, 1981, p. 67.
4. Hans Blumenberg, *Die Arbeit am Mythos*, Frankfurt am Main, 1996, p. 41.
5. Denis de Rougemont, *The Meaning of Europe*, New York, 1965, p. 17.
6. *Ibid.*, p. 18.
7. Denis de Rougemont, *Vingt-huit siècles d'Europe: La conscience européenne à travers les textes — d'Hésiode à nos jours*, Paris, 1961 (1990 edition), p. 8.

namely those who see very far. Already Homer described Zeus as "europos" — an adjective meaning "one who sees very far".[8] For the Greeks, however, Europe was a geographical notion defining a largely unknown territory in the North where the barbarians lived. Yet de Rougemont's work on the idea of Europe — like Federico Chabod's[9] or Jean-Baptiste Duroselle's[10] — was a programmatic attempt to rewrite Europe's history in order to deliver the mythical foundations for a political project of unity. Even as early as the 1950s, this kind of approach had its critics: Denys Hay, for example, noted that, 'there seem to be a number of new myths in the making in the "European idea" books which have recently appeared. Their authors are concerned to promote European unity; they try to do this by invoking great generalizations about the past.'[11] Hay is right: neither the Greeks nor the Romans had in their minds an 'idea of Europe' in the modern sense of the word. The various centres of their world were Mediterranean and ruled the southern parts of what today we call Europe, as well as the Near East and North Africa.

But these appeals would have been meaningless had there not been a real need for European unity and had there not been concrete political steps to institutionalize integration procedures. Opinion polls from the period 1945–50 show that an absolute majority supported some form of a United States of Europe.[12] Thus I would argue that only in a dialectic with the Schuman Plan was the idea of Europe able to become a driving force of integration:

> At the very moment of its announcement the Schuman Plan [...] became an established part of the context of events, a force for change and a myth: The word 'Europe' would never be spoken in quite the same way again. The power of the message impressed even skeptics at the time and has since made it difficult to disentangle the realities of the coal-steel negotiations from the aura envelopping them.[13]

Europe has indeed become a magic formula, a moral concept. It has lost its geographical meaning. Europe is today a synonym of the European Union, thus concealing that Europe is indeed also a geographical term, although we might find it difficult to define clear

8.   *Ibid.*
9.   Federico Chabod, 'L'idea di Europe' in *La Rassegna d'Italia*, 2, 1947, 4, pp. 3–17 and *ibid.*, 5, pp. 25–37.
10. Jean-Baptiste Duroselle, *L'idée d'Europe dans l'histoire*, Paris, 1965.
11. Denys Hay, *Europe: The Emergence of an Idea*, Edinburgh, 1957, p. xvii.
12. See Richard Swedberg, 'The Idea of "Europe" and the Origin of the European Union — A Sociological Approach' in *Zeitschrift für Soziologie*, 23, 1994, 5, pp. 378–87 (384).
13. John Gillingham, *Coal, Steel, and the Rebirth of Europe, 1045–1955: The German and French from Ruhr Conflict to Economic Community*, Cambridge, 1991, p. 231.

borderlines. The magic formula also masks that 'Europe' as a political notion has been constructed in the shadow of the Cold War. In this context, 'Europe' has been stylized as a system of values in which Communism is not included, although Marxism and Communism are genuine European inventions. This exclusion is evident not only in the Pan-European movement of the inter-war period, whose driving force was also a fierce anti-Bolshevism, but also in the bizarre formula of the 'Return to Europe' adopted by many Central and East European intellectuals after the demise of the Soviet Empire. The myth of Europe is a bright narrative of values like freedom, democracy, welfare, solidarity, modern technology and, above all, of high culture. The myth attempts to recreate a 'Golden Age',[14] while repressing the dark side of European history. Dissenting voices, like Bronislaw Geremek's, are rare: 'We have to insist on the fact that Fascism and Communism are not alien to Europe. We should continue to explain how these totalitarian systems are interlinked with our culture. Not only because these ideologies emerged on our continent, but also because they are products of European culture.'[15]

2. History, Culture and the Myth of Europe

Modern myths are stories about secular, not sacred matters. In *Mythologies*, Roland Barthes offers a list of modern myths, including the famous DS car made by Citroën.[16] Thus, in the twentieth century, the myth of Europe's unity has had to be constructed on secular grounds, although Christianity has played a prominent role in European discourses since Charlemagne. One promising foundation for the construction of myths since 1945 has been the cultural heritage of the Occident. Salvador de Madariaga, an important actor in the League of Nations in the inter-war period and a speaker at the legendary Hague Conference in May 1948, concluded his address with the following words:

Above all we must love Europe; our Europe, sonorous with the roaring laughter of Rabelais, luminous with the smile of Erasmus, sparkling with the wit of Voltaire; in whose mental skies shine the fiery eyes of Dante, the clear eyes of Shakespeare, the serene eyes of Goethe, the tormented eyes of Dostoievski; this Europe to whom La Gioconda for ever smiles, where Moses and David spring to perennial life from Michelangelo's marble, and Bach's genius rises spontaneous to be caught in his intellectual geometry;

14. See Anthony Smith's chapter, 'The "Golden Age" and National Renewal', in this volume.
15. Konrad Paul Liessmann, *Der Aufgang des Abendlandes: Eine Rekonstruktion Europas*, Vienna, 1994, p. 57.
16. Roland Barthes, *Mythologies*, Paris, 1957, p. 150.

where Hamlet seeks in thought the mystery of his inaction, and Faust seeks in action comfort for the void of his thought; where Don Juan seeks in women met the woman never found, and Don Quixote, spear in hand, gallops to force reality to rise above itself; this Europe where Newton and Leibniz measure the infinitesimal, and the Cathedrals, as Musset once wrote, pray on their knees in their robes of stone; where rivers, silver threads, link together strings of cities, jewels wrought in the crystal of space by the chisel of time [...] this Europe must be born. And she will, when Spaniards will say 'our Chartres', Englishmen 'our Cracow', Italians 'our Copenhagen'; when Germans say 'our Bruges', and step back horror-stricken at the idea of laying a murderous hand on it. Then will Europe live, for then it will be that the Spirit that leads history will have uttered the creative words: FIAT EUROPA![17]

But as there is no spirit of history, and as humanity has to make history by its own deeds, there is also no 'unity' which mysteriously becomes a subject of history, imposing itself upon the mind and saying 'This is Europe', as de Madariaga suggests in his *Portrait of Europe*.[18] The assumption that the cultural unity of Europe automatically entails the political one is, of course, contradicted by the patent reality of political and cultural differences across the continent. Yet de Madariaga, although conscious of this contradiction, does not look into the nature and dynamics of the differences; while not denying these differences, he wants them 'set [...] in a truer [*sic*] background as *Bêtises que je faisais avant ma naissance*', quoting Victor Hugo. To dismiss three thousand years of European history as 'the foolish things which were being done before my birth' is of course a foolish thing in itself.

It is not foolish, however, to insist on European culture as being probably the strongest link between Europe's different regions. But we have to bear in mind that this is a highly élitist project. Voltaire's vision of a European *res publica litteraria*, in which all European intellectuals of the time should gather (and converse in French) on the grounds of a shared belief in the values of the Enlightenment, was fulfilled for a very short period of time in the second half of the eighteenth century and receded thereafter, when the Napoleonic ambition to impose French hegemony on Europe awakened or consolidated the movements of nationalism throughout the countries his armies had subjugated.

At the very end of the century of Enlightenment, Novalis, the prominent poet of German Romanticism, wrote a speech entitled 'Christendom or Europe'. The text was published only in 1826 because Goethe interdicted its publication in 1799. On its appearance, it was

---

17.　Salvador de Madariaga, *Portrait of Europe*, London, 1952, pp. 2–3.
18.　*Ibid.*, p. 10.

considered by many to be a reactionary pamphlet in the reactionary times of the Holy League. The beginning of the pamphlet states that 'those were beautiful and bright times when Europe was a Christian land, when *one* Christendom lived in this humanly shaped continent; a great common interest linked the most distant provinces of this wide spiritual Empire. *One* leader lacking large mundane properties ruled and united the great political powers.'[19] What follows is a romantic picture of the happiness and greatness of Middle Age Europe being destroyed first by the Protestant revolt against the Roman Church and then by the secularization process of the Enlightenment. And finally Novalis invokes the renaissance of Christianity as the only opportunity for a peaceful Europe: 'From the loins of an honorable European Council (Consilium) Christendom will re-emerge and the business of religious awakening will be carried out following a comprehensive divine plan. Nobody will ever protest against Christian and wordly constraints, because the essence of the Church will be true freedom, and all necessary reforms will be pursued under the leadership of the Church and as a peaceful and formal state process.'[20]

Novalis's text has to be located in the tradition of 'Essays on Europe' which began in the seventeenth century with Sully's *Grand Dessein* (1632) and William Penn's *Essay on the Peace in Europe* (1693), and which was continued by Abbé de Saint-Pierre's *Projet de paix perpétuelle entre les souverains chrétiens* (1756–61), culminating in Kant's *Zum ewigen Frieden* (1795). Yet in these two centuries the idea of Christianity as the foundation stone of European cohesion had slowly withered, giving way to a republican idea of a new European order. With Kant, the notion of federalism came into being. By the nineteenth century, Europe, as a concept of peace and stability, had lost its importance, even among intellectuals. The two important exceptions were Victor Hugo in literature and Giuseppe Mazzini in politics. The mainstream could be summarized in a sentence written by Bismarck to the Russian ambassador in Berlin: 'Who speaks of Europe is wrong. It is a geographic term.'[21] It was the high point of the nation-state and of industrialism. Stability was considered to proceed from diplomacy.

Interestingly, the idea of Europe as a unity based on Christian values has, at least implicitly, been revived since 1945. Most essays on Europe begin with the story of the battle of Poitiers in 732, where Charles Martel defeated the Muslims and stopped their expansion into

19. Novalis, 'Die Christenheit oder Europa: Eine Rede. Abgedruckt' (1799) in *Neue Rundschau*, 107, 1996, 3, pp. 9–25 (9).
20. *Ibid.*, p. 25.
21. Quoted in Timothy Garton Ash, *Im Namen Europas: Deutschland und der geteilte Kontinent*, trans. Yvonne Badal, Munich, 1993, p. 568.

the Christian world, and with the story of Charlemagne, the Frankish king, receiving the imperial crown from the Pope in Rome in 800. I would argue, however, that both events are not constituent elements of Europe's unity as has often been suggested: the rebuff of the Saracens in Poitiers concluded a conflict which was getting increasingly dangerous for the Roman Church, whose position at that time was difficult anyway — Europe was far from being wholly Christianized and far from embodying a consolidation of the Christian dogma. The Roman Church was striving for religious hegemony, not for the unification of Europe. Charlemagne, on the other hand, pursued an empire-building strategy in the tradition of the Roman Empire. He was not primarily interested in Rome: his centre was Aix-la-Chapelle, far in the north of the continent, but the idea of empire was still of Roman coinage. Charlemagne's alliance with the Pope was a genuinely political deal whose success was also due to the fact that the Pope wanted to install and legitimize a Western emperor against the Byzantine powerholder. We know today that Charlemagne had been rather reluctant to be crowned by the Pope. These historical facts challenge the facile conclusions drawn by some modern writers engaged in European myth-construction. But I would be facile if I denied the impact Christianity and Carolingian empire-building had on the emergence of what could be called 'Europeanness'. The concept, however, is a much wider one.

3. The Myth of Europe's Unity between Culture and Economics

In his 1919 essay *La Crise de l'esprit*, Paul Valéry writes that 'every people or race who has been Romanized, Christianized and subjected to the rule of the Greek logos, is deeply European'.[22] In his essay on *Der Aufgang des Abendlandes*, Konrad Paul Liessmann hones this statement further, suggesting that 'as Europeans we are above all Romans', and Rémi Brague stresses the notion of *latinité* as the main characteristic of Europeanness.[23] This is particularly true of European legal thinking, if we limit Europe to the continent. It is not true of England, in which Roman law could never be imposed on common law, which has been deeply rooted in the culture since the Middle Ages. And it is only partly true for the continental countries, because the rule of Roman law could only be forced on the existing law systems in protracted and joint efforts by the German emperors of the

---

22. Paul Valéry, 'La Crise d'esprit' (1919) in *idem*, *Oeuvres*, compiled and annotated by Jean Hytier, Paris, 1957, vol. 2, pp. 988–1014 (1013).
23. Rémi Brague, *Europe, la voie romaine*, Paris, 1993, p. 24.

Holy Roman Empire, and by Italian and French lawyers. The history of French law itself is one of the difficult integration of a special form of case law in the north, and Roman law in the south. Some French lawyers would argue that a mixed system has persisted until today. Interestingly, modern European law is based on the Anglo-Saxon case-law system and not on the Roman tradition.[24] Roman tradition is located in the idea of a republic operating on a system of checks and balances of power and on rational administration in the Weberian sense: 'Rome is the perennial model of the organized and stable power', writes Paul Valéry.[25] Furthermore, Rome was the only ancient state which developed forms of civil rights for its citizens. Every free man could become a *civis romanus* independently of his origin, language, religion or ethnic belonging. Even the prosecution of the apostle Paul had to be carried out within the limits set by his Roman citizenship. Christianity and the Roman Church, after a period of withdrawal from all worldly matters, were able to amalgamate with the Roman system, thus saving and transmitting much of Roman thinking to posterity.

The notion of culture needs to be broadened beyond those works of European art which have been claimed by intellectuals, such as de Madariaga in his *Portrait of Europe* or T.S. Eliot in his essay 'The Unity of European Culture', to be the essence of Europeanness.[26] Poetry or art constitutes but one aspect of a given culture. Economic, political, legal and educational institutions are just as important. And so are food, fashion and feasts, as well as the media. Yet today, with regard to these other elements of culture, there is probably little which could be called genuinely European. When markets and communication systems become global, it is almost impossible to limit influences from outside. The Americanization of European culture is not just a paranoia of French politicians, it is indeed reality.

The main driving force of transnationalization, however, is modern capitalism's (another European invention) striving for ever greater markets. Globalization and interdependence are the well-known concepts of a process which makes it rather difficult, if not impossible, for nation-states and for the European Community to define a clear identity. Thus we have to ask what could provide the basis for the construction — be it by myth or other means — of a European

24. Federico Mancini, 'The Making of a Constitution for Europe' in Robert O. Keohane and Stanley Hoffmann (eds), *The New European Community: Decisionmaking and Institutional Change*, Boulder, CO, San Francisco and Oxford, 1991, pp. 177–94.
25. Valéry, *Oeuvres*, vol. 1, p. 1008.
26. T.S. Eliot, 'The Unity of European Culture' in *idem, Notes towards the Definition of Culture*, London, 1948.

identity. First, it must be argued that globalization is an economic trend more than a comprehensive reality.[27] Second, it can be maintained that globalization does not result in a global political community. As far as we can see, it does not even lead to a real global market but to regional powers, the EU being one of them, NAFTA, ASEAN and Mercosur the others, although these others are not as integrated as the European Union. Given these facts, the main question has to focus on the political organization of these regional powers. Do these co-operative systems tend towards the construction of a new nation or towards empire-building? And if they do, how are the new nations or empires to be politically constituted? Who will be their sovereign? What will be the nature of the body politic capable of legitimizing such a new order? These classical questions of political philosophy have become crucial, particularly for the European Union. All arguments about the frequently quoted democratic deficit can be reduced to them.

In stating that these are some of the real problems of today's Europe, I want to argue that, if a new foundation myth for Europe is needed, it could be found in the great European history of democracy and republicanism ranging from ancient Greece and Rome to the medieval republican city-states and finally to the modern democracies based on parliamentarism and general representation. By this, I am not suggesting that the national systems of democracy could simply be transferred onto the European level. This would be tantamount to the creation of a centralized European state; yet there is no majority of member-state representatives advocating this solution today.[28] This is true not only for Great Britain, but for most of the other member states of the Union as well. But, on the other hand, the praxis of European integration has created a new entity, and a large majority of people are in favour of some kind of unification. Hence models of co-operation based on flexibility and legitimized by a European body politic must be elaborated. This approach implies the thinking of a European constitution based on a Bill of Rights for the individual as being the *zoon politikon*. On these grounds, a reform of European institutions — from the European Council to the European Court of Justice — could be envisaged which would give individuals and their groups a voice in the integration process. The next step should be dedicated to the separation of powers at the European level and, at the same time, at the national and supranational levels as suggested, but never spelled out, by the principle of subsidiarity. The creation of a constitutional

27. See Paul Krugman, *Pop Internationalism*, Cambridge, MA and London, 1996.
28. 'The Union is not and does not want to be a super-state': 'Reflection Group's Report of the Intergovernmental Conference, 1995', SN 520/95, REFLEX 21, p. iii.

assembly, by general vote in all member states, might be one way of initiating such a transformation process and thereby mobilizing public feeling; the effects of this process would be far more potent than any myth construction about a European *Schicksalsgemeinschaft*. Analogous to the American constitutional debate following the revolution in 1776, a European constitutional process might create the We-feeling of an emerging body politic.

One has to be remain sceptical, however, about the opportunities for a constitutional movement in Europe today. In spite of the hopes raised by the actors negotiating the revision of the Treaty of Maastricht, the European constitution is not on the agenda of the political parties, corporate interests, the media, or intellectuals. European integration continues to consist in the operation of executive power in the member states and the supranational institutions. Governing seems easier when democratic accountability is not the main focus of the 'governors'. James Caporaso,[29] Wolfgang Streeck, Dominique Wolton[30] and other scholars analysing European integration have defined European rule as the triumph of the executive over parliaments.

Another source of scepticism is the proposed EU enlargement towards Central and Eastern Europe. Article 0 of the Treaty of European Union states that every European state which so wishes may apply for membership of the Union. This of course complicates the problem of how Europe is defined. While the application of the Visegrad and Baltic states seems more than plausible, others might be more difficult to handle: are Turkey and Morocco European? Morocco's application for EU membership has already been refused on the grounds that Morocco is not a European state. If Christianity is a criterion by which Europeanness is defined, Turkey will also be rejected by the EU. Yet, if having belonged to the Roman Empire is a criterion, the decision will be more difficult to make. And if the criterion is economic performance, even the application of the Visegrad and Baltic states may become unacceptable, not to mention Romania, Bulgaria, Croatia, Bosnia, the Federation of Yugoslavia, Albania, Ukraine, Belarus, and so on. In this case, data on growth, public deficits, interest rates, privatization and other fiscal matters will be much more relevant than discussions about common cultural interests or differences.

29. James Caporaso, 'The European Union and Forms of State: Westphalian, Regulatory or Post-Modern?' in *The Journal of Common Market Studies*, 1, 1996, 1, pp. 29–52.
30. Dominique Wolton, *La Dernière Utopie: Naissance de l'Europe démocratique*, Paris, 1993.

MYTH-MAKING AND NATIONAL IDENTITY: THE CASE OF THE G.D.R.

Mary Fulbrook

Nations are themselves myths. There is no such 'real entity' as a nation: only a social reality, in the Durkheimian sense, when enough people are prepared to believe in the salience of a certain set of characteristics as attributes of nationhood. Such characteristics might include language, culture, religion, belief in common descent or ethnicity. Dominant myths, when institutionalized, however, may become a matter of power, resources and ritual: a stage may come when people no longer have to believe in the myths, but live with the consequences.

The conditions under which such collective beliefs have emerged have puzzled many scholars, from the older discussions of Ernst Renan or Max Weber to the more recent contributions of scholars such as Benedict Anderson, Eric Hobsbawm, Ernest Gellner and others. A sense of nationhood is more likely to occur under certain conditions than others: Anderson, for example, noted the importance of literate élites and what he called 'print capitalism'; the example of anti-colonial nationalism might suggest the importance of political context and struggle based on perceived interest in opposition to others. There is also some connection between the emergence of a system of states in the era of developing industrial capitalism and the replacement of dynastic, hereditary and religious principles of legitimation by belief in a notion of 'nation'. Many scholars have also pointed to the importance of, as Renan classically put it, a would-be nation 'getting its history wrong', or, in the title of a collection of essays edited by Eric Hobsbawm, 'the invention of tradition'. In different ways, myths have been seen as central to the construction of a sense of being a nation.

Myths alone, however, cannot create the necessary conditions for the construction of nations. This chapter explores the limits of myths in the construction of national identity. It takes an example of failure, a case in which politically dominant groups sought to propagate certain myths which failed to achieve true popular resonance: the case of the German Democratic Republic. Before analysing certain aspects of official myths and mass perceptions in the GDR, a few more general remarks are necessary.

What are myths? There are a variety of ways of defining and typologizing myths, as discussed in other contributions to this volume. At their most basic, myths are stories which are not necessarily true, nor even believed to be true, but which have symbolic power. They are constantly repeated, often re-enacted. Myths are, in other words, essentially propagated for their effect rather than their truth value. The extent to which they embody claims to truth varies greatly, from those stories which are widely held to be true and are only revealed as myths when 'exploded' by new 'revelations', to narratives which are of particular exemplary value and may be repeatedly retold or re-enacted as symbolic expressions of important values (the Christian myths of the virgin birth or the Resurrection, for example) irrespective of a general collusion in the knowledge that 'this could not have taken place in this way', in other words, a willing suspension of disbelief.

How do myths relate to the construction of a sense of national identity? It seems to me that, while myths constitute a key and important facet, they are not the only ingredient. Without going into too much detail here, let me present my own definition and theses for the purposes of this chapter:[1] *A sense of national identity is shaped in part by a common past, the perception of shared memories; often a sense of community in adversity; and a sense of a common destiny.*

This cluster includes as one element *a shared history and common memories*. These may include 'collective memory', as well as individual 'real' memories. Even the latter, in any event, are selective remembrances refracted through specific cultural spectacles (including the concepts and evaluations which define and colour remembered events). Myths are clearly a major and important element in this aspect of identity construction: the tales that are told about a nation's past are crucial to embodying an almost anthropomorphic sense of that nation's history as biography. The *sense of community in adversity* and the *sense of common destiny* may also be sustained in part by myths: myths as sustaining and reinforcing values which define Self and Other, and hence the enemy; and myths of history which also entail a sense of future towards which the community is striving, or for which the community may be preordained (as in the notion of God's chosen people).

Myth is, in other words, clearly involved in all levels of nationhood construction. But it is the basic thesis of this chapter that *myths are neither a sufficient condition of nationhood, nor are all possible myths equally effective.* Very often, analyses of myth seek to demonstrate the functionality of particular beliefs in certain contexts (as in much of the mid-twentieth-century anthropology of African or Melanesian or Polynesian non-literate peoples). This chapter seeks to explore the

1. These arguments are explored in greater detail in my forthcoming book, *German National Identities in the Shadow of Auschwitz.*

limits of myth-making, and to examine the ways in which there must be at least some degree of congruence between official myths and popular collective memories and current experiences for a viable sense of nationhood to be articulated.

I take as my specific case-study an example of a failed candidate for nationhood. The German Democratic Republic was founded as a 'provisional state' under the protection of a military occupying power on the ruins of part of Hitler's defeated Third Reich. For the first half of its forty-year existence the GDR — or rather, the leading Communist Party, the SED (Socialist Unity Party) — claimed that the ultimate goal was reunification with West Germany, and that it was only the 'militarist imperialist revanchist' (and so on) forces in the West that stood in the way of national unification. After *Ostpolitik*, however, the goal shifted: in the 1970s, the SED proclaimed a new theory of nation based on class rather than ethnicity, and sought to develop a concept of a GDR nation. The apparent lack of any popular deep-rootedness of this view was revealed when the stampede westwards in 1989–90 precipitated (under favourable international conditions) the voluntary annexation of a disintegrating GDR by West Germany.

In this chapter, I shall examine some of the myths officially propagated in the GDR. I shall compare these with evidence of popular historical consciousness and contemporary experience in order to explore some of the disjunctures between official myths and popular perceptions. Finally, I shall seek to reinsert these reflections into the wider definition of nationhood adumbrated above. I shall proceed by taking three crucial varieties of myth which are relevant to the three aspects of identity construction suggested above: myths of creation; myths of heroes and villains; and myths of a glorious future.

The Common Past: Myths of Creation

Myths of creation, from the biblical creation story and Adam and Eve, to the Roman Romulus and Remus, are arguably universal. When a new people or a new state is founded, it needs a story. Often, too, candidates for nationhood seek to hark back to a 'Golden Age'.

A particular problem for both German states in the shadow of Hitler was the lack of an acceptable history. How, after Auschwitz, was it possible to have any sense of national pride which was rooted in the past? The SED, even in the early years when the officially proclaimed goal remained reunification with West Germany, nevertheless had an apparently perfect solution, providing GDR citizens with a sense of GDR identity and pride. Furthermore, the creation myth of the GDR remained central to its identity throughout the forty years. This was the great anti-Fascist myth. The GDR was a country in which innocent workers and peasants had been oppressed by nasty capitalists and Junkers, imperialists and Fascists, until at last they were liberated by the glorious Red Army of the Soviet Union in conjunction with resistance fighters of other nations.

A very wide range of documents and other materials can be used to explore the ways in which this myth was propagated. Its centrality to GDR identity was evident in the widespread prevalence of modes of its expression. Great attention was devoted to the construction and care of ubiquitous statues and commemoration plaques to resistance fighters all across the GDR and the memorials to Soviet soldiers.[2] The myth was presented to schoolchildren through textbooks and compulsory class visits to exhibitions in the former Nazi concentration camps on GDR soil, such as Ravensbrück, Sachsenhausen, Buchenwald, or the munitions factory at Nordhausen/Dora.[3] It was constantly repeated in popular literature intended for public and international consumption, ranging from straight history textbooks to a range of lavishly illustrated (at least by GDR standards) leaflets and pamphlets about the GDR, repeatedly propagating the notion that the Soviet troops came as liberators of the essentially peace-loving German population from the Fascist yoke of oppression.[4]

Let me take, as a single illustration to stand for many, a quotation from the brochure produced in May 1985, on the occasion of the fortieth anniversary of the ending of the Second World War — a brochure in which there is, interestingly, absolutely no mention of the Hitler/Stalin pact of 1939:

In inconceivably severe battles [...] the Soviet Union brought about the fundamental turn of the war [...], paving the way for the peoples' liberation from the fascist yoke and saving human civilisation. All mankind owes an immortal tribute to the Soviet soldiers and partisans [...].

The fascists had drummed into the German people's brains that defeat in the war would be tantamount to the end of their existence. But in actual fact liberation by the Soviet Union offered the German people a great historic chance. Finally it had become possible to tread the path envisaged by their best representatives throughout the centuries, and for which the fighters of antifascist resistance had fought in deep clandestinity, in the hell of concentration camps and jails and under the bitter conditions of exile —

2.   See, for example, Anna Dora Miethe's contribution in *Gedenkstätten: Arbeiterbewegung, Antifaschistischer Widerstand, Aufbau des Sozialismus*, ed. Institut für Denkmalpflege in der DDR, Berlin and Leipzig, 1974.
3.   See, for example, the official brochure for the 'nationale Mahn- und Gedenkstätte Sachsenhausen'.
4.   See, for example, *Aus erster Hand: Bildchronik 20 Jahre DDR*, ed. Staatssekretariat für westdeutsche Fragen, second edition, East Berlin, 1970; or the less instantly accessible, 839-page long and unillustrated *Grundriss der deutschen Geschichte*, Berlin, 1979.

the path of peace and friendship among nations, humanism and social progress.[5]

The problem for the SED was that, exonerating though these creation myths may have been, they were effectively predicated on a willing suppression of real memories of the past. But such suppression was not entirely effective. Many Germans remembered both elements in this myth — the alleged liberation, and their own exoneration — rather differently.

The moment of their 'liberation' by the Red Army was perhaps the worst experience of their lives up to that point.[6] Many had fled from their homes in territories subsequently taken over by Poland and the Soviet Union, and had been forced on treks through icy conditions with very few possessions, often losing elderly or young relatives and friends who collapsed and died along the way. Rape, plunder, pillage, when not personally experienced, were nevertheless a very lively part of common folk memory and myth about the period. The arrival of the Russians had been experienced by the vast majority with fear rather than relief. Nor had this fear ended with the establishment of more settled peacetime conditions. Worries about missing husbands, fathers and sons in Soviet prisoner-of-war camps went on for many years after the end of hostilities. The presence of brooding Soviet tanks lurking in the forests, patrolling up and down tracks by the side of many through routes, and stationed in large numbers in military garrisons, was hardly conducive to a sense of the officially ordained brotherly love. Even the Free German Youth (FDJ), one of the politically most important mass organizations, provides illustrations of rather traditional anti-Soviet attitudes among East Germans, as when an audience of young people, members of the FDJ, burst into spontaneous applause for Hitler and the German 'Fascist tanks' when watching a Soviet film about the war — applause which was not suppressed by the FDJ officials or other responsible adults present.[7] Probably the first time the Russians were really hailed as liberators was, paradoxically, with the arrival of Mikhail Gorbachev for the fortieth and last anniversary of the GDR in October 1989.

Secondly, there was the implicit lie about the East Germans' own murky or less murky pasts. Degrees of real compromise varied, of course, and the picture is complex; but the simplicity of the official myth of the innocent people was certainly unsustainable. The vast majority of surviving adult males — including, of course, a preponderance of the allegedly innocent workers and peasants, who

5. *Upholding the Antifascist Legacy*, Dresden, 1985, pp. 3–5.
6. See Norman Naimark, *The Russians in Germany*, Cambridge, MA, 1995.
7. See my discussion in M. Fulbrook, *Anatomy of a Dictatorship: Inside the GDR, 1949–1989*, Oxford, 1995 (hereafter *Anatomy of a Dictatorship*), pp. 167–8.

made up the bulk of the German population — had fought in the German army (whatever their personal political opinions), and had colluded in the Nazi regime's condemnation of Communists. Hundreds of thousands of East German adults had been members of the National Socialist German Workers' Party (NSDAP) or its affiliated organizations. They may have been glad when the war, and the suffering it had inflicted, came to an end; but they must have found it hard to recognize themselves, with any degree of honesty, as among the innocent victims of Nazi oppression — particularly when they had lost their jobs and livelihoods, or even been interned in a liberated camp, in the course of denazification processes in the Soviet zone. (As many as 72 per cent of teachers, for example, had belonged to the NSDAP: of these 70 per cent lost their jobs by 1946, although around a quarter were later reinstated.[8] Around 45 per cent of medical doctors had been members of the NSDAP, with a figure as high as 80 per cent in Thuringia.)[9] For those who had played an active role in supporting the Third Reich, subsequent acceptance of official exoneration and collusion in building up a new future in the new regime was one thing; but accepting as true a distorted picture of the past, let alone investing it with any emotional charge, was quite another.

The effective amnesty offered to millions of former Nazis in the GDR, so long as they were prepared to work with the new regime on its terms, was in many ways very helpful for political stabilization and establishment of the new regime. The hypothesis that members of the so-called 'HJ-generation' (those socialized in the Hitler Youth group and brought up in traditions of obedience to authority), were particularly faithful and loyal functionaries in the new state is at least worthy of serious consideration. Certainly, specific illustrations bear out the view that many individuals were quite happy *Wendehälse* (turncoats) after 1945 in the East, just as in the West, and just as, again, after 1990. The case of Herr Lotz, a former informer to the Gestapo on members of the Confessing Church in Thuringia, who readily became an informer to the Stasi in the 1950s, is a single example to stand for an almost infinite number.[10] Nevertheless, new myths and new identities were not quite enough. There were too many distortions and cross-cutting memories which ran at odds with the official myths.

8. Figures taken from Joachim Petzold, 'Die Entnazifizierung der sächsischen Lehrerschaft 1945' in J. Kocka (ed.), *Historische DDR-Forschung*, Berlin, 1993, pp. 88, 102–3.
9. Figures taken from Christoph Klessmann, 'Relikte des Bildungsbürgertums in der DDR' in Hartmut Kaelble, Jürgen Kocka and Hartmut Zwahr (eds), *Sozialgeschichte der DDR*, Stuttgart, 1994, pp. 257–8.
10. For further details, see Fulbrook, *Anatomy of a Dictatorship*, p. 98.

Even among those who had borne little or no part in sustaining Nazism there was a degree of uncomfortable duplicity involved in swallowing the official myth. Reverence for the genuine courage of some of the real anti-Fascist founding fathers of the GDR may have helped to quell potential opposition in some quarters in the early years. But when the humdrum realities and the constant and continued repression of the 1960s and 1970s became the taken-for-granted landscape of everyday life, rumblings from the repressed past began to be heard. The classic illustration of these processes is perhaps best provided in literary form by Christa Wolf. She speaks of the way in which she and many of her contemporaries in the 1950s dared not query the credentials of those who sought to found a new order among the ruins; but, by the mid-1970s, she had engaged in a profound and deep exploration of repressed layers of memory and identity in her own past, in the essentially autobiographical novel *Kindheitsmuster* (A Pattern of Childhood).[11] The process through which Wolf had worked in her highly literary and literate way was arguably paralleled in less articulate manner by millions of others.

Memories of a common past, shared with West Germans, were perhaps more prevalent in the GDR than they were among those fortunate enough to be able to wallow in a degree of amnesia on the more affluent side of the inner-German border. The Wall was a perpetual reminder of the War and its consequences for the division of Germany; and friends and relatives in the West who might be a source of Western currency and goods, as well as nightly watching West German television, were highly important factors in the lives of many East Germans. The founding myths of creation were ever-present — even the official handshake, symbolizing the alleged unity of the Socialist Unity Party, could never be evaded as a visual reminder of a myth — but they were simply too dissonant with other aspects of perception and experience to carry much weight as far as a real sense of separation from West Germany was concerned.

This leads us to the second aspect: the sense of a community in adversity, the sense of common values and common enemies. Here, the official myths were singularly unsuccessful.

A Sense of a Community in Adversity and the Propagation of Values: Myths of Heroes and Villains

The SED itself certainly had a very clear sense of values and enemies. It felt constantly embattled and was deeply paranoid. The *Klassenfeind* (Class Enemy) was ubiquitous, wreaking his ugly work in everything

11. Christa Wolf, *Kindheitsmuster*, Berlin and Weimar, 1976.

from the popular uprising of June 1953 to the occasional incident, such as the defacement of Ulbricht's picture with a Hitler moustache in a works canteen, or the singing of somewhat irreverent words to the tune of the official national anthem. Even the youthful pranks of inebriated teenagers on a school camping trip, or graffiti scratched into desktops by bored apprentices, could be interpreted as evidence of the Class Enemy. The Class Enemy — in some senses the SED equivalent of the medieval Devil — appeared in a variety of more tangible guises, through which the SED sought to propagate a clear sense of Good and Evil, Friend and Foe. The converse of the villains who wrought the work of the Class Enemy were of course the Heroes who struggled (whether they were aware of their role or not) for the cause, or contributed to the forward march of history.

The villains, of course, were not only in the Nazi past — and hence dealt with by the myth of liberation — but also, allegedly, in the contemporary West, and in the traditions on which it sought to build but which the GDR had overcome. Nazism had been a variant of Fascism, carried by monopoly capitalists. The individuals in question (the actual Nazis themselves) and the socio-economic form (capitalism) which had produced them were now safely either exported to, or only still present in, West Germany. The heroes, of course, were, or belonged to, the East. Heroes included the anti-Fascist fighters referred to in the myth of creation, such as Ernst Thälmann; others were contemporary heroes, such as the over-producing manual worker Adolf Hennecke, who, on 13 October 1948, supposedly beat the average daily productivity by a staggering 387 per cent. These individuals, of course, were to encapsulate and embody the more general Class Hero, the workers and peasants in whose name the GDR had been founded. Designation of heroes and villains was constantly shifting, as issues, strategies and tactics changed. In the course of forty years, some heroes and villains were allowed to change roles: Martin Luther and Frederick the Great were notable cases in point, being promoted from the ranks of the castigated to the company of the celebrated, as the regime's propagation of values and foci of identification shifted.

Throughout the forty years of its existence, the GDR was premised on a 'friend/foe' mentality. The definition of a 'them/us' distinction, preferably buttressed by the reality or threat of existential battle, is a classic ploy of rulers seeking to construct a national identity.[12] Military co-operation against a common enemy was a key to the

---

12. As cynical observers might comment on Margaret Thatcher's foreign exploits at a time of very low personal popularity at home — if the memory of the Blitz is fading, a skirmish in the faraway Falklands will do wonders for a notion of British national identity in some quarters. In Thatcher's case, as the results of the 1983 General Election confirmed, this strategy was remarkably successful.

foundation of the German Empire in 1871. Bismarck then devoted considerable attention to the alleged 'enemies within', Catholics and socialists, consolidating a sense of 'small German' identity within the German empire. Wilhelm II, fearing civil war at home, explicitly sought refuge in the fight against the 'enemy without', plunging Germany into the First World War in the hope of uniting the nation at home. Hitler's racial version of the *Volksgemeinschaft* was yet another variant of a 'them/us' distinction, expressed not merely in rhetoric and ritual but effected in the most unimaginable and horrific reality.

Against this backdrop, and in the context of a nation divided not by the decisions of representatives of the people, but as a result of military occupation and the Cold War, the SED faced a formidable task in constructing a new mindset and displacing the old friend/foe mentalities. 'Us' had suddenly to include the former enemy, the Soviet Union, and all it stood for by way of traditional foci of German hatred, including that bogey of conservative nationalists, Bolshevism; 'them' had to include one's friends, relatives, even close family members, in the West. The Federal Republic had to be portrayed as a real and present threat because of all it allegedly stood for (militarism, capitalism, imperialism, Fascism); the German Democratic Republic, by contrast, was presented as peace-loving, genuinely seeking to uphold the unity of the nation (until *Ostpolitik*) or representing essentially a different nation (in the 1970s and 1980s).

Faced with an almost insurmountable catalogue of tasks, a variety of strategies were deployed to present new heroes and villains to displace the old. Memorials and monuments to Soviet soldiers sprang up everywhere; muscular but expressionless statues of giant workers and peasants towered above open spaces; the annual calendar replaced old high days and holy days with new ones, imbued with socialist significance, such as the annual commemoration of the murder of Rosa Luxemburg and Karl Liebknecht. Some old antipathies, such as conservative anti-Americanism, were appropriated and redeployed in campaigns against Western decadence, as evidenced in 'rock'n'roll' or jazz music and blue jeans. Heroes and villains were cast as stereotypes in history books — the classic vehicles for myths and story-telling. The militarization of society was a feature even before the official founding of the 'National Peoples Army' in January 1956, and was a constant presence in the education system, from Kindergarten games onwards. But the inculcation of a friend/foe mentality was not an easy process, and was never entirely successful. It met a range of forms of resistance.

As far as 'foes' were concerned, a widespread antipathy towards war was reinforced by a marked unwillingness to swallow the new designation of the enemy. After the introduction of conscription in 1962, in 1964 the churches wrung the concession of alternative service, without bearing arms, as 'construction soldiers' (*Bausoldaten*). The renewed mini-Cold War following the Western decision to station Cruise Missiles on German soil in 1979, and the Soviet invasion of Afghanistan in the same year, was accompanied by a heightened emphasis on militarization, including the introduction of a compulsory school subject in military education in the GDR already in 1978. Although opposition to the latter was unsuccessful, in the 1980s there was a growing unofficial peace movement in the GDR, making use of the churches as a space for discussion and organization. The tiny minority of activists involved in these unofficial peace initiatives became the kernel of other circles, such as the human rights groups and environmentalist movements of the 1980s, which played a leading role in the 'gentle revolution' of 1989. As far as the more conformist majority was concerned, the myth of the West Germans as enemy rather than friend was never completely accepted. The Wall, supposedly an 'anti-Fascist defence wall', was seen by the majority of East Germans less as self-protection than as self-immolation: incarceration, not defence. A more vibrant sense of common German identity remained alive among East Germans than among their brethren in the West.

If the picture of villains was not so easily internalized, the situation was not much better with respect to the heroes. The workers and peasants delivered a rather unpleasant preliminary verdict on the workers' and peasants' state in the June Uprising of 1953. Thereafter, a variety of strategies were deployed to sustain forms of accommodation, or arrangement, between regime and working masses. Periods of consumerism alternated with periods of austerity; but the implicit concession on the part of the SED entailed recognition of an underlying materialism that would not die away for all the tales of heroic building of socialism (on which more in a moment). Resistance to increased work norms was more prevalent than adulation of Hennecke as hero. Similarly, the ubiquitous slogan 'learning from the Soviet Union means learning to be victorious'[13] was not taken seriously by most East Germans until the accession of Gorbachev to power, accompanied by a marked unwillingness on Erich Honecker's part to admit that he had anything at all to learn from the Soviet Union. Indeed, acquiring a command of Russian only became a serious aim for many (who had maintained a policy of passive resistance through compulsory Russian lessons at school) when the Soviet publication *Sputnik* was suddenly banned (allegedly by the Ministry of Post and Telecommunications!) in November 1988 once it started carrying more critical material.

13. 'Von der Sowjetunion lernen heisst siegen lernen'.

Although the struggling working masses, along with their Soviet friends and liberators, appeared constantly as the heroes of history, something a little more emotive and symbolic was clearly required. After *Ostpolitik*, the SED sought to construct deeper roots for a new sense of GDR patriotism by reappropriating the whole of the German past and making a distinction between 'tradition' and 'legacy' (the so-called 'Tradition/Erbe' debate). Frederick the Great's statue was resurrected on East Berlin's central avenue, Unter den Linden, and Martin Luther was rehabilitated, with the reinterpretation of the Protestant Reformation as the essential precondition for the German Peasants' War.

The Luther example illustrates well the complexities of the situation, and illuminates the ways in which the SED's appropriation of heroes tended to backfire. For many years, Luther had been condemned in the GDR as a reactionary who had supported the princes 'against the robbing and murdering hordes of peasants' (to adopt the title of one of Luther's own more vitriolic tracts, when he had himself just narrowly escaped death in the Peasants' War of 1525). This view of Luther as reactionary was toned down in the later 1970s, as the SED pursued its new, apparently conciliatory policies aimed towards co-opting the Protestant Churches as, effectively, a compliant subordinate partner of the State — a policy that appeared to achieve fruition in the Church/State accord of 6 March 1978.[14] The 'common humanistic goals' of Christianity and socialism (in its Marxist-Leninist version) were presented as mutually compatible, and Christians and Marxists could allegedly walk 'hand-in-hand', as far as their beliefs and activities in the here-and-now were concerned, leaving differences about the afterlife to another day. The culmination of Luther's rehabilitation as not just a Protestant hero, but as a GDR national hero, was reached in the 'Luther year' 1983 — the quincentenary of Luther's birth. It was also, curiously, the centenary of the death of Karl Marx, an anniversary which appeared to be accorded far less significance than one might have expected in a Communist state.

The Luther-year was undoubtedly a success in a number of respects: international tourism and foreign hard currency, as well as prestige and the propagation of the view that the GDR was at least on the way to becoming a more open and tolerant and even partially pluralist society.[15] But it ultimately achieved almost the opposite of what was

14. For further details, see chapters 4 and 8 of Fulbrook, *Anatomy of a Dictatorship*.
15. It was also accompanied by a number of international conferences marked by quite amusing role reversals. The author vividly remembers one such conference at King's College London, at which British neo-Marxists stressed the causal importance of *material conditions* rooted in late feudal relations of production, disagreeing strongly with the East German historians who emphasized the *ideological preconditions* of the Peasants' War in Lutheran thought.

intended. For a small minority of political activists it opened up the churches as a space for the articulation of dissenting views and unofficial organization for reform and change. Even for the vast majority of less active East Germans the resurrection of Luther essentially boomeranged. For the emphasis on an all-German past, and the new willingness to concede importance to great men and to ideas as driving forces in history, only served to underline the continuing real links with West Germany at a time when the easing of travel restrictions and the spread of mass media had made the Iron Curtain ever more porous in any event.

Heroes can also be contested, and symbols can provide the focus of alternative appropriations. For example, a picture of the statue of a man beating 'swords into ploughshares', donated by the Soviet Union to the United Nations building in New York, was appropriated by unofficial peace activists as a symbol on an armband protesting against *all* weapons, Nato and Warsaw Pact, in 1982. This posed immense difficulties for the regime in knowing how to deal with such an infuriatingly conformist symbol of protest.[16] A quotation from official regime heroine Rosa Luxemberg, 'freedom is always the freedom to think differently', was adopted for an unofficial banner by human rights activists in the annual Luxemburg/Liebknecht parade of January 1988.[17] Marx's own writings, and those of some later Marxists, were potent sources for the critiques of the GDR by oppositional spirits such as Wolfgang Harich, Robert Havemann, or Rudolf Bahro. Many writings of neo-Marxists were simply banned. Official myths only work if they are accepted unthinkingly.

Even lived out, ritually re-enacted myths do not always achieve deep or long-lasting effects. They depend on propitious circumstances for their efficacy. While the Wall protected the outer boundaries, the ultimate preconditions of the GDR's existence, the majority of the East German people went through the motions of outward conformity in preference to putting their own personal lives and careers at stake. Sheer habit, conformity with the increasingly taken-for-granted rituals of everyday life, takes over for most people most of the time. Some refused, and paid the price. But the increasing militarization of society, and the attempt to portray the West Germans as deadly enemies rather than relatives and friends, never fully succeeded. Myths of heroes and villains in the GDR *either* never caught on with any real degree of popular enthusiasm (the Hennecke activists were vastly outnumbered

16. See Klaus Ehring and Martin Dallwitz (eds), *Schwerter zu Pflugscharen*, Hamburg, 1982.
17. See Ferdinand Kroh (ed.), *'Freiheit ist immer Freiheit': Die Andersdenkenden in der DDR*, Frankfurt am Main and Berlin, 1988; and, for a personal account by one of the activists, Vera Wollenberger, *Virus der Heuchler: Innenansichten aus Stasi-Akten*, Berlin, 1992.

by those who went on strike against the raising of work norms, not only in 1953 but repeatedly thereafter, though never again with such widespread support or political consequences); *or*, when they did achieve a real degree of popular resonance, they in effect underlined what they had sought to undermine, namely the common heritage with the West.

In the event, the 'community of adversity' became something rather different, something utterly unintended by those in power in the GDR. The realities of a common fate, in which those behind the Wall were subjected to the same daily pressures and constraints, forged common patterns of behaviour and common bonds which did in fact lead to a version of common GDR identity among some at least of the 'community of the oppressed' — but a very different form of identity from that which was officially intended.[18] Such a sense may have been rooted in many popular, perhaps even non-articulated, myths, but it was certainly at odds with the official myths of the regime, and was quite compatible with, indeed in part constructed out of, conformity and participation in the official rituals and ceremonies, such as the annual May Day parades. Mutual complicity in outward conformity was an essential ingredient in this sense of an unofficial GDR identity.

A Community of Destiny: Myths of a Glorious Future

If the past is problematic, and the present is uncomfortable, then there is little to appeal to apart from a glorious future. Myths of a common destiny are vital ingredients of vibrant conceptions of national identity. Even if there is no 'Golden Age' to appeal to in the past, then at least 'at the end of the day' (when the chosen people attain redemption) the battles will not have been fought in vain.

Myths of destiny were vital to official identity construction in the GDR. There were concerted efforts throughout its history to evoke faith in a glorious, even utopian, future as a compensation for the shortcomings of the present. The great advantage of the Marxist-Leninist version of history is that utopia is built into the programme: with the emancipation of the proletariat, the emancipation of mankind in general is assured. All the ills of present and past societies will be resolved in one final synthesis to end all syntheses. When the negation of the negation of all that is truly human has been achieved, then, at one philosophical stroke, humanity will have reached the highest and ultimate stage of history, true Communism.

18 . This unofficial sense of GDR identity has experienced an inchoate afterlife in the 'ostalgia' evident among *Ossis* in the post-unification 'five new Länder', where again there is a common sense of participating in a community of fate, this time against the apparently more affluent, know-it-all, colonizing *Wessis*.

While this ultimate goal remained on the official programme throughout, there were some specific variants of it, the salience of which changed over time in the GDR. Released from imprisonment in Nazi concentration camps, returning from exile in the West or the East, many committed Social Democrats, Christians and other opponents of Nazism could well agree with Communists that the future simply had to be better, and that drastic measures might, in the short term, be necessary to ensure that Nazism could never rear its evil head again. This honeymoon period was not easy, however, and, although its history is fractured, it could be suggested that the decade from 1948 to 1958 saw its death through processes of disillusionment and expulsion. Yet it should be remembered that the importance of building a better future was genuinely believed in as a political goal in the early post-war years by at least a significant minority of committed people. The problem lay in the fact that the specific and politically dominant vision of utopia in the SED under Ulbricht was not that envisaged by many of his contemporaries. The realities of neo-Stalinist repression and stagnation began to displace the dreams of a better future.

As far as more material aspirations were concerned, utopia soon was officially presented as a satisfactory substitute for jam today during the 1950s. The emphasis on sacrificing today in order to overtake the West tomorrow was not an adequate incentive, however, to prevent three million from fleeing to the West while it was still possible, before 1961. Even in the 1960s, under the New Economic System, a tacit postponement of utopia and emphasis on the present, more characteristic of the Honecker period, began to be apparent. In the early Honecker years there was a much higher emphasis given to the satisfaction of consumer needs in the here and now, when the utopia of tomorrow began to recede as an attainable and realistic goal. Having replaced utopia on the immediate political programme by a crass materialism worthy of Western capitalism, the SED found the economic difficulties of the 1980s a shade embarrassing.[19] As the streams of refugees to the West in the summer of 1989 were to show, loss of the myth of a glorious future left no reason to remain in a near bankrupt present.

On the whole, the record of the GDR suggests that myths of the glorious future really only worked for the already committed. There is some evidence, for example, to suggest that even top Party apparatchiks were somewhat discomforted by such a blatant violation of human rights as the erection of the Berlin Wall; but they persuaded

---

19 . Some scholars have interpreted the resurrection of German national heroes at a time of economic difficulty in the 1980s in this way; see, for example, Harold James, *A German Identity, 1700–1990*, revised edition, London, 1990.

themselves to accept it as an essential short-term measure in order to achieve long-term goals (and their self-persuasion was mightily helped along by the processes of Party discipline).[20] The ends justified the means.

But not for ever, and not under every conceivable circumstance. In the 1980s, substantial numbers of apparatchiks began to get increasingly uneasy about the unwillingness of Honecker and his gerontocracy even to admit, let alone address, the mounting economic, environmental and political problems of the GDR. For a brief historical moment, Gorbachev appeared to hold out the hope, yet again, of a better future, particularly among genuinely reformist SED functionaries such as Hans Modrow. Even for cynics like Honecker's short-lived successor Egon Krenz, Gorbachev at least appeared to offer apparently reformist tactics and an acceptable public face behind which the SED could regroup and recover its hold on power. But in the event, *perestroika* and *glasnost´* could only come packaged in Western clothes; as rule by the SED and the Stasi collapsed in the face of candles and prayers, the majority ensured that a glorious future was abandoned in favour of a West German present.

Conclusions: Not Quite a Nation

Myths are not all there is to the construction of a nation. Official myths did not resonate well in the GDR, not only because of disjunctures with popular collective memory (and popular myths, however partially suppressed), but also because the associated values and goals were not widely shared. The GDR was not based on a shared consensus: it was based on complicity, collusion, the threat or reality of coercion, a degree of ambivalence and apathy. East Germans retained a sense of a common past with the West, even as their patterns of behaviour, their attitudes and assumptions, and their styles of life radically diverged from those prevalent in a West Germany which was also changing. It is from this curious background that the fault lines and fractures in 'unified' Germany must be understood.

It is, however, possible to engage in some more general reflections, or hypothetical ruminations. Had international and economic conditions been otherwise, and had the Soviet bloc, including the GDR, not collapsed, with the passage of time the Federal Republic might eventually have conceded full recognition to the GDR, including retraction of the right of East Germans to automatic citizenship in West Germany. It is just about possible that, with the passing of generations, eventually the founding myths would no longer have

---

20. See, for example, Günter Schabowski, *Das Politbüro*, Hamburg, 1990, for a relatively plausible retrospective attempt at self-justification along these lines.

appeared so absurd, the dissonances between reality and myth would have lessened or at least become less salient. Myth would have become a matter of unexamined rhetoric and ritual.

The role of myths may be highly important as far as certain political élites with the will to form a nation are concerned. But it is essentially *politics* which determines whether a 'nation-state' will be formed, and what precise shape it will take. The history of modern European nation-states suggests that a combination of factors (including economic and military ones) are crucial in the essentially contingent processes of nation-state formation. Once the self-proclaimed nation-state itself is securely established, a variety of institutions, practices and symbols will help to propagate a particular version of its identity, with varying degrees of resonance among different groups in the population.[21] And the success of the state — or at least its establishment against serious challenge — will help to secure the success of its myths.

The limits of the SED's attempts at the propagation of myths reveal in part the limits of its attempts to create a new socialist nation. But, as Karl Marx should have been able to tell the SED leadership, ideology is never quite enough. There needs to be, as Gramsci more perspicaciously pointed out, a degree of recognition of the people's own views and experiences, however fragmented and incomplete, for the more coherent bodies of thought articulated by organic intellectuals to attain truly hegemonic status. Myths may be essential to the construction of nations; but they are not all there is to nation-building, and not all myths are equally available for effective appropriation.

21. Obviously this paragraph relates to a whole host of questions about nation- and state-building which go beyond the scope of this chapter, and cannot be discussed further in this context.

MAKING HISTORY: MYTH AND THE CONSTRUCTION OF AMERICAN NATIONHOOD

Susan-Mary Grant

'Fiery the Angels rose, & as they rose deep thunder roll'd
Around their shores: indignant burning with the fires of Orc.'
(William Blake, *America: A Prophecy*, 1793)

Introduction

At its most simple, the construction of America as a nation can be viewed as a process comprising two distinct phases: creation and consolidation. The first of these, the American Revolution, was a product of the eighteenth century and the second, the Civil War, of the nineteenth. Of the two, however, it was the latter which created the American nation *qua* nation, and in the process transformed the original act of creation into one of the founding myths of national construction. In effect, nineteenth-century Americans, in an attempt to realize what they regarded as the legacy of the Founding Fathers, replaced their colonial and revolutionary past as it was with the past as they wished it to be. The result was two contradictory interpretations of that past, Northern (Puritan/Yankee) and Southern (Cavalier), two differing ideologies that eventually led to a war which, according to some, transformed a 'Union' into a 'Nation'. However, the victory of the Northern/Yankee variant of American ideology has not only obscured the process of national construction in the nineteenth century, but has hindered our appreciation of the central function of myth in the construction and consolidation of the American nation. This chapter will seek to unravel the process of American national construction in order to show not only how Americans came to regard themselves as a separate nation, but what kind of nation they intended to be.

The eighteenth-century poet and mystic William Blake portrayed the emergence of the American nation in mythic terms. His imaginative account of the battle between George Washington and 'The Guardian Prince of Albion' located the revolt of the thirteen colonies against George III within a 'larger impulse towards spiritual rebirth and revelation'.[1] In both his understanding of the idealism of the Founding Fathers and his sense of what kind of nation America hoped to be,

---

1.   P. Ackroyd, *Blake*, reprint, London, 1995, pp. 169–71.

Blake was ahead of his time. He remains so over two hundred years later. Towards the end of the twentieth century, scholarly interest in nationalism is on the increase, yet the dominant nation of this century remains on the sidelines in nationalism studies. In light of the fact that several of the most prolific writers on the subject of nationalism — including Walker Connor and Benedict Anderson — work in the United States, it is all the more difficult to understand why the process of national construction in America remains so neglected. Some explanation for this general unwillingness on the part of nationalism scholars to engage with the American case has been put forward by Parish, who sees it as a result of the combined forces of academic specialization, ideological inclination and Eurocentrism. As he points out, however, nationalism scholars are the losers. America offers the prime example of the voluntaristic nation as defined by Gellner, and 'was well ahead of the field in meeting many of the conditions — political democracy, education, mobility, and so on — for the creation of the kind of "imagined community" which Anderson describes'.[2]

A similar point is made by the author of the only recent full-length study of American nationalism, Zelinsky, who further suggests that, given 'the extraordinary character of its inception', America may have more to teach us about 'the essential nature of nationalism and statism than any other example'. In America, he argues, 'we have as close a simulation to a controlled laboratory experiment as the vagaries of history will permit'.[3] The laboratory metaphor is questionable. In a nation of immigrants which experienced a remarkable period of diversification and expansion in the nineteenth century, the hygienic clarity of the laboratory metaphor soon breaks down. Nevertheless, the essential point remains. Scholars of nationalism can learn much from the American example, particularly when it comes to the myths that support the collective existence of a nation. America is closer to the past than many of the older, European nations. The forces that constructed the American nation — military, social, religious, economic and political — remain sharp and distinct, unblurred by time. This has served to hinder rather than help America achieve and sustain a strong sense of nationhood. It is 'uncomfortable to be reminded of the forced nature of one's national genesis', yet for a country born in Revolution and matured in Civil War, such discomfort can hardly be

---

2. P.J. Parish, 'Confidence and Anxiety in Victorian America' in *Uppsala North American Studies Reports*, no. 6, Uppsala, 1991, pp. 227–8; S.-M. Grant, 'When is a Nation not a Nation? The Crisis of American Nationality in the Mid-Nineteenth Century' in *Nations and Nationalism*, 1996, 2, pp. 108–12.
3. W. Zelinsky, *Nation Into State: The Shifting Symbolic Foundations of American Nationalism*, Chapel Hill, NC and London, 1988 (hereafter *Nation Into State*), pp. 6, 15.

avoided.[4] Consequently, many of the myths that support the American nation focus on these events, and interpret them in such a way as to produce unity from disunity, consensus from conflict. America provides us with the opportunity to examine this process. In the American case it is possible to isolate the myths that, over the years between the nation's supposed inception in 1776 and the victory of the Union forces in 1865, served both to consolidate and undermine the development of the largest, as well as the most neglected, democratic civic society of the modern period.

Nationhood Achieved?

Initially, the American colonists invoked not myth but solid legal argument in support of their national ambitions. Usefully, for nationalism scholars, a founding document, the Declaration of Independence, was the result. On the question of separate nationhood, it was unequivocal: 'these United Colonies are, and of right ought to be, Free and Independent States', it asserts. As far as the actual process of the political construction of the American nation is concerned, it was the Constitution, rather than the Declaration of Independence, which established the framework of government, but it was, and is, the Declaration of Independence that Americans invoked as their first and most powerful national symbol. They supported its philosophical constructs and ideological ambitions with additional symbols: the national flag; the eagle; the Great Seal, with its classical allusions, 'Incipit Novus Ordo Saeclorum', derived from Virgil and drawing a deliberate parallel between the newly formed United States and the Christian mission on earth; and 'E Pluribus Unum', which was never, in fact, approved by Congress as the official national motto. 'In God We Trust' is, in fact, the national motto, proposed in 1861 as the nation faced civil war, but not ratified until 1956. Zelinsky,[5] in particular, provides a sustained analysis of these symbols, although he neglects to mention that the eagle was almost a turkey. But, so far as the myths of national construction are concerned, one needs to consider more closely how Americans responded to the discrepancy between what was being invoked and what was being practised.[6]

---

4.   David L. Miller, *On Nationality*, New York, 1995, p. 34.
5.   Zelinsky, *Nation Into State*, pp. 117–27.
6.   For further discussion of the Great Seal, see Conor Cruise O'Brien, *God Land: Reflections on Religions and Nationalism*, Cambridge, MA, 1988, p. 62. Benjamin Franklin was opposed to the adoption of the eagle as the national bird, believing it to be too aggressive a symbol. He favoured instead the turkey.

The Declaration of Independence actually lends a false clarity to the process of American national construction. Zelinsky[7] argues that, as far as American national development is concerned, 'we can pinpoint most watershed events with precision, sometimes down to the very day and street address (e.g. July 2, 1776, 550 Chestnut Street, Philadelphia, Pa.)'. This is a gross over-simplification of a complex process which was neither begun nor concluded in a single day in a house in Philadelphia. The title of a recent textbook on the American Revolution expresses a similar confidence in its subtitle, 'Nationhood Achieved, 1763–1788'.[8] However, the construction of the American nation, and the development of the belief that Americans were a distinct and separate people, was the result of a lengthy process comprising philosophical, ideological, mythological, religious and political constructions and reassessments carried out over many years. As far as historians of the United States are concerned, most would agree that, in the American case, the 'nation was the child, not the father of the revolution', yet one needs to go further, because this was a child that took many years to develop and at great social, economic, political and, finally, military cost.[9] It was not a process that was completed, or even deemed to be completed, by 1788, and, whilst we can identify with some accuracy the date and location of the signing of the Declaration of Independence, this in itself does not help explain why this was a 'watershed' event nor how it even came to take place. In any case, as with so many American 'national' documents, the Declaration of Independence would have turned out to be so much worthless rhetoric had it not been accompanied by eventual military victory at Yorktown. In America, as elsewhere, professions of national sentiment would have rung hollow indeed, and been long since forgotten, had the point not been carried with a bayonet or a rifle.

This may seem rather an obvious point, yet it is one which goes straight to the heart of one of the central myths of American national construction, namely that the ultimate victory of the Americans over the British and, later, the North over the South, was in some way pre-ordained, that a nation destined to provide guidance for the rest of mankind could not have failed to emerge in the way it did. This is the foundation myth of the unique origins of the United States, as a nation 'under God', as a 'Redeemer Nation' or a 'City on a Hill'. It presents the Revolution not as a military victory, but rather as the natural product of an Enlightenment philosophy which found its fullest and

---

7.   Zelinsky, *Nation Into State*, p. 15.
8.   H.M. Ward, *The American Revolution: Nationhood Achieved, 1763–1788*, New York, 1995.
9.   E.S. Morgan, *The Birth of the Republic, 1763–89*, revised edition, Chicago, IL and London, 1977, p. 100.

best expression in a populace physically and intellectually honed by the rigours of the frontier experience to be receptive to new, republican ideas. One could argue that America was a nation spurred into existence by the behaviour of the British government, who saw — long before the colonists themselves did — the implications of American nationalism.[10] Yet the myth of American exceptionalism, the idea that America represents 'an ideological construct, the materialization of novel ideas that had been smouldering among the intellectually and religiously disaffected far and wide within the Atlantic community', has greater appeal.[11] It is a myth that resonates down through American history, from the arrival of the Pilgrim Fathers on Plymouth Rock to the stories of the Oregon Trail and the opening of the West. It rests on an idealized version of the New England Puritan past, virtually ignores the Southern colonies, and downplays the extent of the disagreements and differences between the colonists themselves, since what is frequently overlooked is the fact that the Revolutionary War, like the later Civil War, was a war fought between neighbours, and not just against British forces. As one observer noted at the time of the Revolution: 'It matters little whether the Americans win or lose. Presently this country is the scene of the most cruel events. Neighbors are on opposite sides, children are against their fathers. Anyone who differs with the opinions of Congress in thought or in speech is regarded as an enemy and turned over to the hangman, or else he must flee.'[12] Historians are, of course, well aware of the reality behind the war fought for American independence and the position of the loyalists at that time, some 60,000 of whom were forced to flee to Nova Scotia, Canada, New Brunswick or back to Britain. Yet the myth of American consensus against the British oppressor is hard to shake, and the popular image of the Revolution remains quite distinct from the events that actually took place. Writing just before America's bicentennial celebrations of 1976, Shy reflected that:

the Bicentennial itself, and [American] anxiety about it, is a continuation of the national myth which began in the 1780's, when the elation of ultimate victory combined with the sour memories of widespread human weakness and depravity as revealed in the seven-year struggle, to produce a wonderfully creative period in American politics. The ink was barely dry on

10. *Ibid.*, pp. 100–2.
11. Zelinsky, *Nation Into State*, pp. 16–17.
12. Undated letter quoted in Ernst Kipping, *The Hessian View of America, 1776–1783*, trans. B.A. Uhlendorf, Monmouth Beach, NJ, 1971, pp. 34–5, also quoted in J. Shy, *A People Numerous and Armed: Reflections on the Military Struggle for American Independence*, revised edition, Ann Arbor, MI, 1990 (hereafter *A People Numerous and Armed*), p. 23.

the Treaty of Paris before myth and reality about the Revolutionary War were becoming entwined.[13]

So, far from an event in which Americans rose up as a man against the wicked British oppressor, Americans served in the Revolutionary War in as haphazard a way as they did in the later Civil War. Following an initial burst of enthusiasm, war-weariness and disillusion both took their toll. As Shy notes, this is not the way in which Americans like to think about the beginnings of their nation, yet for the Revolutionary generation itself there was little alternative. They could hardly avoid the lessons of a war that had ended 'not with Napoleonic victories or massive defections from the enemy armies, but with ragged unpaid American soldiers drifting down the Hudson valley to sign on as sailors in the ships which were evacuating British forces, while American officers back at Newburgh half-heartedly planned a coup d'état to get the money owed them by Congress'.[14] All too aware of the precariousness of their new political experiment, aware, too, that the reality of its achievement did not coincide with the ideals it proclaimed, the Americans' search for unifying, 'national' symbols began almost at once.

Zelinsky sums up America's problem bluntly: 'Before 1776', he points out, 'the new nation was symbolically impoverished, lacking its own music, literature, art, native costume or cuisine, and homegrown heroes.' The most pressing problem, but the one which it was in the American power to address, was the creation of eidolons — mythical ideal figures — as unifying symbols for a nation newly conceived, if not quite yet born. The history of America shows 'just how vital to the forging of a nation it is to have a lively set of eidolons', particularly if one is seeking to create 'a strong sense of nationhood in a hurry'. The first such ideal figure was, of course, George Washington, the 'Father of his Country', and much has been written about the uses to which the image of Washington has been put over the years. It is Washington, along with Jefferson and Lincoln, who symbolizes the American 'nation', and this is made nowhere more obvious than in the memorials that have been erected in Washington, DC. When one considers the achievement of American nationhood, many would agree that Washington's 'actual deeds and, perhaps more to the point, his numinous symbolic presence were absolutely central elements in the success of this unprecedented project'.[15]

---

13. *Ibid.*, pp. 25–6. Shy's essay was originally written in 1974 and revised in 1975. Figures for the number of loyalists who fled are also taken from this source (pp. 245–61).
14. *Ibid.*, pp. 22–3, 25.
15. Zelinsky, *Nation Into State*, pp. 21, 30–4.

As an eidolon, however, Washington incorporated contradictory features. Certainly he sought to direct his countrymen toward the path of successful nationhood, most notably in his 'Farewell Address' (1796) to the new nation he had done so much to create. The dominant theme of this was the overwhelming need to avoid sectional disagreement, to foster national unity. In his 'Farewell Address' Washington encouraged Americans 'to see themselves as an entirely new breed in a young and rapidly evolving land'.[16] This was a theme that encapsulated the ambitions of the fledgling nation, the idea of universal participation in the republican experiment, of a people bonded not by ethnic or historical ties, but through political inclusiveness and, most importantly, by choice.[17] This was clearly a nation which, if it had not yet achieved the unity of true nationhood, nevertheless harboured a strong desire to do so. Although 'Early political discourse in the USA preferred to speak of "the people", "the union", "the confederation", "our common land", "the public", "public welfare", or "the community" in order to avoid the centralizing and unitary implications of the term "nation" against the rights of the federated states', these constructions were understood in singular, as well as in plural terms.[18] It did not occur to the colonists to construct thirteen separate nations, indeed, '"independent states" must have been intended to convey a singular as well as a plural meaning, for it was Congress, the central government of the nation that levied war against Great Britain, contracted an alliance with France and concluded peace'.[19]

Washington himself saw the central importance of the Union. Only this, he asserted, could ensure the future safety and success of America. Yet in part Washington himself laid the groundwork for the one issue that would prove the Union's temporary undoing. Like the author of the Declaration of Independence, Thomas Jefferson, the 'Father of his Country' was a slaveholder. Washington went to war for liberty, yet perpetuated slavery. Historians have devoted considerable effort towards understanding and explaining the phenomenon that came to be termed the 'Jeffersonian paradox': how a people who declared that 'all men are created equal, that they are endowed by their Creator with certain unalienable Rights, that among these are Life, Liberty and the pursuit of Happiness' could justify the retention of a system of unfree labour. These are not arguments that I wish to reiterate here. What is of

16. R.N. Smith, *Patriarch: George Washington and the New American Nation*, Boston, MA and New York, 1993, p. 280.
17. K. Malik, *The Meaning of Race: Race, History and Culture in Western Society*, London, 1996 (hereafter *The Meaning of Race*), pp. 133–4; E.J. Hobsbawm, *Nations and Nationalism Since 1780: Programme, Myth, Reality*, reprint, Cambridge, 1991, pp. 18–20.
18. Malik, *The Meaning of Race*, p. 18.
19. Morgan, *The Birth of the Republic*, p. 102.

interest in an assessment of the myths that supported the creation and consolidation of the American nation, is how this paradox worked against the construction of a successful and unifying national myth, creating instead divisive, sectional myths that drove the nation apart.

Nationhood Contested

Between the Revolution and the Civil War, Americans struggled to draw out of their history the myths they required for national stability. It fell to the generation born after the Revolution to 'give meaning to the American past, present, and future [...] to discover for themselves in a shifting environment what it meant to be an American and what the destiny of America was'.[20] Consequently, American history itself became the new national preoccupation. This is not surprising. 'An aesthetically and emotionally satisfying myth of origins is not only a necessary ingredient of an evolving national identity but a prerequisite for a sense of future direction and development.'[21] When Americans in this period turned to the past they were trying to clarify it, to establish what, exactly, its lessons were. This was not an easy task. As one nineteenth-century New Yorker noted, 'We are so young a people that we feel the want of nationality, and delight in whatever asserts our national "American" existence. We have not, like England and France, centuries of achievement and calamities to look back on; we have no *record* of Americanism and we feel its want.'[22] Ante-bellum Americans were, in effect, attempting to create a 'record of Americanism', which would provide them with a blueprint for the future. History was not, therefore, studied for its own sake, but rather used to invoke a precedent. One minister reminded his flock:

how dearly the Fathers prized the right of free discussion. It was for this one purpose mainly that they left their native land, and pitched their tents in an untrodden wilderness. It was on this one point more than all others that they took issue with the despots of the old world. Authority and prescription could not bind their conscience. The decrees of Synods and Popes could not control their mind. The edicts of aristocracies and oligarchies could not manacle their opinions. They held to free speech and a free press [...]. Free thought and free speech are fundamental to this

---

20. F. Somkin, *Unquiet Eagle: Memory and Desire in the Idea of American Freedom, 1815–1860*, Ithaca, NY, 1967, pp. 3–4.
21. J.V. Matthews, '"Whig History": The New England Whigs and a Usable Past' in *The New England Quarterly*, 51, 1978, p. 193.
22. George Templeton Strong, diary entry for 8 November 1854, reproduced in Allan Nevins (ed.), *The Diary of George Templeton Strong: The Turbulent Fifties, 1850–1859*, New York, 1952, pp. 196–7.

Republic. Our whole scheme of government and religion is built upon them.[23]

This kind of argument was typical of the period, and almost entirely mythical. Whilst some colonists might well have been motivated to migrate for the reasons the minister describes, many were far less idealistically inclined. As a result, colonial society was both varied and, to a very great extent, violent, since 'these were dangerous times, with violent people and tough leaders who felt the dangers keenly and were ready to use violence themselves'.[24] Equally unsettling was the establishment of a racial divide in the Chesapeake colonies. Such unsavoury elements were, however, written out of the story by the first historians of America, who preferred instead to focus on the myth of progress. As Appleby points out, not only was the greed, violence and general incompetence of the colonial past conveniently ignored, but, as told by the first historians, 'the settlement of America has all the simple rhythms and repeated choruses of a popular ballad [...]. The story begins with English Pilgrims fleeing persecution and ends with Lincoln's fervid hope that "government of the people, by the people and for the people shall not perish from the earth".' She warns, however, that one should be careful not to scoff at this mythologizing of the American past, for it was much 'more than a literary production'. Its focus on progress and on industrious migrants on the New World frontier served to obscure the potentially embarrassing 'memory of those uprooted Africans and cast-off Europeans who had also become Americans'.[25]

More significantly, the early historians of, and spokesmen for, America did not confine themselves to whitewashing the nation's past, but often rewrote it with a distinctly sectional slant. This was nowhere more true than in the Northern states in the nineteenth century, where hardly an opportunity was missed to make sectional capital out of the national past. For individuals so inclined, however, there was a potential problem. Southerners had played a fairly central role in the creation of the new nation, especially in the leadership sense. Zelinsky reminds us that a 'large, perhaps disproportionate, share of early American patriot heroes were Southerners',[26] from the presidents Washington through Jefferson, Madison, Monroe, to military heroes such as Richard Henry Lee and Patrick Henry. Northerners responded to this fact in one of two ways. They either acknowledged it, and used it

23. Edin B. Foster, *A Sermon on the Crime Against Freedom*, Concord, 1856, pp. 4, 6–9, 20.
24. Shy, *A People Numerous and Armed*, pp. 274–5.
25. J. Appleby, *Liberalism and Republicanism in the Historical Imagination*, Cambridge, MA, 1992, pp. 4–5, 6–7.
26. Zelinsky, *Nation Into State*, p. 127.

to support their argument that the South enjoyed, and had done from the outset, too much power in the nation, or they queried it, and argued instead that the South had not shared the burden of the Revolutionary struggle equally with the North. Between North and South in the ante-bellum period, the past became yet another bone of contention, as Franklin has shown. Southerners reacted strongly against the Northern analysis of the Revolutionary period. They detected a tendency on the part of Bancroft — the first American historian, and a Northerner — and Northerners in general 'to glorify the deeds of the heroes of their section', and concluded that 'southerners could not entrust to northerners the responsibility of recording something so important as the South's role in the American Revolution'. The South, of course, responded in kind, and argued that it was they, not the North, who had done more to secure the Revolution's outcome. Here 'was a strange spectacle indeed. Here were two sections that were virtually at war with each other in the 1850s, not merely over the current problems that beset them but also over their comparative strengths and weaknesses during the war for independence.'[27] It was a ludicrous, not to say wholly anachronistic argument, but both sides took the matter very seriously. In this spirit of sectional antagonism, the New York *Tribune* advised its readers that from 'the origin of our National history, the North has been steadily loyal and devoted to the Union, while every formidable opposition to it has derived its impulse and power from the South'. Naturally inclined towards loyalist, Tory politics, it asserted, the South had been a hindrance rather than a help to the nation during its Revolutionary struggle.[28]

Supporting these alternative views of the Revolutionary past was the belief that North and South had different ethnic origins, that they were not, and never had been, one and the same people in genealogical terms. One Northerner argued that the North had been settled by the Anglo-Saxon race, which was 'farther advanced in civilization, more enterprising and persevering, with more science and art, with more skill and capital, and with the advantage in the main of a homogeneous population'. The South, by contrast, constituted 'a lower civilization'.[29] One New York minister, likewise, attempting to guide his flock toward 'the national idea which will create our national character', advised them that 'Virginia and Massachusetts were an

27. J.H. Franklin, 'The North, the South, and the American Revolution' in *The Journal of American History*, 62, 1975, pp. 8, 17.
28. *New York Daily Tribune*, 9 October 1856.
29. Samuel Nott, *Slavery, and The Remedy*, New York, 1856, pp. 20–1.

extension of the Cavalier and Puritan into the Western continent'.[30]
The myth of the 'Cavalier' and 'Yankee' has been extensively studied
by Taylor,[31] who argues that Northerners, alarmed at the pace of
nineteenth-century change, looked to the South as an ordered,
aristocratic society with its roots firmly in the Old World. As such, it
represented stability in an uncertain world. However, for an increasing
number of northerners at this time, this version of the South —
whether it consoled them or not — represented the past. It was a
romanticized past, a literary construction, as inaccurate historically as
it was comforting psychologically. The Cavalier myth, with its clear
reference to the England of the seventeenth century, was an
anachronism in the nineteenth-century world that ante-bellum
Americans inhabited. This was a view shared by Northerners who did
not find much to admire in the South, who were, in fact, openly
hostile to it and to the system of slavery that it both maintained and
defended. For them, the South represented the past, a redundant past
that had no place in America's future.

For an increasing number of ante-bellum Americans, therefore, the
past became ammunition in the war over the future. Again, this is not
surprising. As Malik points out, national loyalty was especially
difficult to create and sustain in the 'new nation-states such as Italy or
the USA, where nationhood imposed a sense of collectivity upon
disparate peoples, who had not previously considered themselves to be
part of the same collective'.[32] He sees this as a post-bellum
phenomenon, but it is clear that the argument applies far more
successfully to ante-bellum American thought. As Parish has argued,
one of the strategies employed by Americans 'for overcoming the lack
of a long history was to focus attention upon the national future', and
this, combined with 'the strong postmillennial emphasis in American
Protestantism gave an extra dimension to the concept of the
missionary nation'.[33] Time and again, Americans were reminded of
their national mission to act as an example to all mankind. 'The
wonderful progress of this country in population and wealth, has
excited the astonishment of the world', one paper exulted. 'The friends
of free institutions everywhere, have watched this progress with
admiration, and have adduced the success which has attended our

30. Rev. A.D. Mayo, sermon delivered on 23 November in New York State (no
     location given, but probably Albany), and printed in the *Albany Evening Journal*,
     24 November 1856.
31. William R. Taylor, *Cavalier and Yankee: The Old South and American National
     Character*, Cambridge, MA, 1961, reissued 1979.
32. Malik, *The Meaning of Race*, p. 138.
33. P.J. Parish, 'An Exception to Most of the Rules: What Made American
     Nationalism Different in the Mid-Nineteenth Century?' (hereafter 'An
     Exception') in *Prologue*, 27, 1995, p. 222.

experiment, as a triumphant illustration of the capability of the people for self-government.'[34] Ultimately, however, more was at stake than the admiration, or recognition, of the rest of the world. The very idea of America was rooted in this experiment in self-government. As the New York *Tribune* argued, American nationality was 'a thing of ideas solely, and not a thing of races. It is neither English nor Irish, nor Dutch, nor French; it is not Puritan nor Cavalier; it is not North nor South; our nationality is our self-government, our system of popular liberty and equal law [...] aside from the identity of our national principles we have no national identity, nor shall we for centuries.'[35]

Yet as the ante-bellum period progressed, the disparate elements of America which the *Tribune* had identified — Puritan and Cavalier, North and South — were pulling in opposite directions as far as the national mission was concerned. For post-Revolutionary Americans, the interpretation of their national ideals represented the root of the problem. The central ideals of the national myth of America can be summed up in two simple words — Liberty and Equality — as in the first sentence of Lincoln's Gettysburg Address: 'Four score and seven years ago our fathers brought forth on this continent, a new nation, conceived in Liberty, and dedicated to the proposition that all men are created equal.' Yet, in the formative period of the American nation what did Americans understand by these concepts? In the middle of the Civil War, Abraham Lincoln summed up the problem for many Americans when he observed that 'The world has never had a good definition of the word liberty, and the American people, just now, are much in want of one. We all declare for liberty; but in using the same *word* we do not all mean the same *thing*.'[36] For Northerners, Lincoln went on, liberty was understood to mean the ability to control one's own life and labour; but Southerners took it to mean the ability to control the lives and the labour of others, their slaves. Equality, likewise, meant many things to many people, and the opening line of the Declaration of Independence, that all men are created equal, was to prove an even more contentious issue than the question of what, exactly, was meant by 'liberty'. Yet it was an idea with strong, and lasting, appeal. Pole reminds us:

The idea of equality, in its varying manifestations, had thus revealed since the nation's founding hours a tenacity which afforded a peculiar glamor to American claims and pretensions, and some justification to the offer, or threat, of social justice which America had always claimed to hold out to

34. *Albany Evening Journal*, 23 January 1847.
35. *New York Daily Tribune*, 7 November 1854.
36. Abraham Lincoln, 'Address at Sanitary Fair, Baltimore, Maryland', 18 April 1864, in *The Collected Works of Abraham Lincoln*, New Brunswick, NJ, 1988, vol. 7, pp. 301–2.

the common people in the face of the empires, monarchies, priesthoods, social hierarchies, and all their attendant prejudices, of the Old World.[37]

Americans began their life as a new nation — or a nation-in-waiting — theoretically united by these ideas. They represented a new people, and out of the diversity of their plural colonial past they would construct a new, singular future — *E Pluribus Unum*. Further, they would construct a new, secular state, *Incipit Novus Ordo Saeclorum*, unencumbered by the trappings of religious proscriptions. Yet the glaring discrepancies between what was professed and what existed were too fundamental to ignore, and the myths that Americans constructed to support their national experiment proved insufficient to the task at hand. Rather than pulling the nation together, the myth of liberty and equality served to drive it apart. The sectional fault lines that were to rupture the Union in 1861 were present from the outset, as Washington well realized, and gave the lie to the *E Pluribus Unum* idea. The new secular nation preserved its unity by portraying itself as a chosen land, a chosen people. If the idea of God had been removed from government, it was nevertheless invoked everywhere else. In effect, the new American nation had been constructed on ground that was fertile, but unstable, and nowhere was that instability more apparent than in the myth of liberty and the reality of slavery. It is hardly overstating the case to argue that the consolidation of slavery as a labour system in the South 'may have been one of the most important, enduring, and paradoxical legacies of the Revolutionary War'.[38]

Following their Revolution, Americans could not identify the common ground necessary for the construction of nationhood, because the revolutionary process itself had removed that ground from them. Liberty and equality, from the outset, meant very different things to each section, and so the myth diverged. American nationalists, in common with nationalists elsewhere, 'rewrote the past to establish the idea of an organic nationhood stretching back through time'. As elsewhere, too, this 'historical rewriting [...] was buttressed by the invention of national traditions'.[39] What was especially divisive in America is that these national traditions ceased, in the course of the ante-bellum period, to find truly national expression. Both North and South believed that they, and not the other, were faithful to the ideals of the Founding Fathers. Both believed that Freedom and Equality found their best expression in their section, and did not exist in the other. In the mid-nineteenth century, the myths of American national

37. J.R. Pole, *The Pursuit of Equality in American History*, revised edition, Berkeley, CA and Oxford, 1993, pp. 4–5.
38. Shy, *A People Numerous and Armed*, p. 257.
39. Malik, *The Meaning of Race*, p. 140.

construction became weapons which North and South, increasingly, turned on each other.

Nationhood Enforced

Ultimately, of course, North and South traded verbal weapons for real ones and, by 1865, the questions over the validity of American, as opposed to Southern, nationalism had, at least nominally, been settled. The Civil War was the event that most would argue established the existence of the American nation and validated the republican experiment in self-government. One should not, perhaps, express any surprise at this. It is, after all, war 'which turns a people into a nation', according to the nineteenth-century military historian Heinrich von Treitschke.[40] Civil wars are, however, a different matter. It is in the peculiar, and internecine, nature of such wars that they are neither lost nor won, and simultaneously both lost and won by one nation and by the same people. In the American case, von Treitschke's statement does, initially, seem to make sense. By preventing the South from leaving, or destroying, the Union, the North had succeeded in making a nation. However, the Civil War 'compromised the voluntary principle at the root of the American nation by the resort to compulsion in order to save the Union'.[41] In order to re-establish the nation in the aftermath of such a conflict, Americans had to construct an entirely new set of myths and a new pantheon of ideal figures, as well as reinforcing the old ones.

The focus of the new national myths was, of course, the Civil War itself, and its role in the achievement of American nationality. Here, too, Americans had precedents to inform them. As Shy has argued, the whole notion of warfare is 'tightly bound up with American national identity'.[42] Furthermore, he suggests that, from the Seven Years' War (1754–63) onwards, a similar pattern of defeat, rallying, endurance and ultimate victory can be recognized. In each case, 'the very existence of American society was seen to be at stake', and in each case America emerged victorious. Surprisingly, he concludes that the Civil War did 'little to change basic American patterns of thought and action'. Yet the Civil War, like the three previous wars that Shy identifies — the Seven Years' War, the Revolution, the War of 1812 — fits into this same pattern. Seen from the Northern — ultimately the victorious — perspective, the initial defeat at Bull Run was followed by four years of increasingly brutal conflict and an eventual series of victories over the

40. Quoted from Heinrich von Treitschke in David Potter, *The South and the Sectional Conflict*, Baton Rouge, LA, 1968, p. 56.
41. Parish, 'An Exception', p. 226.
42. Shy, *A People Numerous and Armed*, p. 284.

Confederacy which led to military victory and the consolidation of nationhood. The Civil War, more than any other, had strong and obvious links with the Revolutionary conflict of the eighteenth century, and of all the wars fought by America, it was the Civil War in which the very existence of America was at stake. For Americans at the time and since, the Civil War holds a special place in the national consciousness; it was America's 'jihad'.[43]

Both North and South, in addition, used the Revolutionary conflict as justification for their respective positions. The South's defence for its actions, and the right of secession itself, was derived from the statement in the Declaration of Independence that 'it is the Right of the people to alter or to abolish' any form of government that ceases to guarantee their liberties, 'and to institute new Government, laying its foundation on such principles and organizing its powers in such form, as to them shall seem most likely to effect their safety and Happiness'. The North's defence of the Union, likewise, was predicated on the lessons of the past — or the past as the North and Lincoln interpreted it. The Civil War, for many in the North, was a re-enactment of the Revolutionary conflict, and was presented by Lincoln as the achievement of America's destiny. If Americans truly were a chosen people, an example for the rest of mankind to follow, then it was imperative that the Union not be broken, that the South not be permitted to secede, that national forces were victorious. Of course, at the time these forces, and these ideas, were not national, but strongest in the Northern states. Increasingly during the ante-bellum period, and openly once the war broke out, the North took to itself both the symbolism and the ideology of American nationality, and denied to the South full participation in the American idea except on Northern terms.

History is written by the winners, and the North's victory in the Civil War not only secured the existence of America as a nation, but defined how that nation, and the war which created it, would be interpreted. The whole question of sectional interaction in the ante-bellum period is dominated and overshadowed by the Civil War that came in 1861. Without becoming too involved in a discussion of the causes of the American Civil War, it is nevertheless worth making the point that historians, in the main, regard the Northern position as reactive, the Southern as proactive in their discussions of the issues involved. Certainly it was the South that seceded, and some historians have attributed this to the development, from *c*.1830 onwards, of 'Southern nationalism'. The construction of the argument, at its most simplistic, is that Northerners consistently supported the Union,

---

43. T.P. Lowry, *The Story the Soldiers Wouldn't Tell: Sex and the American Civil War*, New York, 1994 (hereafter *Sex and the American Civil War*), p. 7.

whereas a small, but increasingly influential, group in the South did not. Eventually this group of extremists, led by South Carolina, left the Union, and the North took up arms in order to hold the nation together. The outcome we know. The North won, the slaves were freed, and a new era of American history inaugurated. Southern nationalism had proved itself insufficient to the task at hand. It was, therefore, not a true nationalism, but an aberration, a myth, an ideology too weak to keep men in the field by 1865. American nationalism, the 'real' nationalism, triumphed.

As a further consequence of Union victory in 1865, and in part too because of his assassination in the same year, Lincoln joined the pantheon of American eidolons, taking his place alongside Washington and Jefferson in national mythology. Yet the apotheosis of Lincoln has, to a great degree, obscured the reality of the Civil War for subsequent generations. Lincoln's personal identification with the Union, his decision to issue the Emancipation Proclamation, and his invocation of the American nation in the Gettysburg Address have been taken as sufficient proof that America as a whole subscribed to such ideas. Of course it did not, a fact that Lincoln was well aware of. He recognized, for example, that the major flaw in the national fabric, the issue of slavery, had to be addressed, but it was a far from straightforward matter. If the North had actually been, as it eventually proclaimed to be, devoted to the ideals of freedom and equality, then the question of emancipation would not have had to have been addressed in the roundabout, and ultimately unsatisfactory, manner that it was. The necessity of trying to achieve emancipation in a nation where few supported the idea meant that the Emancipation Proclamation, when it came, did not encompass the Union states, retained slavery among those who were loyal to the Union, and sought to affect it only in those areas where the Union was not in control. The fact that the slaves themselves interpreted it in a more liberal sense was surely intended, but that does not detract from the fact that Lincoln could not advocate emancipation openly, but rather had to effect it covertly. The portrayal of the Civil War as a war for freedom, therefore, is extremely misleading. This is nowhere more obvious than in the construction of the anti-slavery myth, the legend, as Woodward describes it, 'that the Mason and Dixon Line not only divided slavery from freedom in antebellum America, but that it also set apart racial inhumanity in the South from benevolence, liberality and tolerance in the North'. More significantly, 'the myth-makers credited the North with the realization in its own society of all the war aims for which it fought (or eventually proclaimed)'.[44] Ultimately, Americans succeeded in squaring

44. C.V. Woodward, 'The Antislavery Myth' in *The American Scholar*, 31, 1962, 2, p. 316.

the circle of the myth of liberty and the reality of slavery by making a national crime sectional, by placing the blame for racial injustice, inequality and the outbreak of the Civil War itself on the South alone. Yet, as a myth of national reconstruction, it had limited applicability, since the re-establishment of the South's racial and social order was achieved in a very short period of time after Appomattox, thereby undermining much of what Lincoln had worked to achieve. As a nation, post-bellum America failed to live up to the example of its most recent national hero, and yet constructed the myth that it had, in fact, done so. Given that the South, with its racial ideology, had been forced back into the nation, this is not surprising. The American state had proved itself sufficiently strong to enforce loyalty, but the ideologies of the South were unlikely to be affected by military defeat. Defeat, indeed, served only to strengthen Southern ideology, as the myth of the 'Lost Cause' makes very clear.

A brief consideration of the myths that surround the two opposing generals in the Civil War — Grant and Lee — clarifies this point. Of the two, it was Grant, clearly, who fought for the preservation of the American nation, but it is Lee who, to a considerable degree, has been better treated by history. Far from being portrayed as a noble warrior, Grant was, for many years, known as 'butcher Grant', a man profligate with the lives of his men, a general who achieved victory at considerable cost, and an alcoholic. Yet this picture of Grant, misleading as it is, was not the immediate one to emerge after the Civil War. When approving the embossing of a medallion bearing the images of Washington, Lincoln and Grant, and inscribed 'pater, liberator, salvator', Hamilton Fish (Grant's Secretary of State) expressed the hope that 'it will not be considered irreverent to say that Washington, Lincoln and Grant will be regarded as a political trinity'. Yet by the early twentieth century, as his biographer notes, Grant 'was valued less and the Lost Cause of the Confederacy, in particular, was celebrated more and more. In the shadow of the vanquished nobleman Robert E. Lee, "butcher Grant" did not appear as heroic as he once had.'[45] Lee, by contrast, was presented as a cavalier *sans peur et sans reproche,* a man torn between love of his country and loyalty to his state, unable to resolve the tensions between nationalism and sectionalism in his own life. In a recent study of the American Civil War, one historian has commented that, 'just as Charlemagne was the matter, the central motif of France and King Arthur the matter of Britain, so, too, is Robert E. Lee the matter of Dixie', and, to some degree, of America as a whole.[46]

45. W.S. McFeely, *Grant: A Biography,* reprint, New York and London, 1982, pp. 274, 522.
46. Lowry, *Sex and the American Civil War,* p. 7.

In these contradictory, and changing, images of Grant and Lee one can detect the process whereby Americans sought to rewrite the history of their Civil War, in order both to make it palatable to the opposing sides and to diminish the actual horror and bloodshed of the conflict. Ultimately, America is a nation not only defined, but actually created, by war. This in itself does not make her unique, but given the high idealism of the American national myth, with its voluntaristic ethos, it is an uncomfortable fact for Americans to live with. Furthermore, for a nation whose destiny it was to influence the world, the recognition that nationality can only be achieved at gunpoint cannot be an encouraging one. The American response was, and has been, to focus on the nobler sentiments as expressed by Lincoln in the Gettysburg Address, and on its mythical invocation of the nation. It is a point frequently made that between Lincoln's First Inaugural in 1861 and the Gettysburg Address in 1863 one can trace the shift from the concept of a voluntaristic Union to the concept of a nation. In the First Inaugural Lincoln did not use the word nation, but did refer twenty times to the 'Union'. By the time of the Gettysburg Address the word 'nation' is stressed — Lincoln uses it five times — whereas Union is not mentioned once.

The Gettysburg Address, in many respects, goes to the heart of the American national myth, with its evocation of the 'fathers' of the nation and its recollection of the ideals of liberty, equality and government of, by and for the people. O'Brien has recently argued that, as a nation, America only survived because its leaders devised, quite deliberately, an 'integrating language of race, blood and ancestry'. Lincoln, in the Gettysburg Address, he reminds us, 'is mystical about the consecration provided by the dead', and the speaker who preceded him, Edward Everett of Massachusetts, likewise invoked 'the bonds that unite us as one people — a substantial community of origin, language, belief, and law [...] common national and political interests; a common history; a common pride in a glorious heritage'.[47] In the final assessment of the myths that worked to create the civic nationalism of America, however, it is as well to bear in mind two things. First, Lincoln and Everett were not addressing a national audience, but were speaking to Union supporters in 1863, during and not after the Civil War. Second, the occasion of the address was the dedication of the cemetery at Gettysburg, the scene of some of the bloodiest fighting of that war. The mythologizing of the Civil War, the reverential approach that Americans adopt towards it and towards Lincoln, like that accorded the Revolution and Washington, should not blind us to the fact that the American nation may have been invoked by myth, but it was created in battle. In the Gettysburg Address,

47.   M. O'Brien, 'Angry is Good' in the *Times Literary Supplement*, 9 February 1996, p. 9.

Lincoln was preparing the way for the future, for the achievement of nationality, for unity with the South, and for a re-dedication of America as a nation to the ideals set out in the Declaration of Independence. When he spoke, however, victory was not assured, and neither he nor Everett were expressing truly national ideals. Theirs was a Northern variant of the American national myth. For the myth to have national resonance, Americans have to overlook this fact. That they have chosen to do so should not surprise us. As Renan indicated, in the creation of a nation what people select to forget about their historical past is as important, and as revealing, as what they choose to remember.[48]

---

48.   E. Renan, 'What Is a Nation?', translated by H.K. Babha in Babha (ed.), *Nations and Narration*, London, 1990, p. 11.

THE MYTH OF DIVINE ELECTION AND AFRIKANER ETHNOGENESIS

Bruce Cauthen

Throughout history, the concept of chosenness has been a potent catalyst for social mobilization and national coherence. Chosenness consists in the idea of a particular people who have been especially anointed by the Deity to discharge a mission and whose destiny is divinely and cosmologically determined; they may also collectively possess a divine warrant to subdue 'heathens' and propagate the faith in a heathen land. When the cause of a people is conceived to be the very will of God, the collectivity is infused with a powerful sense of purpose that transcends more mundane considerations of social organization. Theirs is a calling to which all members of the community must respond. Failure to realize the collective vocation may incur the wrath of the Deity, lead to the dismemberment of the people and — for its individual members — the prospect of eternal damnation. The very land on which the group dwells is thought to be hallowed ground as it is believed to be deeded exclusively to them as a consecrated parcel from the Almighty Himself. This mystically sublime stewardship acquires an increasingly emotive dimension when the soil has been soaked with the blood of ethnic kinsmen.[1]

The classic example of a chosen people is, of course, the ancient Israelites whose epic narrative of election, exodus, exile in the wilderness, and ultimate redemption has been related to successive generations through the Old Testament. As the nomadic wandering of the Jews of antiquity was in preparation for their eventual occupation of the Promised Land, the physical habitation of this sacred homeland by the Israelites was essential for the realization of their election and the establishment of their corporate identity.[2]

Many peoples have identified themselves as instruments of providential design or have interpreted their national history or destiny

---

1. This observation is suggested in part by N. Smart in P.H. Merkl and N. Smart (eds), *Religion and Politics in the Modern World*, New York and London, 1983, p. 21. For a similar discussion of the emotive symbolism of 'blood and soil' and one which is directly related to the Afrikaner experience, see D. Chidester, *Shots in the Street: Violence and Religion in South Africa*, Cape Town, 1992, pp. 1–12.
2. See S. Grosby, 'Religion and Nationality in Antiquity: The Worship of Yahweh and Ancient Israel' in *European Journal of Sociology*, 32, 1991, pp. 242–3. D. Novak, *The Election of Israel: The Idea of the Chosen People*, Cambridge, 1995, provides an extensive consideration of the myth of divine election and the Jews.

as the will of God.[3] Of course, such sublime self-conceptions tend to create collective attitudes of moral superiority, although, as Anthony Smith cautions, there is a distinction to be drawn between chosenness and ethnocentrism:

A myth of ethnic election should not be equated with plain ethnocentrism. Ethnic communities have quite commonly regarded themselves as the moral centre of the universe and as far as possible affected to ignore or despise those around them. A myth of ethnic election is more demanding. To be chosen is to be placed under moral obligations. One is chosen on condition that one observes certain moral, ritual, and legal codes, and only for as long as one continues to do so. The privilege of election is accorded only to those who are sanctified, whose life-style is an expression of sacred values. The benefits of election are reserved for those who fulfil the required observances.[4]

Although the concept of chosenness may seem somewhat anachronistic in the presumably modern, rational and secular world of today, the resurgence of religious fundamentalism and, particularly, religious nationalism[5] clearly indicates that the myth of divine election is a phenomenon whose contemporary socio-political relevance can hardly be discounted. Until quite recently, however, the notion of a chosen people has received remarkably scant scholarly attention — at least from a comparative perspective. Moreover, much of the contemporary research has been of a decidedly deconstructionist approach, which tends to dissect and ultimately dismiss a people's historical myth of divine election as little more than a quasi-religious programme, fabricated and manipulated by a nationalist élite, and imposed on the masses as a vehicle for political mobilization. In this regard, the concept of chosenness is often interpreted as merely a sanctimoniously contrived ideology, retroactively interjected back into history, to justify a dubious record of ethnocentrism, racism, territorial aggrandizement, warfare, enslavement or worse.

3. Conor Cruise O'Brien, for example, states that, historically, 'Christians in general considered themselves successors to the Jews as a chosen people, but it soon appeared that some Christians were more chosen than others' (C.C. O'Brien, 'Why do Some Nations Still See Themselves As The Chosen People?' in *The Times*, 25 June 1991, p. 14). In this regard he identifies the Franks, the English Puritans, the Reformed Germans and the Muscovite Russians.

4. A.D. Smith, 'Chosen Peoples: Why Ethnic Groups Survive' (hereafter 'Chosen Peoples') in *Ethnic and Racial Studies*, 15, 1992, 3, p. 441.

5. For respective discussions of the contemporary threats posed to the secular state by the resurgence of religious fundamentalism and religious nationalism, see G. Kepel, *The Revenge of God: The Resurgence of Islam, Christianity and Judaism in the Modern World*, Cambridge, 1994, and M. Juergensmeyer, *The New Cold War: Religious Nationalism Confronts the Secular State*, Berkeley, Los Angeles and London, 1993.

This has certainly been the case with a number of recent studies which have examined the Afrikaner concept of ethnic election. Yet, generally, as the ecclesiastical historian William Hutchinson counsels, 'appeals to popular ideas of chosenness, whether these were offered by literary figures or by politicians, probably cannot be dismissed out of hand as cynical constructions. The evidence suggests that policymakers in nineteenth-century Europe and America, like their successors in various world societies of today, were dependent for some of their support on religiously derived beliefs that they did not need to construct — beliefs that, for good or ill, were really there.'[6]

Afrikaner Ethnic Election

In certain ways the Afrikaners seem to illustrate the model of a people conspicuously and self-consciously committed to follow that which they see as the will of God. It may well be argued that a distinct sense of collective piety (which some may dismiss as nothing more than religiosity, sanctimony and hypocrisy) has traditionally pervaded the Afrikaner psyche. Deep religious devotion was characteristic of the early Boers and, even in the present day, Christianity remains a powerful force in Afrikaner society. The traditional Afrikaans' churches — particularly the predominant Dutch Reformed Church, which has maintained an 'official character'[7] since the inception of the Dutch colony at the Cape — remain pivotal social institutions, and membership levels of Afrikaners are comparatively high for any industrialized society. Even Leonard Thompson, whose writings have hardly been sympathetic to Afrikaner religious belief, concedes that,'despite the inroads of urbanization and capitalism, religion continues to be a determining influence over the personal beliefs, corporate behavior, and the self-justification of Afrikaners'.[8]

Christian conviction has certainly been a defining factor of Afrikaner identity.[9] Afrikaners, both élite and ordinary, of all political

6.   W.R. Hutchinson, 'Introduction' in W.R. Hutchinson and H. Lehmann (eds), *Many Are Chosen: Divine Election and Western Nationalism*, Minneapolis, MN, 1994 (hereafter *Many Are Chosen*), p. 25.
7.   See A. Hastings, 'Politics and Religion in Southern Africa' in G. Moyser (ed.), *Politics and Religion in the Modern World*, London and New York, 1991, pp. 162–3, for a discussion of the Church's authority.
8.   L. Thompson, *The Political Mythology of Apartheid*, New Haven, CT and London, 1985, p. 215.
9.   In this regard, Johan Kinghorn observes that, 'the religious dimension was integral to the internal discourse on ethnicity in Afrikaner circles. It was not for nothing that Afrikaner ethnicity presented itself as *Christian Nationalism*' (J. Kinghorn, 'Social Cosmology, Religion and Afrikaner Ethnicity' in *Journal of South African Studies*, 20, 1994, p. 394). Templin concurs that 'the Afrikaners saw themselves in terms more glorious than many other nationalisms. Their

persuasions, continue to invoke the name of God, and dramatically employ biblical and apocalyptic imagery just as their ethnic forebears did in days past. The Afrikaner vigorously equates his cause as a providentially defined mission.[10] Certainly, Andries Treunicht, the late leader of the Conservative Party and a clergyman by profession, encapsulated his political message within a theological discourse. Eugene Terre'Blanche of the notorious Afrikaner Weerstanbeweging (AWB) regularly denounces all enemies of the Boer people as anti-Christ. However, the public articulation of fervent religious conviction is an activity which is hardly confined to conservative Afrikaners: when the well-known Afrikaner dissident Beyers Naude broke with the National Party in the 1970s, he did so denouncing apartheid as a sin and a doctrinal heresy, and he named his anti-apartheid organization 'The Christian Institute'. And when former State President F.W. de Klerk was recently asked why he had abolished apartheid, his response was that God had instructed him to do so.

Given this intensely religious atmosphere which, even today, continues to infuse Afrikanerdom, it is hardly surprising that approaches which have emphasized the socio-cultural influence of religion have proven such a dominant theme in the literature and have been continually employed, even by recent researchers, to analyse the growth of Afrikaner ethnic identity and of Afrikaner nationalism. Yet although this perspective, known as the Calvinist paradigm,[11] has remained a prevalent and enduring approach, the school of thought is not without its detractors. In this regard, the most vocal and consistent critic of the Calvinist paradigm has been the Afrikaner political scientist Andre du Toit.[12]

"cause" was God's cause, and their nation was an elect people, called out from others in the area for a unique task' (J.A. Templin, *Ideology on a Frontier: The Theological Foundation of Afrikaner Nationalism, 1652–1910*, Westport, CT and London, 1984 [hereafter *Ideology on a Frontier*], p. xi). In a recent study of the Afrikaners, it was noted that, 'Many Afrikaners still cling to the belief that they are a special or "chosen" people whose survival is somehow more important than that of other nations in the world': G. Leach, *The Afrikaners: Their Last Great Trek*, London, 1988, p. 50.

10. See H. Zille, 'The Right Wing in South African Politics' in P.L. Berger and B. Godsell (eds), *A Future South Africa: Visions, Strategies, and Realities*, Cape Town, 1988, pp. 66–8.

11. For analyses of the Calvinist paradigm, see I. Hexham, 'Dutch Calvinism and the Development of Afrikaner Nationalism' in *African Affairs*, 79, 1980, and D.J. Bosch, 'The Roots and Fruits of Afrikaner Civil Religion' in J.W. Hofmeyer and W.S. Vorster (eds), *New Faces of Africa: Essays in Honour of Ben Marais*, Pretoria, 1984.

12. See A. du Toit, 'No Chosen People: The Myth of the Calvinist Origin of Afrikaner Nationalism and Racial Ideology' (hereafter 'No Chosen People') in *American Historical Review*, 88, 1983, pp. 920–1; *idem*, 'Puritans in Africa? Afrikaner "Calvinism" in Late Nineteenth-Century South Africa' (hereafter

It should prove instructive to consider in some detail the objections registered by du Toit and evaluate the cogency of his critique before we examine the historical development of the concept of Afrikaner chosenness. One tenet of du Toit's argument is located in drawing a sharp ideological distinction between the English Puritans who settled in New England and the Dutch who colonized the Cape. Du Toit asserts that the well-educated Puritans commanded a sophisticated theological knowledge of the set of complex Calvinistic principles and envisaged the establishment of a new society founded upon their intellectual understanding of Calvinism. In contrast, the territorial interest of the Dutch was purely commercial; they also lacked the rich theological and rigorous intellectual traditions of Puritanism, and were largely unconcerned with the construction of a religiously defined society.[13] The Puritans — prior to their landing at Plymouth Rock — perceived themselves as a people chosen to build *the city on the hill*, the New Jerusalem; according to du Toit, however, the Dutch laboured under no such mystical or sublime imperative. To substantiate this point, du Toit points not only to the theological marginalization in the Cape Colony, but also to the lack of social — especially ecclesiastical — organization on the frontier as the trekboers, or nomadic farmers, began to migrate eastward in the eighteenth century:

Linked only tenuously with the market and the cash economy based on the Cape, without regular schools, for the most part outside the reach of the few functioning congregations and subject to only the flimsiest of administrative controls, the *trekboers* outside of the western Cape were in fact for generations without most of the institutional constraints or socializing agencies which could have been instrumental in retaining and transmitting intellectual and social conditions. In such circumstances it becomes questionable in what sense one could expect to find any theological tradition at all, let alone such a systematic and sophisticated doctrine as that of Calvinism.[14]

'Puritans in Africa?') in *Comparative Studies in Society and History*, 27, 1985, p. 213; and *idem*, 'The Construction of Afrikaner Chosenness' in Hutchinson and Lehman (eds), *Many Are Chosen*, p. 118.

13. See du Toit, 'No Chosen People', p. 922 and *idem*, 'Puritans in Africa?', pp. 211–12. R. Ross, 'The Fundamentalisation of Afrikaner Calvinism' in H. Diederiks and C. Quispel (eds), *Onderscheid en minderhied: Social-historiche opstellan oer dicriminatie en vooroordeel aan geboden aan professor Dik van Arkel bij zijn afscheid als hoogleraar in de ociate geschiedenis aan de Rijksunivversiteit te Leiden*, Hilversum, 1987, largely concurs with du Toit's perspective: Ross describes the early settlers at the Cape as the *dregs* of European society and concludes 'The development of Afrikaner social and religious self-identity [...] is a historical construct of relatively recent date' (p. 202).

14. Du Toit, 'Puritans in Africa?', p. 212. It is interesting to note that Hexham is another dissenter from the Calvinist paradigm; he suggests that the religious practices of the Boers underwent numerous mutations on the frontier. Although

There is an implicit insinuation, then, in du Toit's work that the
Dutch settlement of the Cape was essentially devoid of any genuine
religious devotion and that, as the Boer migrated eastward, his faith —
already minimal and inauthentic — was subjected to a continual
erosion on the frontier.

Du Toit argues that no distinct ideology of Afrikaner chosenness was
articulated until nearly a century and a half after the colonization of the
Cape. He recalls that travellers, who left written accounts of their
expeditions, did not detect any psychological inclinations among
Afrikaners to suggest that they conceived of themselves as a people
with a providentially ordained calling. It was not until the renowned
English missionary David Livingstone visited South Africa in the late
1850s that the idea of Afrikaner election began to gain currency. Du
Toit makes the point that Livingstone was 'the first writer who
directly attributed specific notions of divine mission to Afrikaners as a
historical explanation of their racial views and practices'.[15] Yet, says du
Toit, it was not until the 1940s that the ideology was most vigorously
promoted when the National Party attempted to provide a theological
justification for their racial policies; and, he warns, 'To read the
situation of the mid-twentieth century back into the earlier period is,
however, anachronistic.'[16]

One is left with the question, nevertheless, of why a people's
corporate belief in their ethnic election must so crucially depend on a
profession of Calvinist theology. There are certainly numerous
historical cases of pre-Calvinist and non-Calvinist Christian ethnic
communities which identified themselves as chosen peoples.[17]
Moreover, numerous non-Christian peoples have espoused myths of

Hexham admits that Boer 'folk religion' was definitely Protestant in character, he
argues that it contained a number of features which were certainly not Calvinist.
Hexham contends that the primitive Christianity of the Afrikaners incorporated
exotic elements from indigenous animism and Malay Islam, including
clairvoyance, spirits and genie, healing, witchcraft, and magic. Although there
may well have been evidence of occultism in the relatively few isolated cases
which he discusses, Hexham asserts the highly speculative thesis that such was
the religion of the majority of the rural Afrikaners until the nationalist élite
imposed a more conventional form of Calvinism on the masses prior to the
Second World War. See A. Hexham, 'Modernity or Reaction in South Afrika:
The Case of Afrikaner Religion' in William Nicholls (ed.), *Modernity and
Religion*, Waterloo, Ontario, 1987, pp. 62–88.

15. Du Toit, 'No Chosen People', p. 939. Du Toit reiterates that 'the origins of these
     latter notions of Afrikaner chosenness may be located in the historical context of
     the turn of the century with respect to the discourses of (Christian) mission and
     empire that were paramount at that time': 'The Construction of Afrikaner
     Chosenness', p. 124.
16. *Ibid.*, p. 116.
17. See O'Brien, 'Why do Some Nations Still See Themselves As The Chosen
     People?'.

divine election.[18] Even within the Protestant tradition, it was identification with the Israelites of the Old Testament, more than any other factor, which seemed so powerfully to influence the crystallization of the myth of divine election. As Conor Cruise O'Brien observes, a significant religious practice of the Reformation — the rejection of allegorical, in favour of literal, exegesis of the Old Testament —was instrumental in enabling Protestant communities to realize a corporate sense of ethnic election.[19] All that was necessary for a popular identification with the ancient Israelites was a very basic understanding of the historical narrative of the Old Testament and a recognition that this narrative corresponded with one's own.

The historian Donald Harman Akenson also emphasizes the significant relevance of the Old Testament narrative of the Israelites in the formulation of an ideology of chosenness — or a *covenantal culture*, as he calls it.[20] As du Toit suggests, the globally co-ordinated evangelism of the late nineteenth century had important religious implications for South Africa.[21] However, even during this historical period of evangelical proselytism and imperial expansion, Hartmut Lehmann and William R. Hutchinson attribute the divinely sanctioned nationalisms of the day to 'the chosen people model as it was derived, accurately or not from the Hebrew scriptures. Indeed, without such symbols as the "Old Testament" account of a chosen people, a people united under God, the powerful union of nationalism and Christianity might well have been less feasible.'[22] And, as we will see below, the Bible — particularly the Old Testament — was a central element of Afrikaner life.

Du Toit's assertion that the myth of divine election was not explicitly stated until the late nineteenth century is shared even by those analysts who have emphasized the concept of chosenness as an approach for explaining the process of Afrikaner ethnic identity formation.[23] Templin suggests, however, that the notion of chosenness '"blundered into being" from a particular cultural matrix. The roots of the idea of a particular people selected by God for a particular destiny were deeply imbedded in the cultural development of the nation even before the ideas were enunciated, certainly before any attempt was made

18. See Smith, 'Chosen Peoples'.
19. C.C. O'Brien, *God Land: Reflections on Religion and Nationalism*, Cambridge, MA, 1988, p. 25.
20. D.H. Akenson, *God's Peoples: Covenant and Land in South Africa, Israel, and Ulster*, Ithaca, NY and London, 1992 (hereafter *God's Peoples*), chapter 1.
21. See Hastings, 'Politics and Religion in Southern Africa', p. 162, for a discussion of this point.
22. See Hutchinson and Lehmann (eds), *Many Are Chosen*, p. 289.
23. See Templin, *Ideology on a Frontier*, p. 289, and Akenson, *God's Peoples*, p. 60.

to systematize them.'[24] Yet, even if one was to accept du Toit's tenuous assumption that Afrikaner ethnic election was a largely latter-day nationalist construction to justify apartheid, one suspects that there must have been pre-existing sentiments of divine purpose which had some degree of resonance in the Afrikaner psyche.

To dismiss adequately the misconceptions of du Toit and others, it is necessary briefly to examine the early history of the Cape Colony and of frontier expansion with regard to the important role which religion — and an increasing identification with ancient Israel — actually played. Moreover, to fully appreciate the evolving concept of Afrikaner chosenness, one must carefully consider the ethno-historical significance of three events which instilled and reiforced the myth of divine election in the collective consciousness of the Afrikaners.

The Prominence of Religion at the Cape and on the Frontier

Although the Dutch colonists who first arrived at the Cape of Good Hope in 1652 were dependents of the Dutch India Company (VOC) — which was attempting to establish a re-provision station along the maritime route to the East Indies — and not religious pilgrims *per se*, mid-seventeenth-century Holland was characterized by an intensely charged religious environment. The Dutch had steadfastly maintained the Reformed faith against the encroachment of Catholic Spain.[25] Among some of the Dutch visitors to the Cape, there was a distinct sense of being among the elect[26] and this confidence was considerably reinforced when they encountered the non-Christian inhabitants. For example, Wouter Schouten recorded the following in his journal in 1665:

It is lamentable that among mankind such folk (as we are now told of) are to be found, who, although descended from our father *Adam*, yet show so little humanity that truly they resemble more the unreasonable beasts than reasonable man, living on earth such a miserable and pitiful life, having no knowledge of GOD nor of what leads to their Salvation. Miserable folk, how lamentable is your pitiful condition! And Oh Christians, how blessed is ours! if we are true Christians. GOD be eternally thanked therefor, honoured and exalted, in that he has called us from this abyss of miserable

24. Templin, *Ideology on a Frontier*, p. 8.
25. A.R. Colquhoun has noted that 'The faithfulness of the Hollanders to the reformed faith had been intensified by the persecutions of the Spaniards': Colquhoun, *The Africander Land*, London, 1906, pp. 185–6.
26. Templin argues, 'The Dutch in the far-flung reaches of the commercial empire of the Dutch East India Company took with them the assumption that their "divinely" chosen princes of Orange and their Reformed doctrine of divine election were closely related': Templin, *Ideology on a Frontier*, p. 6.

darkness [...] God [...] must be thanked, praised, and exalted by us for ever.[27]

Some historians have suggested that, even among the very first colonists, there was a sense of mission to Christianize the indigenous peoples.[28] There are accounts — such as that of Pieter Van Hoorn of 1663 — of African children being baptized alongside Dutch infants.[29]

Furthermore, as suggested previously, the established church of the Colony was the Dutch Reformed Church and its predominance and authority were profound, 'From the earliest days it exercised great influence not only on the minds, but on the lives of its members.'[30] Although the Church was structurally subordinated to the State, the colonial authorities resolutely promoted religion among the settlers.[31] On one occasion, when an officially appointed ecclesiastical official neglected to perform the ministerial duties that were expected of him by the community, the faithful organized a vigorous protest.[32] Moreover, there was substantial opposition from the religious community to the government's decision to sanction civil marriage ceremonies.[33] The Cape Colony was indeed characterized by an intensely religious atmosphere and an overwhelming sense of genuine religious devotion seemed evident in the laity.

Towards the end of the seventeenth century, groups of French Huguenots — who had fled their homeland after the revocation of the Edict of Nantes and settled initially in Holland — began to immigrate to the Cape. The Huguenots were also intensely devout.[34] They repeatedly beseeched the colonial authorities for the right to establish their own separate congregation, which was later finally granted. There was a relatively prompt assimilation, however, of the French refugees into the larger Dutch community. Some scholars have explained that

27. Quoted in R. Raven-Hart (ed.), *Cape Good Hope 1652–1702: The First Fifty Years of Dutch Colonisation as Seen by Callers*, Cape Town, 1971 (hereafter *Cape Good Hope*), p. 85.
28. See, for example, A. Wilmont, *History of the Colony of the Cape of Good Hope*, Cape Town, 1869, p. 32.
29. See Raven-Hart, *Cape Good Hope*, p. 32. However, the initial paternalistic mission of proselytism was not consistent and eventually declined; see R. Elphick and R. Shell, 'Intergroup Relations: Khoikhoi, Settlers, Slaves and Free Blacks, 1652–1795' in R. Elphick and H. Giliomee (eds), *The Shaping of South African Society, 1652–1795*, Cape Town, 1979, pp. 117–26.
30. Colquhoun, *The Africander Land*, pp. 185–6.
31. See P.J. Idenburg, *The Cape of Good Hope at the Turn of the Eighteenth Century*, Leyden, 1963 (hereafter *The Cape of Good Hope*), p. 60.
32. See Wilmont, *History of the Colony of the Cape of Good Hope*, p. 120.
33. See Idenburg, *The Cape of Good Hope*, p. 61.
34. One historian remarked that,'the French refugees brought with them an earnest religious feeling, which became contagious, and was soon spread to all the other settlers': A.H. Keane, *The Boer States: Land and People*, London, 1900, p. 164.

this rather rapid assimilation was greatly facilitated by a common subscription to a Calvinist creed.[35] In the early eighteenth century, an increasing number of single German males — also of the Reformed faith and in the employ of the VOC — settled in the Cape. These colonists took Dutch wives, and their offspring learned Dutch instead of German. This German contingent was also readily incorporated into the evolving Cape Dutch culture.[36]

In the eighteenth century, the trekboers began to migrate eastward into the hinterlands. Yet, although they may have left the established institutional structure of the Church, they hardly forsook its religious teachings. The lack of the support of congregations and of pastors, as well as the hardships endured on the frontier, caused the Boers to rely even more strongly on the Bible, which they carried with them into the wilderness. Templin describes the Bible as central to their way of life, 'As frontiersmen moved farther to the east, the Bible and the Psalter were often the only books they had'.[37] Walker suggests that, although the Bible may not have been for the Boers 'in the most literal sense The Book, the only book, they must have been drawn towards it, and towards the Old Testament in especial, because there was the story of a pastoral, semi-nomadic people very like themselves'.[38] Although it was not unusual for rural Afrikaners to travel great distances to attend church services,[39] the home became the primary locus for a daily, family-oriented devotional service in which Bible-reading, particularly from the Old Testament, was an integral component.

It has been suggested, by Templin for example, that the distinct lack of ecclesiastical organization and concomitant shortage of professionally educated clergymen resulted in the development of a 'fundamentalistic popular piety' and the emergence of an 'egocentric folk theology', which increasingly shaped the religious convictions of the rural Boers; consequently, many 'situational interpretations' were incorporated into their belief system.[40] Perhaps the most profound

35. See M. Nathan, *The Huguenots in South Africa*, Johannesburg, 1939, and C.G. Botha, *The French Refugees at the Cape*, Cape Town, 1970. Although Nathan and Botha — and they are by no means the only researchers who share this view — are probably quite correct that mutual adherence to the Calvinist faith accelerated the coalescence of the French into the Dutch society at the Cape, it should be recalled that in colonial South Carolina, during the same historical period, the Huguenots also readily assimilated into the larger community of English settlers from Barbados and England, all of whom were overwhelmingly Anglican.
36. See Templin, *Ideology on a Frontier*, pp. 30–1.
37. *Ibid.*, p. 281.
38. E.A. Walker, *The Great Trek*, London, 1934, p. 59.
39. See W.E.G. Fisher, *The Transvaal and the Boers*, London, 1900, p. 50; see also Walker, *The Great Trek*, pp. 56–7.
40. Templin, *Ideology on a Frontier*, p. 4.

theological deviation was the Afrikaner propensity to base his faith on a literal interpretation of the Old Testament, which showed him 'an angry jealous Deity ready to pounce on him if he does not perform certain ceremonial rites, and providing a man-made moral code which might be interpreted as one willed provided its letter be accepted'.[41] Moreover, there was a corporate and self-conscious identification with the ancient nation of Israel itself. In the 1770s, some Boers reached the Fish River Valley and felt that they were physically retracing the historical path of the Israelites.[42] 'Since there was a strong stress on the Old Testament [...] and since the Afrikaners were a pastoral people with a strong patriarchal social structure, the analogies even increased in the Afrikaner ethnic consciousness.'[43] Yet, if there was already a basic identification of the trekboers with the Israelites, the parallels were to assume an even greater relevance when larger and co-ordinated migrations of Boers made their exit from the Colony during the mid-1830s.

The Great Trek

Of all the momentous events of Afrikaner history, surely none occupies a more central place and celebrated status than the Great Trek.[44] The year 1834 began the historic mass-migration of Afrikaners from the vast frontier region of the Cape Colony. Numerous Boers made the drastic decision to bargain away their cherished farms, to abandon their long-standing homes, to uproot their families, and to retreat into the wilderness. They gathered up all of their worldly possessions and, together with their servants and livestock, prepared for a distant relocation.[45] As the first oxwagon[46] convoys began to depart from the Cape for the long overland journey which lay ahead, the Afrikaners travelled into a formative stage of their collective consciousness.

41. Colquhoun, *The Africander Land*, p. 203.
42. See Walker, *The Great Trek*, pp. 55–6, and S. Patterson, *The Last Trek: A Study of the Boer People and the Afrikaner Nation*, London, 1956, p. 177 — particularly the footnote.
43. J.H. Coetzee, 'Formative Factors in the Origins and Growth of Afrikaner Ethnicity' in B.M. du Toit (ed.), *Ethnicity in Modern Africa*, Boulder, CO, 1978, p. 249.
44. See B. Cauthen, 'The Great Trek, the Search for the Promised Land and the Afrikaner Ethnoscape' in *ASEN Bulletin*, 11, 1996, from which excerpts in this section concerning the Great Trek are taken.
45. See J. Fisher, *The Afrikaners*, London, 1969, p. 63.
46. For descriptions of the standard type of wagon which was employed during the Great Trek, see Walker, *The Great Trek*, pp. 36–7; Fisher, *The Afrikaners*, pp. 64–5; and G.H. Mason, *Life with the Zulus of Natal South Africa*, London, 1855, facsimile reprint, London, 1968, pp. 122–4.

Hermann Giliomee is perhaps correct to point out that it was a band of free burghers, not an ethnic group, which undertook the Trek.[47] By that time, there was, however, a significant divergence between the frontier Boers and the rest of colonial society in terms of their concept of law, attitudes towards indigenous peoples, theological conviction, even attire; and 'as the differences became evident Boers tended to draw together to maintain their separate traditions'.[48] In any event, the collective wilderness experience — fraught with many hardships and much danger — was instrumental in fostering an increased sense of Afrikaner ethnic identity, not only for the Voortrekkers, but, particularly, for their progeny. Vernon February describes the Afrikaner migration as 'seen mostly in heroic-epic proportions. It produced for the Afrikaner a mythology on which he could firmly base his nationalism.'[49] Moreover, no other historical episode (except perhaps the Covenant itself which occurred during the migration) did more to implant firmly the intense identification of the Afrikaners with the children of Israel and, hence, reinforce and magnify the sense of election — for the present and especially successive generations — which already existed in the popular imagination. The Great Trek was their exodus; their wandering in the wilderness; their communion with Jehovah; their journey beneath the pillar of fire; their triumph against the Midianites; and their slow, yet sure, journey to the Promised Land.

Three decades of British control of the Cape — which brought with it large-scale immigration from Britain, as well as policies which ultimately attempted to prescribe the exclusive use of the English language in the Colony — presented a series of socio-political challenges to the Afrikaners, particularly the rural, agrarian communities, and laid the foundation for the fateful conflict between Brit and Boer which would persist, and tragically intensify, throughout the remainder of the century. The increasing encroachment of the British colonial state upon the flourishing Boer settlements along the eastern frontier resulted in much unwelcome interference, supervision, and regulation of the distinctively self-reliant social institutions and fiercely independent life-styles of the rural Afrikaners. It was feared that the bucolic Afrikaner arcadia was in danger of imminent destruction by the forces of British imperialism. The Boers realized that the colonial administration would make the acquisition of additional acreage increasingly difficult as the new land policies favoured grants to British immigrants.[50] Despite this economic threat to their agrarian society, it

47.   H. Adam and H. Giliomee, *Ethnic Power Mobilized: Can South Africa Change?*, New Haven, CT, 1979, p. 100.
48.   Templin, *Ideology on a Frontier*, p. 86.
49.   V. February, *The Afrikaners of South Africa*, London and New York, 1991, p. 42.
50.   See Fisher, *The Afrikaners*, pp. 60–1. For informative discussions of the numerous causes of the Great Trek, see H. Cloete, *The History of the Great Boer Trek and*

was the socio-legal challenge to the rigidly defined racial order which the Boers seemed to find most perilous.[51]

During the years of frontier expansion, the Europeans began to refer to themselves as exclusively Christian and to the Africans as *heathen*.[52] This was essentially the same attitude exhibited by the first Dutch visitors; yet the initial impulse to Christianize the indigenous people seemed quickly to dissipate. Indeed, as the trekboers began to encounter the various native peoples — to whom they immediately attributed a shocking lack of not only culture, but, particularly, Christianity — the religious exclusiveness of the Afrikaners began to intensify, and they saw themselves as 'chosen by God to protect and control the "benighted heathen"'.[53] Walker also discerns a distinct element of racial bigotry inherent in the religion of the frontier and a conscious effort to maintain distance from the African *heathens*.[54] The Boers therefore felt that they had a God-given right to subdue the land, its inhabitants — and, at times, their livestock — and, consequently, became embroiled in a series of skirmishes with the Xhosas, between 1834 and 1835, known at the time, derogatorily, as the Kaffir Wars.[55] The Boers suspiciously regarded Cape Town and London as unwilling to put an end to this internecine strife, which resulted in extensive property loss, and to protect their interests against the so-called Bantu; the rural Afrikaners became increasingly convinced that their best defence was to flee.[56]

The Afrikaners were particularly hostile to the various activities of the clergymen and schoolteachers dispatched to the Cape by the London

the Origins of the South African Republics, London, 1900, pp. 33–74, and E.A. Walker, *A History of Southern Africa*, London, 1935, pp. 196–200. See also G.S. Were, *A History of South Africa*, London, 1982, pp. 54–62.

51. See Akenson, *God's Peoples*, p. 62.

52. See Patterson, *The Last Trek*, p. 9, and Templin, *Ideology on a Frontier*, p. 39, for a discussion of the hardening of the attitude of the settlers towards the indigenous peoples. See also J.H. Coetzee, 'Formative Factors in the Origins and Growth of Afrikaner Ethnicity' in du Toit (ed.), *Ethnicity in Modern Africa*, pp. 245–8.

53. Templin, *Ideology on a Frontier*, p. 39.

54. Walker, *The Great Trek*, pp. 57–8. However, in his recent and monumental history of the Xhosas, Mostert argues that the religiously motivated racial exclusiveness of the later Voortrekker communities was not necessarily characteristic of the lone trekboer of the early eighteenth century, who enjoyed a less adversarial relationship with the Xhosas: N. Mostert, *Frontiers: The Epic of South Africa's Creation and the Tragedy of the Xhosa People*, London, 1992, pp. 778–81.

55. These clashes are now referred to as the *Frontier Wars*. For a descriptive account of the latter stages — which are referred to above — of this persistent and spasmodic conflict, see J.B. Peires, *The House of Phalo: A History of the Xhosa People in the Days of their Independence*, Berkeley, Los Angeles and London, 1982, pp. 145–60.

56. See Fisher, *The Afrikaners*, pp. 60–2.

Missionary Society to proselytize, educate and alleviate the plight of the indigenous peoples. The Afrikaners saw this as not only interference with their labour supply, but as a plan to expel the Boers from their farms by attempting to organize the natives against them.[57] Moreover, the Boers could not tolerate any attempt to subvert the socio-racial basis of frontier society — the economic and cultural implications were far too grave to contemplate. The diaspora, beginning in 1835, of more than 10,000 Afrikaners from the Cape Colony can hardly be described as the flight of the faithful from an apostate or doctrinally discriminatory state. Even after the British capture of the Cape, the Dutch Reformed Church retained its prominence.[58] Moreover, the Church's hierarchy disavowed the Trek and discouraged its clergy from participating. Certainly economic, strategic and socio-political concerns figured prominently in the catalogue of grievances which the Voortrekkers themselves registered as their reasons for escaping the British colonial authorities.[59] Yet the motivation for the Trek, at least according to the Voortrekkers themselves, is hardly devoid of a religious dimension. The articulation of the grievances is liberally infused with religious fervour — indeed moral indignation — that the *heathen* should be elevated to the station of the *Christian*. A distinctive characteristic of a chosen people (particularly an emigrant one) — or even of an ethnic community in which a myth of divine election is beginning to take root — is its separation from indigenous peoples.[60] J.N. Boshof complained in a newspaper editorial that, 'The blacks are encouraged to consider themselves upon an equal footing with the whites in their religious exercises in church or community, [...] thereby showing a disrespect for the religious institutions of the people.'[61] A contemporary journalist remarked of the Voortrekkers that they considered themselves to be under divine guidance.[62] As Akenson explains:

57. See Templin, *Ideology on a Frontier*, pp. 74–5, and Patterson, *The Last Trek*, pp. 12–13. J.S. Galbraith, *Reluctant Empire: British Policy on the South African Frontier 1834–1854*, Berkeley and Los Angeles, 1963, provides an informative discussion of the activities of the London Missionary Society in Southern Africa: see pp. 79–97.
58. See Hastings, 'Politics and Religion in Southern Africa', p. 162.
59. Piet Retief, a prominent leader of the Trek, published his 'Manifesto' in the *Grahamstown Journal*, 2 February 1837. There are excerpts of his Manifesto in both Patterson, *The Last Trek*, pp. 20–1, and Templin, *Ideology on a Frontier*, pp. 100–1.
60. See Smith, 'Chosen Peoples', p. 449.
61. 'J.N. Boshof to the editor, *Grahamstown Journal*, February 17, 1839' in J. Bird, *The Annals of Natal*, vol. 1, Pietermaritzburg, 1888, p. 504. Quoted (and secondary reference) in Templin, *Ideology on a Frontier*, p. 100.
62. See Walker, *A History of Southern Africa*, p. 200.

it was the Hebrew scriptures that legitimated the notion that outside peoples were inherently inferior: the scriptural references extended from the story of Ham to the repeated, almost incantatory scriptural denunciations of local native tribes. These racial aspects of the scriptural code were intertwined with all the other aspects of the covenantal system — the Land, the Law, and so on — so the need for racial purity was given moral justification and the obtainment of that purity was sacralized.[63]

This sentiment is perhaps evident in the words of Anna Steenkamp — the niece of Piet Retief, the Voortrekker leader — who insisted that the primary precipitant of the Trek was the native 'being placed on an equal footing with Christians, contrary to the laws of God and the natural distinction of race and religion, so that it was intolerable for any decent Christian to bow down beneath such a yoke; wherefore we rather withdrew in order to preserve our doctrines in purity'.[64]

And so, like the Israelites of old, the Voortrekkers embarked on their arduous and historic journey to the Promised Land — in their case, Natal. Boer explorers had previously described the region as a 'land of milk and honey' which they believed to be largely uninhabited.[65] Natal was to be the Afrikaner Zion. Here the Boers could restore unto themselves a Christian society which excluded both the British and the Africans.[66] In the omnipresent idiom of the frontier — the language of the Old Testament — the Afrikaners conceived their mass migration.[67] It has been argued that the Old Testament imagery of the Exodus was employed by the Voortrekkers to vindicate the massive flight.[68] This sacred and monumental analogy must have exerted a powerful influence

63. Akenson, *God's Peoples*, pp. 75–6.
64. Anna Steenkamp, 'Record of Migration' in Bird, *The Annals of Natal*, pp. 459–68. Quoted (and secondary reference) in Templin, *Ideology on a Frontier*, pp. 100–01.
65. See Patterson, *The Last Trek*, p. 21. Patterson explains that the seemingly sparse demographic patterns of indigenous peoples in Natal at that time were the temporary result of the decimation and dispersal of the local tribes by the Zulus under Shaka. This view, although contentious, is substantiated by E.J. Krige, *The Social System of the Zulus*, London, 1934, pp. 12–14.
66. Templin, *Ideology on a Fronter*, p. 101.
67. Both Akenson (*God's Peoples*, p. 61) and O'Brien ('Response' in Hutchinson and Lehmann [eds], *Many Are Chosen*, pp. 142–3) gleefully point out the sceptical and deconstructionist Andre du Toit's concession that the frontier Boers' use of biblical language and imagery was 'ubiquitous': see his 'Captive to the Nationalist Paradigm: Professor F.A. van Jaarsveld and the Historical Evidence for the Afrikaner's Ideas on His Calling and Mission' in *South African Historical Journal*, 16, 1984.
68. Templin, *Ideology on a Frontier*, p. 286. S.G.M. Ridge suggests the Voortrekkers employed 'a cluster of metaphors relating to Israel's experience to give some tentative form to their own view of themselves: a form which became less tentative as they faced emotionally taxing crises'. See Ridge, 'Chosen Peoples or Heirs of Paradise: Trekkers, Settlers, and Some Implications of Myth' in C. Malan (ed.), *Race and Literature*, Pinetown, 1987, p. 106.

on the Boers and served to intensify their sense of election. Furthermore, the myth of divine election was soon to acquire an even more overt significance — and, indeed, a corporate and contractual dimension — when, on the eve of a decisive military victory over an indigenous people, the Afrikaners made a covenant with God.

The Covenant

First of all, it should be reiterated that the Great Trek did not represent an all-inclusive, unitary Afrikaner migration. Although it was originally intended that the different gatherings of emigrants should converge at the Blesberg near present-day Bloemfontein,[69] various bands of Boers exited the Cape Colony at intervals, each under the direction of different Voortrekker leaders. Moreover, although in the minds of many Afrikaners distant Natal signified the Promised Land, its destination was not pursued by all with equal determination. Some of the less adventurous Afrikaners relocated only as far as what was to become the Orange Free State, where extensive colonies of trekboers had already previously settled.[70] Even among those Voortrekkers who envisaged Natal as their ultimate dwelling place, settlements — both of a permanent and semi-permanent nature —were established en route.

A harrowing — yet socio-culturally significant — experience which was common to the farther migrations of the Great Trek was the increasing conflict with the African tribes which the Voortrekkers encountered as they pushed eastward. The settlers in the Transvaal, led by Andries Potgeiter and Pieter Uys, confronted the fierce Ndebele (Matabele). And the larger column of Voortrekkers which continued on towards Natal, under the guidance of Piet Retief and Andries Pretorius, fatefully engaged the Ndebele's even more martial cousins — the Zulus. In both situations, an eventual crushing defeat of the heathen enemy electrified the Afrikaners' collective sense of election and convinced them that they somehow constituted the terrestrial partner in a strategic alliance with the Deity.

The initial flashpoints of major conflict erupted in October 1836, when Ndebele warriors surprised a Boer hunting party and attacked two separate Voortrekker encampments in the central Transvaal. In subsequent clashes, the primitive weapons of the Ndebele were to prove no match for the superior firepower of the Afrikaners and their makeshift — yet highly effective — defensive position (known as the

---

69. See Fisher, *The Afrikaners*, p. 68. Fisher provides a very useful account of the often confusing chronology of the departures of the numerous Voortrekker migrations from the Cape and of the course of their various trajectories: see *ibid.*, pp. 66–9.
70. Patterson, *The Last Trek*, p. 23.

laager), in which the oxwagons were circled to form a fortification to impede the enemy's advance. Consequently, the Africans were to sustain very heavy losses in contrast to relatively slight Boer casualties.[71] Sarel Cilliers, who was widely regarded as the movement's chaplain, — and who prior to Veg-kop beseeched the Almighty for support and deliverance — attributed the impressive Voortrekker victories to the intervention of the hand of God. These military successes did much, no doubt, to convince the scripturally oriented Afrikaners of their divinely warranted invincibility. However, as Templin points out, in both engagements the Afrikaners were aided by the Rolong — a hospitable African tribe which were visited by Wesleyan missionaries and which had been the traditional foe of the Ndebele; moreover, much of the Afrikaner livestock either perished or was captured during the battles.[72]

Piet Retief — who was determined to settle with his followers in Natal — intended to pursue a more pragmatic approach in dealing with the more formidable and numerically superior opponent which was embodied in the Zulus, who were ruled, at that time, by the fierce Dingaane.[73] Retief ingratiated himself in an interview with Dingaane and obtained the King's assurance of land in exchange for Zulu cattle which had been stolen by Sikonyela (a Batlokua chieftain) and, preferably, the culprit as well. Retief had been warned by Robert Owen, an Anglican missionary who served as an interpreter to Dingaane, to be wary, as this land included the same tracts which Dingaane had previously ceded to the British settlers in Natal.[74] In the mean time, however, Retief — citing the downfall of Mozelikatzi, chief of the Ndebele — sent a written injunction to Dingaane, advising him of the Almighty's terrible justice which was meted out to wicked kings; and, this certainly must have been interpreted by the Zulu

---

71. At the Battle of Veg-kop, on 16 October, more than four hundred Ndebele were slain as compared to only two Afrikaner fatalities. And, when the same Voortrekker colony again engaged the Ndebele the following January, the body-count was nearly identical — although this time it was even less costly to the Afrikaners.
72. Templin, *Ideology on a Frontier*, pp. 105–6.
73. For an interesting description of Zulu military organization and prowess, as well as a vivid portrait of Dingaane, see the following: P. Becker, *Rule of Fear: The Life and Times of Dingaane King of the Zulu*, London, 1964; D.R. Morris, *The Washing of the Spears: A History of the Rise of the Zulu Nation under Shaka and its Fall in the Zulu War of 1879*, London, 1966; J.D. Omer-Cooper, *The Zulu Aftermath: A Nineteenth-Century Revolution in Bantu Africa*, London, 1966; J. Selby, *Shaka's Heirs*, London, 1971; B. Roberts, *The Zulu Kings*, London, 1974; and S. Taylor, *Shaka's Children: A History of the Zulu People*, London, 1994. Each of these sources also provides an informative account of the events leading up to the Battle of Blood River.
74. See Fisher, *The Afrikaners*, p. 79.

monarch as a warning.[75] Dingaane was definitely disturbed by the awesome military strength of the Afrikaners which had decimated the mighty Ndebele. He was also alarmed by the increasing numbers of Voortrekkers which were already beginning to settle in Natal.[76] This grave concurrence of events intensified Dingaane's fear of an impending invasion and he reinforced his capital with several thousand troops.

As promised, Retief recovered the stolen herd, and with a seventy-man force of Voortrekker volunteers, and thirty Coloured attendants, made his way back to Dingaane's royal kraal at Umgungundhlovu. Retief, however, had no intention of accommodating his potential enemy's ultimate demand for firearms and horses; and, apparently, word of this had reached the King, who was infuriated.[77] When Retief and his men arrived at the Zulu capital, they were disarmed by an amenable Dingaane, who deeded them Natal. While they were being lavishly entertained by their Zulu hosts in the royal kraal, a royal pronouncement ordered 'Kill the wizards' and the Voortrekkers met their demise, as did the Coloured retinue which was stationed at the gate.

Several days later — before the news of Dingaane's treachery had reached the Voortrekkers — Zulu warriors or *impis* then set upon the vulnerable archipelago of Boer encampments situated along the banks of the Blaauwkraans, Bushman and Mooi rivers and, under the cover of darkness, continued the bloodletting initiated in the royal kraal. In what is known as the Blaauwkraans Massacre, nearly three hundred pioneers were murdered, a disproportionate majority of whom were women and children. There was also a considerable loss of livestock. When the dead were counted, and the reality of Retief's terrible fate began to crystallize in their minds — as might be expected from a people who took literally the 'eye for an eye' justice of the Old Testament — there was a public outcry for retribution. One of the female survivors denounced Dingaane and proclaimed, 'God will not leave him unrecompensed nor will our men acquit him.'[78]

The Voortrekker encampments were consolidated into three protected laagers to ensure mutual defence until an effective retaliation could be launched. Potgieter and Uys came from the Transvaal to offer their support. Because of dissension among the leadership of the Voortrekkers, the first attempt at reprisal — conducted in concert with a band of English settlers — failed. Although not particularly costly in terms of Voortrekker casualties, it was a strategic blunder and a great

75. See Templin, *Ideology on a Frontier*, p. 108, which also provides the text of this letter.
76. See Fisher, *The Afrikaners*, p. 79.
77. See Walker, *The Great Trek*, p. 163.
78. See *ibid.*, p. 168, from which this quotation is taken.

psychological defeat for them. The Zulus continued to attack the Afrikaner positions. When, in August 1838, after three days of heavy fighting the attacking Zulus finally retreated, Retief's niece declared, 'Thanks and praise are due to the Lord, who so wonderfully has rescued us out of the hands of our numberless and blood-thirsty foes, and granted us the victory [...] The Lord strengthened us and weakened our enemy.'[79] Although the Voortrekkers had confronted a tragic series of reversals, 'An assurance of God's favor, however, sustained this small band of pilgrims where those of a lesser faith would have perhaps turned back to their former security.'[80] Even if the faith of the Voortrekkers had wavered in recent months, by the end of that same year it would be very much restored.

Andries Pretorius, an affluent cattle rancher from Graaf-Reinet, arrived in November and filled the leadership vacuum. Pretorius, who had volunteered in the campaigns against the Ndebele, was enthusiastically welcomed by the community. He was determined to launch a decisive punitive strike against Dingaane. He knew too that he must act quickly as the British colonial authorities at the Cape were becoming increasingly alarmed about the political instability in Natal.[81] There were reports that he was welcomed by the Voortrekkers as a champion sent from God; and Pretorius himself admonished the people that they should prepare for battle with prayers and must rely on the Almighty for victory.[82]

The hectic preparations for war were suspended on 9 December for the strict observation of the Sabbath; and on that day Sarel Cilliers, who had invoked the name of the Deity prior to the campaigns against the Ndebele, administered the following vow to God:

My brethren and fellow countrymen, at this moment we stand before the holy God of heaven and earth, to make a promise, if He be with us and protect us, and deliver the enemy into our hands so that we may triumph over him, that we shall observe the day as an anniversary in each year, and a day of thanksgiving like the Sabbath, in His honor; and that we will build a temple to His honor where we may worship Him; and that we shall enjoin

79. Steenkamp in Bird, *The Annals of Natal*, p. 463. Quoted in Templin, *Ideology on a Frontier*, p. 110.
80. *Ibid.*, p. 110.
81. See Fisher, *The Afrikaners*, p. 83, and Walker, *A History of Southern Africa*, p. 209. It should be noted that there had been two campaigns launched by English settlers — with the aid of anti-Dingaane Zulus — from Port Natal against the Zulu strongholds. Both expeditions accomplished little more than exciting Dingaane's warriors to further violence: see Walker, *The Great Trek*, pp. 173–4.
82. See Templin, *Ideology on a Frontier*, p. 110, for a discussion of the religiously charged atmosphere prior to battle.

our children that they must take part with us in this, for a remembrance for our prosperity.[83]

Thus a cosmic bargain was struck by the Voortrekkers with the Almighty. If God would lead the *kommando* to victory over the Zulus, they would build a sanctuary to His glory and remember the date of their triumph as an occasion of solemn remembrance. The Covenant, which was later to figure so prominently in nationalist discourse and to bind the Afrikaners together as a nation, had been established.

A week was to pass before the Voortrekker *kommando* — which numbered approximately 460 men now on manoeuvre in the field — was finally to engage the enemy. As the Boers marched off to battle, aware that they would confront a far more populous enemy, they identified themselves as the Israelites, and Pretorius as their Joshua.[84] There are also reports that the vow was recited again each night up until the fateful day.[85] Pretorius offered peace if Dingaane would return the horses and guns of Retief's party. His proposal was rebuffed amid clashes with Zulu patrols. On Saturday, 15 December 1838, as the *kommando* camped on the banks of the Ncome River in order to prepare for the next day's religious observation, Pretorius was confident that God had selected this readily defensible position as the *holy* site for the Afrikaner victory.[86] And after the Armageddon erupted on the following day, the Afrikaners were assured of the Lord's intervention, for when the battle ended more than 3,000 Zulu *impis* lay dead; the Voortrekkers had not suffered a single fatality, with only three wounded.[87]

The Voortrekkers emerged from the awesome contest relatively unscathed while the field was littered with the corpses of the vanquished 'heathen' foe; torrents of blood from the fallen Zulus supposedly spilled into the river, turning its water red. The Afrikaners were convinced that the Almighty had delivered His 'elect' and made them triumphant in an encounter against overwhelming odds. Many messages — celebrating the glorious, divine victory — poured in from

---

83. This is Cilliers's own recollection of the Covenant quoted in *ibid.*, p. 110. Thompson, however, points to inconsistencies concerning the wording and adminstration of the oath in the recollections of the participants: see Thompson, *The Political Mythology of Apartheid*, pp. 166–8.
84. See Templin, *Ideology on a Frontier*, pp. 110–11.
85. See D. Harrison, *The White Tribe of Africa: South Africa in Perspective*, London, 1981 (hereafter *The White Tribe of Africa*), p. 17.
86. See Walker, *The Great Trek*, pp. 186–7.
87. However, it should be noted that the Afrikaners were not alone in the victory. Sources indicate that they were aided by several Englishmen and a contingent of black troops from Natal; also there is evidence that Coloured grooms and black herdsmen accompanied the *kommando*. See Harrison, *The White Tribe of Africa*, p. 17, and A. Cowell, *Killing the Wizards: Wars of Power and Freedom from Zaire to South Africa*, New York, 1992, p. 146.

kinsmen in the Cape, echoing these same sublime sentiments.[88] In keeping with the holy oath affirmed one week before, a church was soon erected in Pietermaritzburg — the new Afrikaner citadel of Natal.[89]

Kruger and the Renewal of the Covenant

Regardless of its immediate impact, the historian Leonard Thompson contends that the concept of the Covenant faded quickly into cultural oblivion.[90] Although Thompson concedes that there were private commemorations of 16 December during the past, it was not until the 1880s, in Kruger's Transvaal Republic, that the anniversary of Blood River was celebrated as a major public holiday,[91] and therefore, in his view, exploited for political purposes. He argues that before then it could not have resonated very powerfully with the Afrikaner masses, although he admits that it remained a very important occasion for some of the ageing Voortrekkers, including Sarel Cilliers, and was remembered in private observances. Thompson notes that it was two Dutch Reformed clergymen — both originally from Holland — in Natal, in 1864, who were instrumental in reviving public interest in the Covenant.

Conor Cruise O'Brien puts the fading prominence of the Covenant into the context of a culture no longer threatened:

For the various peoples who have at different periods identified themselves as chosen peoples, the idea — probably always knocking around at the back of their minds — tended to become explicit and urgent only at times of national crisis [...] The Covenant had done its work, and no need was felt to go on about it in more relaxed times [...] But the fact that these ideas have left little or no explicit record in times of relatively little pressure does not demonstrate that they did not remain around in the folk mind, available to be called upon in times of trouble.[92]

Moreover, one must wonder to what extent the devout would wish to subject the observance of such a supremely religious event to public display. In any event, the idea of the Covenant assumed an increasingly

88. See Templin, *Ideology on a Frontier*, pp. 112–13.
89. See Walker, *A History of Southern Africa*, p. 209.
90. See Thompson, *The Political Mythology of Apartheid*, chapter 5. Du Toit emphasizes the same point: see 'The Construction of Afrikaner Chosenness', pp. 131–2.
91. Yet the anniversary actually became a public holiday in the Transvaal in 1865, although its commemoration was relatively subdued: see Akenson, *God's Peoples*, p. 66.
92. O'Brien, 'Response', pp. 142–3. O'Brien goes on to remark that the situation was essentially the same with the Ulster Protestants who also only explicitly avowed their *chosenness* during periods of crisis.

overt socio-political dimension when British imperialism again threatened Afrikanerdom in the late nineteenth century.

Although the ever-encroaching British Empire was never far behind, the Afrikaner striving for collective freedom and independent statehood was finally — albeit temporarily — realized with the establishment of the South African Republic (known as the Transvaal) in 1852 and the Orange Free State in 1854. Loubser considers the motivation to be 'gaining control of the polity to institute the divine order in society as a whole'.[93] The New Jerusalem had been founded and its republican survival, as well as that of the culture and liberty of its citizens, was dependent on the ordinance of the Almighty, whose plan the people so plainly discerned.

In many ways Stephanus Johannes Paulus Kruger exemplified the Boer ideals of independence, pastoralism and, particularly, piety. The Kruger family was one which had embarked upon the Great Trek in the 1830s. Of German extraction, the Krugers were congregants of the doctrinally orthodox Gereformeerde Kerk, known as the Doppers. The Doppers constituted the most conservative of the Afrikaans' churches, and, advocating a life of sanctity and asceticism, were described by one historian as the 'Puritans of the Boer community'.[94] The young Paul Kruger quickly matured as the oxwagons rolled into the interior, and at an early age he took up farming and ranching in the Boer city-states of Rustenburg and Potchestroom. During his mid-twenties, Kruger — like the patriarchs of old — experienced a dramatic conversion,[95] and from that day forward his life was characterized by an intense, fundamentalist Calvinist faith and an unshakeable certainty of divine purpose. One of Kruger's biographers describes the early sense of Messianism on which Kruger built his career, 'everything that happened to him was seen in terms of the will of God, the key to the phenomenon of Kruger was his implicit belief that he was *called* by God'.[96] Kruger was destined to play a prominent role in the socio-political affairs of the Transvaal — first as part of a wartime triumvirate which rebelled against British occupation in 1880, and then as the Republic's president following his election in 1883. The devout

---

93. J.J. Loubser, 'Calvinism, Equality, and Inclusion: The Case of Afrikaner Calvinism' in S.N. Eisenstadt (ed.), *The Protestant Ethic and Modernization: A Comparative View*, New York and London, 1968, p. 374.

94. M. Nathan, *Paul Kruger: His Life and Times*, Durban, 1941, p. 37.

95. For a description of Kruger's conversion experience, see R. Statham, *Paul Kruger and His Times*, London, 1898, pp. 39–41, and Nathan, *Paul Kruger: His Life and Times*, pp. 38–9. J. Fisher provides a vivid glimpse of Kruger's adolescence and early adulthood on the frontier: see Fisher, *Kruger: His Life and Times*, London, 1974, pp. 12–20.

96. J. Meintjes, *President Paul Kruger*, London, 1974, p. 6.

Kruger left a profoundly theological imprint on the Transvaal during his years of public service.

If Kruger had a personal vocation, his people had a collective one. They had been guided from the Cape by the Almighty who had tried them in the wilderness; and, in Kruger's recollection, God had delivered them when they had placed their faith in Him and He had ultimately granted them liberty.[97] After the discovery of diamonds, however, the collective freedom of the Transvaal Afrikaners was again jeopardized as Imperial designs on the territory became increasingly apparent. When the British annexed the Transvaal in 1877, Kruger was convinced that God was chastizing the nation for forsaking the Covenant.[98]

As Afrikaner exasperation at British domination intensified and began to assume a more militant character, several thousand Boers assembled at Wonderfontein in 1879 and again made a covenant with God that their liberty might be restored. During the year which followed, more than ten thousand Afrikaners gathered at Paardekraal. In an extended meeting, infused with religious revivalism, the Boers defiantly reasserted their independence; and, like the Israelites of old, erected a great monument of stones as a symbol of their steadfast faith. Kruger attested to the congregants, 'I stand here before you called by the People. In the voice of the people I have heard the voice of God, the King of Nations, and I obey!'[99] And as the Afrikaners prepared for the inevitable confrontation with the British, they did so with the fervent expectation that God would protect their republic.

Several days later, tensions erupted into armed conflict and the First Anglo-Boer War — the First War of Independence, according to Afrikaners — was well under way.[100] In a series of skirmishes at Bronkhorstspruit, Laingsnek and Ingogo, the British were routed and suffered heavy losses; Afrikaner casualties were few. It was said that, upon hearing news of the initial triumph, Kruger prostrated himself in the dust and thanked God for His intervention.[101] The Boers' successful

97. See H. Giliomee, 'The Development of the Afrikaner's Self-concept' in H.W. van der Merwe (ed.) *Looking at the Afrikaner Today*, Cape Town, 1975, p. 17.
98. See T.D. Moodie, *The Rise of Afrikanerdom: Power, Apartheid, and the Afrikaner Civil Religion*, Berkeley and Los Angeles, 1975 (hereafter *The Rise of Afrikanerdom*), p. 27.
99. Quoted in Meintjes, *President Paul Kruger*, p. 106.
100. D.M. Schreuder provides a detailed narrative of the war: see Schreuder, *Gladstone and Kruger: Liberal Government and Colonial 'Home Rule' 1880–1855*, London, 1969, pp. 99–168. See also R.I. Lovell, *The Struggle for South Africa 1875–1899: A Study in Economic Imperialism*, New York, 1934, pp. 25–33, and C.F. Goodfellow, *Great Britain and South African Confederation 1870–1881*, Cape Town, 1966, pp. 198–203. For a captivating account of the decisive victory, see A.J.P. Opperman, *The Battle of Majuba Hill*, Johannesburg and Cape Town, 1981.
101. See Meintjes, *President Paul Kruger*, p. 110.

military momentum culminated in their stunning victory at Majuba Hill in February 1881. An armistice was brokered and independence was restored under the suzerainty of the Queen. Again, the Afrikaners had prevailed in the midst of an overwhelming foe; and, in the minds of many Boers, divine assistance and the inherent righteousness of their cause seemed to be the decisive factors in the determination of victory: 'They were convinced that the Lord had delivered the British hosts into their hands and could be relied on to do so in any future conflict.'[102]

Thousands of Afrikaners returned to Paardekraal in December 1881 to express their collective jubilation at the war's successful outcome in a patriotic celebration, which culminated in a religious service on 16 December.[103] Kruger admonished his constituents — to whom (at least those of Afrikaner extraction) he now referred as 'God's People' — that it was the Deity who had restored their freedom.[104] Clergymen of the Dutch Reformed Church revived public interest in the annual commemoration of the anniversary of the Covenant at Blood River — now popularly known as Dingaane's Day[105] — and it assumed ever-increasing prominence as Afrikaners reflected upon their ethno-history. The sublime conviction of divine election which had developed in the collective consciousness of the Voortrekkers was now solemnly pronounced by the Kruger regime and its significance was reinforced by the annual public celebration of the Covenant. The myth of ethnic election and the observance of the Vow constituted the fundamental tenets of a burgeoning nationalism which Moodie has described as the

---

102. See Fisher, *The Afrikaners*, p. 118.
103. Curiously, Thompson and du Toit insist that the festival at Paardekraal in 1881 and those which followed there for the next decade did not explicitly emphasize any historical continuity with the Covenant of 1838, but rather refocused public attention on the republican assembly which met on the same site in 1880. See Thompson, *The Political Mythology of Apartheid*, p. 171, and du Toit, 'The Construction of Afrikaner Chosenness', pp. 132–3. They argue that Kruger's political rhetoric at the time contained no direct references to Blood River. This view is, however, contradicted by F.A. van Jaarseld in his extremely controversial essay which recommended that the Day of the Vow be discontinued as a public holiday: see van Jaarseld, 'A Historical Mirror of Blood River' in A. Konig and H. Keane (eds), *The Meaning of History*, Pretoria, 1980, p. 27. Certainly, the parallels between Blood River and Majuba Hill must have been very much on the minds of Kruger and other Boers gathered at the celebration. Indeed, M. Juta reveals that, as a child, Kruger was deeply impressed by Cilliers's public prayers prior to the Boer victory at Veg-kop and became increasingly convinced that corporate supplication would bring divine favour: see Juta, *The Pace of the Ox: A Life of Paul Kruger*, Cape Town and Pretoria, 1975, p. 97.
104. See van Jaarsfeld, 'A Historical Mirror of Blood River', p. 27.
105. See Thompson, *The Political Mythology of Apartheid*, pp. 171–3; du Toit, 'The Construction of Afrikaner Chosenness', pp. 132–3; and van Jaarsveld, 'A Historical Mirror of Blood River', pp. 27–8.

Afrikaner 'civil religion'.[106] As Templin notes, 'During and following the war, patriotism, nationalism, hero worship, and theological assurance that the Boers were God's elect went hand in hand.'[107] The myth of divine election had been firmly implanted in the Afrikaner psyche.

Conclusion

The myth of divine election took root very early on in the course of Afrikaner ethno-history and exercised a profound influence on Afrikaner ethnogenesis. Even after the crushing Boer defeat in the Second Anglo-Boer War in 1902, the concept of chosenness — which resonated so powerfully in the popular imagination — persisted, if not intensified, and provided a very effective stimulus for socio-political mobilization prior to the electoral victory of the National Party in 1948. Afrikaner ethnic election, with its emphasis on racial exclusivity, also tragically facilitated the rise of apartheid after the nationalists captured state power. Although the South African state is no longer under the control of Afrikanerdom, the concept of chosenness which electrified the early Boers remains a potent force in Afrikaner politics. Even today, the myth of divine election continues to infuse Afrikaner nationalism.

---

106. See Moodie, *The Rise of Afrikanerdom.*
107. Templin, *Ideology on a Frontier*, pp. 212–13.

NATIONAL MYTHS IN THE NEW
CZECH LIBERALISM

Kieran Williams

It is well known that events since 1989 have allowed a reassertion and exploration of Slovak national identity. They have also, however, permitted a rethinking of Czechness in which myth plays a central part. New liberals (or 'liberal-conservatives') in the two main successor parties to Civil Forum, while usually associated primarily with economic transformation strategies, have taken part in this attempt at nation-shaping; indeed, a mythopoeic vision of the Czech nation is an essential component of the liberal revolution.

Nationalist mythopoeia may seem incompatible with the intentions of this liberal revolution, which is usually portrayed as rationalist, critical and self-critical, with an aversion to Romantic revolution's reliance on the emotional impulses of national culture.[1] In those rare instances that contemporary liberal theorists have tried to accommodate ideas of nationhood and nationality, they stress that nations are 'evolutive social realities' that emerge spontaneously through undirected interactions. Given the organic, evolutionary nature of the nation, they argue, it would be futile to try to impose a 'guided behaviour' on it.[2]

Guided behaviour, however, is exactly what new Czech liberals, especially Prime Minister Václav Klaus (on whom I will focus), hope to achieve through the use of myth in contemporary political discourse. The apparent paradox arising here is similar to that obtaining in the economic transition: new liberals are using precisely the constructivist devices so loathed in much liberal theory, in the belief that they will deliver the country to a purported condition of spontaneous, undirected order.

Motives

The reasons for this outwardly constructivist undertaking are several and various. The Czech liberal tradition, like those in many countries of Central Europe, always included concern for the fate of the nation as

1. Bruce Ackerman, *The Future of Liberal Revolution*, New Haven, CT, 1992, pp. 7–8.
2. Jesús Huerta de Soto, 'A Theory of Liberal Nationalism' in *Il Politico*, 60, 1995, pp. 583–98.

well as for individual freedom; in the nineteenth century the idea of a single, unified community of nationally conscious individuals was embraced as the vehicle for progress.[3] The Czech school of liberal political economy that flourished between 1890 and 1925, represented by Albín Bráf, Jozef Kaizl, Alois Rašín and Karel Engliš, combined principles of free trade, careful spending and restrained (but heartfelt) nationalism.[4] The young Rašín, whom Klaus has often cited as an inspiration, was so radical in his demands for recognition of the historical rights of the Bohemian state in the 1890s that he was imprisoned for two years, and during the First World War was sentenced to death for treason, a sentence commuted by the last Habsburg emperor.[5]

A second source of sensitivity to nationhood is the activity of a circle of independent intellectuals that originally assembled around the periodical *Tvář* in the mid-1960s and covertly re-convened in 1978. The group included Klaus (writing on economics under the pseudonyms Zdeněk Dvořák and Jan Řehák), Tomáš Ježek, Bohumil Doležal, Emanuel Mandler and Jan Strásky. Unlike the better-known group around Charter 77, this circle, which developed in the 1980s into the Democratic Initiative, connected a liberal concern for human rights to questions of nationhood and the national condition. In 1985 they devoted a whole collection of *samizdat* articles to the issue of Czech identity; Klaus did not participate, but Doležal and Ježek, who would serve as close advisers to Klaus after 1989, did.[6] It can be stated, therefore, that from an early point the core of the Czech liberal community linked issues of nationhood to those of individual emancipation.

Finally, a reason can be found in the very goal of the liberal revolution: to eliminate institutions and practices that distort the spontaneous ordering abilities of the market. It is deemed necessary that the individuals who will interact in pursuit of their ends do so with minds cleared of certain expectations and instilled with certain values. New Czech liberals assume that, just as a market of sorts always existed even under central planning, so certain values and inclinations have survived in Czech society which, with encouragement, can facilitate the transition to an open economy. So, as Václav Klaus has admitted:

---

3. Otto Urban, 'Český liberalismus v 19. století' in Milan Znoj, Jan Havránek and Martin Sekera (eds), *Český liberalismus: Texty a osobnosti*, Prague, 1995, pp. 16, 20.
4. For excerpts of their writings, see *ibid.*, pp. 460–95.
5. František Vencovský, *Alois Rašín: život a dílo*, Prague, 1992.
6. *Hledání naděje 1978–1987: Výber z ineditních sborníků*, Prague, 1993.

I believe in Adam Smith's invisible hand and in Hayek's spontaneously arising system of human interactions. At the same time, I am aware that it is necessary, especially in the initial construction of this system, to maintain certain, not insignificant, regularities and certain sequential rules, and that it is therefore necessary in this phase to grant a large 'constructing' role to the economic centre, to the institution whose role in a time of normal conduct of this conceived system must otherwise be minimal.[7]

In other words, Klaus has admitted that, during the transition to the free market, the state must help create the necessary conditions. This means not only the creation of certain institutions, intervention in market processes (wage, price and rent controls), and the illusion of private ownership (via investment funds and banks in which the state retains a controlling share), but also the formation of identity, appetites and aversions.

New Czech liberals enlist myth to present a vision of the Czech nation as Europeans naturally inclined to democracy, hard work, commerce and self-reliance. A mythologized reading of Czech history serves to erase awkward facts, such as the times when Czechs were inclined to pan-Slavism and looked away from Western Europe,[8] or acquiesced to authoritarian rule, either by foreigners or compatriots. Liberals also seek to establish a profile and programme distinct from that of President Havel and of the original Civil Forum. Above all, they must confront the fact that socialism and Communism, including Stalinism, had genuine support in the Czech working class and intelligentsia before 1948,[9] and that the Left still commands a following.

Choice of Myths

Roughly seven common myths are relevant that can be found in Czech literature, political discourse and popular imagination, as identified by Robert Pynsent,[10] Jiří Rak,[11] Vladimír Macura[12] and Ladislav Holy.[13]

7. Václav Klaus, *Česká cesta*, Prague, 1994, p. 74.
8. Jiří Rak, *Bývali Čechové: České historické mýty a stereotypy*, Jinočany, 1994 (hereafter *Bývali Čechové*), pp. 99–126.
9. Jacques Rupnik, 'The Roots of Czech Stalinism' in Raphael Samuel and Gareth Stedman-Jones (eds), *Culture, Ideology and Politics: Essays for Eric Hobsbawm*, London, 1982.
10. Robert B. Pynsent, *Questions of Identity: Czech and Slovak Ideas of Nationality and Personality*, London, 1994 (hereafter *Questions of Identity*), especially pp. 148–210.
11. Rak, *Bývali Čechové*.
12. Vladimír Macura, *Masarykovy boty a jiné semi (o) fejetony*, Prague, 1993.
13. Ladislav Holy, *The Little Czech and the Great Czech Nation: National Identity and the Post-Communist Social Transformation*, Cambridge, 1996.

The list is not exhaustive and these myths are not necessarily compatible; nor do they feature in every mythopoeic scheme.

1. The foundation myth of the Czech nation, when it entered the Bohemian lands led by Forefather Čech, who looked down from the Říp hill (just north of today's Prague), and viewed the Promised Land.

2. The myth of the natural democratic spirit of the Czechs. This myth is fuelled by legend or by readings of the medieval Bohemian kingdom, and leads to further assumptions that the Czechs are naturally individualist, love freedom and peace, and incline to civic virtue and to liberalism itself.

3. The myth of Slav reciprocity, especially of fraternity with Slovaks, which is portrayed as a time-honoured way to avoid or escape from ethnic, cultural and political isolation. There is a competing myth, however, of Slavs as prone to disunity and petty squabbling, rendering themselves vulnerable to foreign domination.

4. The myth of the special Czech mission, the great contribution to the spiritual liberation of Europe and all humanity, be it Charles IV's Gothic Arcadia, a Hussite purification of Christianity, 'socialism with a human face', or Bohemia as a bridge spanning the divide between East and West. This myth quietly supports arguments of Czech distinctness from (even superiority over) its neighbours, and of having different needs, aims and talents to theirs.

5. The myth of long-running conflict with certain neighbours, especially Germans, and of the unreliability or duplicity of the mightier nations of Western Europe.

6. The myth of a dark age (*temno*) of national dormition, especially after the skirmish of the White Mountain in 1620, which ties into the preceding myth of threats to identity from foreign domination.

7. The myth of realism, centrism (and being at the centre of Europe) and pragmatism as national virtues, the accepting of certain constraints and making the best of them. It can also be seen as a myth of mythlessness, of being a rational nation (again, unlike Poles, Slovaks and Hungarians) that is too honest and self-deprecating to sustain precisely the sorts of myths listed above.

Myths in Action

First, Klaus justifies his own rethinking of Czechness as a part of democratization and economic transformation by equating it to the original national revival that took place in the late eighteenth and early nineteenth centuries.[14] Just as that time has come to be presented as the rebirth (rather than invention) of Czech identity, so too Klaus masks

---

14. Klaus, *Česká cesta*, p. 26.

his revolution as the return to what is natural. The Communist period is portrayed as an age of darkness like that following the White Mountain, in that the nation and all of its members were degraded:

In the period of Communism we were oppressed individually [...] but we were equally oppressed as a nation. Under the banner of proletarian internationalism, we lost our national (and state) identity and now we are in the process of its repeated definition, in the process of the new formulation of our state and national interests.[15]

Klaus's most histrionic use of myth came in September 1993, when he delivered a speech from the summit of Říp. This is the hill in northern Bohemia from which the nation's mythical forefather, Čech, like Moses from Mount Nebo, looked over the lands below, then descended to tell his people, 'See, this is the land which you have sought. I have often spoken to you of it and promised that I will lead you into it. This is the Promised Land, full of beasts and birds, flowing with honey. You will have abundance in everything and it will be a good defence against enemies.'[16] In his speech Klaus referred to this tale simply as a legend, yet invoked what he considered truly resonant associations with Říp as the vantage point for foreseeing a happy future. He praised the hill as a symbol of 'the traditions of our ancestors', of their 'devotion to the ideas of national and civic freedom'. He reminded his audience that it was on Říp that a Czech prince built a chapel in the twelfth century to celebrate the Bohemian victory over the (German) Holy Roman Emperor Lothar, a battle — claimed Klaus — that affirmed the Czech state's distinct identity. (It should be noted, however, that the name Říp is probably Celtic or Germanic in origin.)

Klaus then looked over the landscape below Říp and reminded his audience of all that the Czechs had accomplished since 1989, assuring them that 'we are not threatened by the events which we have seen in recent days in Russia', since the Czech Republic, alone among post-Communist states, had made the transition to a market economy without social upheaval. Thanks to the 'practical, active patriotism' of every Czech today, he predicted, future generations would praise their achievements and would recall the poet Jaroslav Seifert's line, 'How nice it is here at home.'[17]

In the course of this short speech, Klaus combined myths of origin and destiny, interwove allusions to Czech feelings of superiority over other nations, presented a patriotism of constructive, non-conflictual civic work, and suggested that he was the new Forefather Čech,

---

15. Václav Klaus, *Dopočítávání do jedné*, Prague, 1995, p. 122.
16. As recounted by Alois Jirásek, *Staré pověsti české*, Prague, n.d., p. 11.
17. Klaus, *Česká cesta*, pp. 9–11.

surveying the glittering Promised Land of a successfully transformed society.

Though he is usually less histrionic, Klaus frequently employs mythical or mythologized characters from Czech history to reinforce a message about contemporary policy. For example, although it was decided not to make St Václav's (Wenceslas) Day (28 September) a state holiday, Klaus gave an address in September 1992 in which he attempted to rehabilitate his namesake as a forgotten national figure who symbolized the values that the new state should endorse. Though Klaus admitted that little is known of the historical Václav, apparently assassinated in 935, traditions tell of:

a prince basically more humane and educated than were his still semi-barbarian surroundings; a prince who, in the spirit of the faith that he took literally and seriously, to the letter, strove to elevate and cultivate these surroundings; who felt that from the West come not only attackers and conquerors but also, perhaps primarily, bearers and communicators of values in which the life of the individual and the existence of the state can be reliably anchored [...]. It is a tradition of Czech statehood — I emphasize Czech and I emphasize statehood. It is a Christian tradition that pushes certain values to the fore, such as humaneness and culture. It is a tradition linked with Europe.[18]

Klaus noted that Václav's apparent willingness to make an alliance with the Germans was misused by the Nazi Protectorate to encourage collaboration, and that this turned Czechs away from the values of Václav into the clutches of 'Communist Russia'. Now, when Czech statehood had been renewed, he proposed a return to the values represented by the Václav cult to provide a 'common language' to facilitate 'a basic and deep consensus in everyday life'. This return to course can include a *modus vivendi* with Germany, and to justify this relationship Klaus offered a Bavarian audience a benign, mythologized account of medieval Bohemia's suction into Germano-Roman Christianity, away from Byzantine Orthodoxy, a story he felt had to be told today since forty years of Communist rule had obscured the Czechs' 'natural' belonging to Europe.[19]

Klaus has displayed indifference to Jan Hus and, without directly attacking the Hussite movement, he has noted that religious conflicts in the early modern age were marked by violence and intolerance on all sides.[20] When accepting the Conrad Peutinger prize in 1993, he observed that Peutinger had travelled in Bohemia in the sixteenth century and had criticized Hussitism for allegedly endorsing common

18. Klaus, *Rok — málo či mnoho v dějinách země*, Prague, 1993 (hereafter *Rok*), p. 68.
19. Klaus, *Česká cesta*, p. 131.
20. *Ibid.*, p. 110.

ownership, and Klaus added that he himself views 'Hussite utopianism' as simply another third-way illusion, 'which in this regard differs little from Communism'.[21]

Instead, Klaus offered some thoughts in 1993 on the Counter-Reformation cult of Jan Nepomucký (St John of Nepomucene) on the 600th anniversary of his murder. Klaus did not attempt to explode the myth of Nepomucký, a German-speaking ecclesiastical functionary who was killed for asserting the jurisdiction of the Church against the State. A Nepomucene cult was then fostered by the Bohemian clergy in the eighteenth century to dispel the Czechs' international reputation as heretics and ease their return into the Catholic fold, and thereby restore national self-confidence and respect.[22] Instead, Klaus chose to present Nepomucký as the victim of 'the long battle between spiritual and secular powers. This battle is not only the framework within which were born the basic values of European civilization and thus of the Czech nation. It is also the basic feature of European democracy.' Klaus claimed that the resistance of the Church to State domination prevented the complete absorption of the spiritual realm into the political, and thus prevented the rise of something like Byzantine caesaropapism, which, he pointed out, had suffered prolonged decline, and had produced successor states (much of Eastern Europe) which remain backward and corrupt.

Having again found a chance to distance the Czech Republic from most of the post-Communist world, Klaus reflected on the divisive effect of the Nepomucene cult in Czech society as yet another example of an alleged Slav tendency to in-fighting, which he claimed only facilitates foreign domination and inhibits social integration. Klaus warned that today, 'at the moment of the advent of the new Czech state', the emergence of sharp cleavages in society 'would be something very dangerous'. He claimed that the Nepomucene cult has much in common with that of Hus, and that together they could offer a package of values around which Czech society should unite: justice and truth, public right and freedom of individual conscience. 'In the months and years ahead', he warned:

when we must put our devastated economy in order, renew basic moral and political values, and place our newly arisen independent state on a firm foundation, let us proceed aware of that division of which I have spoken, and which is still so prominently embodied in the dispute over Jan Nepomucký. We stand before a basic task: to search and find what binds all of us, all citizens of this state, regardless of nationality, religious or

---

21. *Ibid.*, p. 131.
22. Pynsent, *Questions of Identity*, pp. 201–2.

political persuasion. This means searching for a common Czech patriotism.[23]

In this way, a fourteenth-century clergyman can be enlisted to serve a twentieth-century politician keen to inhibit the emergence of social cleavages.

Myths of Czech uniqueness combine with myths of Czech realism in discussion of European integration. When asked whether he is a Eurosceptic, Klaus replied that he prefers to subscribe to 'Euro-realism', which he explains as a position 'that accepts reality, attempts to live in it and, at the same time, maximizes the effect that we can have from it'. This rules out what he dubs '*a priori* scepticism and any blocking of reasonable activities'.[24]

Such characteristic realism, Klaus explains, should also direct Czechs to remain modest in their self-perception: he told one interviewer that Czechs should have no illusions that they are in a position to make some great contribution to Europe, that they are somehow the navel of the world.[25] Yet, in almost the same breath, Klaus makes pronouncements that conform perfectly to myths of national mission. He tells his countrymen that they can make a great contribution to Europe just by being a free people.[26] What this means is that Czechs, located (he claims) equidistant to Maastricht and Sarajevo, can use their experience of Communism to warn the world against the constructivist conceit. In particular, Czechs can warn Europe against the dangers of the trend that Klaus claims to see in the West of pursuing vaguely left-wing, interventionist policies, both nationally and supranationally in Brussels:

The Czech Republic has the chance — in the historical period of which we are speaking — to warn against this danger. We have behind us the experience of Communism and this makes us very sensitive to certain things which the West does not feel so keenly.[27]

It is thus the Czech mission to save Europe from its own unhealthy inclinations, those deep-rooted leanings of which Hayek warned, towards socialism, planning and constructivism. In the service of this liberating mission, Klaus castigates Brussels for maintaining protectionist barriers to trade with East-Central Europe, which he scorns as 'a clear example that neither the idea of the free market nor the idea of Europeanism as such have yet triumphed'.[28] It is the Czech

23. Klaus, *Rok*, p. 70.
24. Vladimír Mlynář, 'Rozhovor s Václavem Klausem' in *Respekt*, 1994, 21.
25. Antonín Přidal, *Z očí do očí*, Brno, 1994, p. 161.
26. *Ibid.*
27. Mlynář, 'Rozhovor s Václavem Klausem'. See also Klaus, *Česká cesta*, pp. 148, 164.
28. Klaus, *ibid.*, p. 136. See also Klaus, *Dopočítávání do jedné*, pp. 141–5.

lot today, he suggests, to teach Europe the true meaning of both, to be a bearer of freedom.

In arguing this point, he has no qualms about comparing himself to Konrad Adenauer, who simultaneously acted as head of government, head of the main German right-wing political party, and as a driving force for European integration.[29] At the same time, Klaus has rebuked Adenauer for rejecting the possibility of positive national sentiments and for espousing a Europe of blurred national boundaries. It is part of the Czech mission to promote a vision of Europe in which national identity, especially the newly rediscovered identity of the Czechs themselves, would not be submerged. Lest Czechs forget the dangers that can accompany dealings with larger nations, such as the British, French and Germans, Klaus periodically reminds them of the ways these peoples have failed the Czechs at crucial moments in the past.[30]

Impact

To date, Klaus's use of myth in guiding Czech behaviour has had limited results. As noted earlier, a key motive for the use of myth is to deter voters from registering their sympathy with parties of the Left. Despite such efforts, in the 1996 elections to the lower house of parliament, the Social Democrats received 26.4 per cent, and the relatively orthodox Communists 10.3 per cent. Another 8 per cent of the vote went to the Republican Party, whose ultranationalism has little in common with the liberal view of Czechness. Although Klaus was able to assemble a minority government, the vote tally showed that a very large share of the participating electorate did not want to conform to the Czech stereotype promoted by the coalition.

Looking ahead, however, liberals may find a more willing audience as new school textbooks engrain in children a nation-centred (rather than class-centred) approach to Czech history. David Čaněk concludes a recent analysis of textbooks with the claim that a clear mythicization of the nation and the national movement can now be detected. The history of the nineteenth century in Bohemia and Moravia is taught exclusively as the history of the Czech national movement, with non-Czech groups (Roma, Jews, Germans) either completely omitted from school history or vilified.[31] Imbued with a view of history in which Czech national assertion plays a central part, the next generation of voters may prove more receptive to the political power of myth.

---

29. Klaus, *Česká cesta*, p. 149.
30. See his musings on Munich, for example, in *ibid.*, pp. 20–2.
31. David Čaněk, *Národ, národnost, menšiny a rasismus*, Prague, 1996.

POLISH NATIONAL MYTHOLOGIES

Norman Davies

Everyone needs myths. Individuals need myths. Nations need myths. Myths are the sets of simplified beliefs, which may or may not approximate to reality, but which give us a sense of our origins, our identity, and our purposes. They are patently subjective, but are often more powerful than the objective truth — for the truth can be painful.

Some nations have more need of their myths than do others. Imperial nations invent myths in order to justify their rule over other peoples. Defeated nations invent myths to explain their misfortune and to assist their survival. Poland may well have belonged to this latter category, as political adversity over many generations seems to have created the sort of imaginative climate in which myths can flourish. Polish culture, and in particular literature, art and historiography, is full of instances where the national imagination triumphs over realism.

A facetious piece of evidence to support this point of view may lie in the fact that the Polish word for 'myth' is *mit* — pronounced like the English 'meat'. In the days of food shortages in the 1970s and 1980s, when Poles would stand in line for hours on end for the most basic of supplies, they used to pass the time telling jokes. One hoary teaser asked: 'What word has the same sound and meaning in both English and Polish?' The answer was, of course, '*mit*'.

More seriously, it is important to remember that, in modern times, the Poles have had to compete with the mythology of other stronger nations who have often given a pejorative twist to Poland's image. In the national mythology of Russia, for example, the Poles are usually cast in the role of the eternal Western enemy, the traitor to Slavdom, the religious foe of the Orthodox Church, the main resort of scheming foreigners, who constantly conspire to invade Russia and to undermine her traditional values. Russians love to remember the one occasion, in 1612, when a Polish army occupied the Moscow Kremlin. They conveniently forget the far more numerous occasions when Russian armies have trampled over Poland. It so happened that Russia's national identity was crystallizing in the mid-nineteenth century, in the very era when the two great Polish Risings of 1830–1 and 1863–4 shook the tsarist empire to its core. The opposition between noble Russian and ignoble Poland was fixed for the duration. One has only to watch one of the wonderful Russian operas of that era, such as

Another version of this paper was presented in February 1996 as the Milewski Lecture at New Britain, CT.

141

Glinka's *A Life for the Tsar* or Mussorgsky's *Boris Godunov*, to see how deeply Russians are imbued with a negative stereotype of Poland. It was no accident that Dostoevsky gave Polish names to many of his criminal characters (notwithstanding that his own name was of Polish origin).

The Zionist myth, too, casts Poland in a negative role. It has gained widespread publicity due to the unparalleled tragedy of the Jewish Holocaust and to powerful American support for the state of Israel. In essence, it holds that the stateless condition of the Jewish people in pre-war Europe left them so vulnerable to persecution that the creation of a separate Jewish state in Palestine was the only viable solution. Unfortunately, since Poland was the European country where most European Jews had settled and where the German Nazis chose to perpetrate the Holocaust, an exclusively hostile image of Poland has become a central feature of the Zionist programme.

Germans have looked on their eastern neighbours much as the English once looked on the Irish. Just as Ireland proved to be the only obviously discontented part of the United Kingdom in the nineteenth century, so the Poles stood out as the most substantial and troublesome minority in the German empire. What is more, Poland provided the most accessible pool of cheap labour for German industries, and millions of poor migrants flocked westwards into the rapidly expanding cities. As a result, the widespread sympathy for Poland, which had been manifested in the era of the *Polenlieder* of the 1830s, faded away; and for at least a century German and Polish nationalism were irreconcilable. According to the hostile German stereotypes, 'Polack' summoned up images of hopeless romantics, feckless workers, undesirable tramps, and anti-German conspirators. *Polnische Wirtschaft* (literally 'Polish economics') became a standard German idiom for 'a right old mess'. So-called 'Polish Jokes', which type-cast all Poles as primitive and stupid, were a close parallel to the 'Irish Jokes' retailed in England. The long tradition of disdain for everything Polish provided a ready-made ingredient for the later Nazi policies of German racial supremacy, where Poles were officially included in the class of *Untermenschen* — 'sub-humans'.

There is no way that the riches of Poland's national mythology can be reduced to the space of one short chapter. They can be illustrated, however, from a number of different examples drawn from a variety of historical periods. In the exposé which follows, seven separate myths will be examined.

1587

In 1587, the memorable *Annales sive de origine et rebus gestis Polonorum et Lithuanorum* was published in Cracow by the Calvinist nobleman, Stanisław Sarnicki. This treatise on 'The Origins and Deeds of the Poles and Lithuanians' was by no means the first of its kind. Sarnicki had several prominent rivals in the historical profession of his day, including the Bishop of Warmia, Marcin Kromer (1512–89), whose famous chronicle, *De origine et rebus gestis Polonorum*, had been printed more than thirty years earlier. Sarnicki is remembered for giving a new twist to an old tale.

Ever since the Jagiellonian court historian, Canon Jan Długosz, writing in the previous century, most Polish writers had held to the theory that the Polish nation could trace its roots to the ancient Sarmatians, a nomadic Indo-Iranian people who had settled the plains of Eastern Europe before the Christian Era. The classical division of the Eurasian steppes into *Sarmatia europea* and *Sarmatia asiatica* with the boundary on the River Tanais or Don was still current in Renaissance Europe. Sarnicki's contribution was to claim that the Sarmatians were ancestors not of the Poles as a whole, but only of the Polish nobility. Henceforth, it was the *szlachta* alone who claimed Sarmatian descent. Very soon, *nobilis-Polonus-Sarmata* became synonyms for members of a 'Sarmatian race'. Non-nobles, burghers, Jews and peasants were not even counted as Poles. The 'Polish nation' was seen to consist exclusively of nobles.

Such was the haughty arrogance of this noble racism that it may be compared to the notorious *limpieza de sangre*, the belief in the purity of noble blood which flourished in Spain in the same period. Polish nobles were taught to believe that they were biologically different from the rest of the population, and that their privileges depended on 'the defence of their blood'. Miscegenation with the lower estates was treated as a crime. Walerian Nekanda Trepka, author of the *Liber chamorum* or 'Book of Hams' (1620), spent much of his life rooting out thousands of families of ignoble origin who, having fraudulently wormed their way into the *szlachta*, were busily diluting the race. For him, and his like, it was impossible to think without distaste of nobles and non-nobles marrying or breeding:

Balsam, when added to tar, ceases to be balsam but turns to tar; and weeds, when sown in the finest fields, will not become wheat [...] so, if a noblewoman marries a peasant, she will certainly give birth to an ignoble child. For what purity can come from such impurity, what perfume from such a stench! It is a wise proverb: Nightingales are not born from owls.[1]

Poland's 'Sarmatian Myth' has many parallels in other European countries. It has much in common, for example, with the Normanist Theory in Russia, which held that the founders of 'Kievan Rus'' and their kin in the modern Russian aristocracy were the descendants not of Slavs but of Vikings. What is more, like the Normanist Theory, it evolved over time. In the seventeenth century, in the era of Poland's closest contacts with the Ottomans, it helped to bolster the Oriental style of dress and armour which the Polish nobility adopted. In the eighteenth century, it underlay the conservative philosophy of 'Sarmatism' which favoured the complacent view that everything in Poland, including the 'Golden Freedom' of the *szlachta*, was unique and superior. By that time, on the eve of the Commonwealth's demise, the racial overtones of the ancestral myth had mellowed; and large numbers of Jews, for example, were able to buy their ennoblement without difficulty.

The question remains whether Poland's 'Sarmatian Myth' contains any grain of historical fact. Most historians have treated it as a colourful fantasy, a genealogical invention as eccentric as that of Polish nobles who claimed to be descended from Noah or from Julius Caesar. The evidence is certainly thin. But that does not stop scholars from trying. One intriguing curiosity lies in the passable resemblance which exists between the emblems of Poland's unusual system of heraldry and the *tamgas* or 'pictorial charges' of the ancient Sarmatians. Given that a tribe of Sarmatian Alans was said to have disappeared into the backwoods of Eastern Europe in the fourth century, it is nice to think that there might have been some sort of ancestral link between the most efficient cavalrymen of the Roman Army and the most distinguished cavalrymen of early modern Europe. Sobieski's 'Winged Hussars' were still carrying the same enormous lances, and riding the same oversize chargers, that had made the Alans famous more than a thousand years before.[2]

1620

On 11 March 1620, the Crown Chancellor of Poland, George Ossoliński, paid a visit to London, and read a Latin peroration before King James I in Whitehall Palace. He brought news of the latest

1. From W.N. Trepka, *Liber Generationis vel Plebeanorum* (Liber Chamorum), ed. W. Dworaczek, Wrocław, 1963; 'Proemium' quoted by Norman Davies, *God's Playground*, 2 vols, Oxford, 1981, vol. 1, p. 233.
2. See Tadeusz Sulimirski, *The Sarmatians*, London, 1970, discussed by Neal Ascherson, *Black Sea*, London, 1995, pp. 230–43.

invasion of Poland's eastern borders by the Ottoman Turks, and appealed to the English King for aid against the infidel. After all, as he explained, Poland was 'the most trusty rampart of the Christian world':

Tandem erupit ottomanorum iam diu celatum pectore virus [...] et publico barbarorum furore, validissimum christiani orbis antemurale, petitur Polonia.

[At last, the poisonous and hidden plan of the Ottomans has been revealed, and Poland, the most trusty rampart of the Christian world, has been assailed by the vulgar fury of the barbarians.][3]

The myth of Poland's role as the 'Bulwark of Christendom', the *antemurale christianitatis*, had a very long career. Initially inspired by the wars against Turks and Tartars, it was later employed to justify Poland's defence of Catholic Europe against the Orthodox Muscovites, and later against Communism and Fascism. It was still very much alive in the twentieth century, in the Polish–Soviet War of 1920, for instance, or in the spiritual sense, in Solidarity's stand against the decaying Communist regime of the 1980s. Not surprisingly, it inspired the name of a very distinguished academic journal, published in Rome.[4]

The myth of the *antemurale* does indeed encapsulate many splendid sentiments, but it can hardly be taken at face value as a perfect reflection of historical reality. For one thing, the Poles were not alone in seeing themselves as the watchmen of the Catholic world. Hungarians and Croats boasted very similar views, and used the same terminology. For another, it is not realistic to think of Poland's strategic role over half a millennium exclusively in terms of static defensive emplacements. On many occasions, the Poles did man the ramparts. On other occasions, they sallied forth and stormed other people's ramparts. It may have been something of an exception to the general rule, but the sight of Polish soldiers manning the walls of the Moscow Kremlin in 1612, or marching with Napoleon into Russia exactly 200 years later, is not what the *antemurale* was meant to signify. It is a sad fact that different European nations remember different historical dates.

3. *A True Copy of the Latin Oration of the excellent Lord George Ossolinski .[...] as it was pronounced to his Majestie at White-hall by the said Embassadour [...]* (London, 1621); printed in W. Chalewik (ed.), *Anglo-Polish Renaissance Texts*, Warsaw, 1968, pp. 247–62.
4. *Antemurale*, Journal of the Polish Historical Institute in Rome (1954–).

1655

In 1655, the Commonwealth of Poland–Lithuania had been overrun
from all sides. The Russians had taken Minsk and Wilno, and were
marching on Kiev. The Swedish armies of Charles X had advanced on
two fronts, from Pomerania in the West and from the Baltic provinces
in the East. They captured Warsaw and Cracow. The Pauline monastery
of Jasna Góra near Częstochowa was one of the very few fortified
positions in the country to hold firm. Protected by its holy icon of the
'Black Madonna', the *Matka Boska Częstochowska*, it resisted all
attempts to seize it. As the monks intoned their prayers to the Blessed
Virgin, and the Prior stood on the battlements hurling defiance, the
Swedish cannonballs bounced harmlessly off the roof, and Swedish
muskets backfired into the musketeers' faces. The monastery proved
impregnable. After months of futile siege, the Swedish King sounded
the retreat. Poland was saved. Indeed, she recovered so quickly that,
within two years, the Polish armies of Hetman Stefan Czarnecki were
advancing across the Baltic into Sweden. In recognition of the
country's deliverance, the Polish King, John Casimir, vowed to
dedicate his whole kingdom to the Virgin Mary. At the moving
ceremony held in the cathedral of Lwów, the *Śluby lwowskie*, in 1656,
the Virgin Mary was solemnly crowned as the 'Queen of Poland'.
Henceforth, Catholic Poles were taught not just to revere the Mother
of God as their patron, but increasingly to regard Catholicity as the
touchstone of their national identity. Here was a key moment in the
growth of myth of the *Polak-Katolik*, 'the Catholic Pole' — the belief
that if you weren't a Roman Catholic, you somehow didn't qualify to
be a true Pole.

Given that anything between one third and one half of Poland's
population consisted of non-Catholics — Protestants, Orthodox,
Uniates, Jews and Muslims — the growing association of Polishness
and Catholicity was to prove extremely divisive. The divisions became
most intense in the era of nationalism in the late nineteenth and early
twentieth centuries, when each of Poland's numerous minorities
developed strong national and ethnic identities of their own. It was no
accident that the journal of Poland's most nationalistic political
movement, the *Stronnictwo narodowe* or 'National Democracy' of
Roman Dmowski (1870–1939), took the name of *Polakatolik*. It
would have been news to Polish nationalists of that persuasion to learn
that the Teutonic Knights, and the Kingdom of France, had both
adopted the patronage of the Virgin Mary long before Poland did.

Even so, for generations of Poles, the serene and sorrowful face of
the *Matka Boska* has been the source of great solace. The power of the
Black Madonna of Częstochowa, and her counterpart in Lithuania, the
Matka Boska Ostrobramska, is celebrated in liturgy and literature alike.

Best loved, perhaps, is the invocation which occurs in the opening lines of the national epic, *Pan Tadeusz* by Adam Mickiewicz:

> Panno święta, co Jasnej bronisz Częstochowy
> I w Ostrej świecisz Bramie! Ty, co gród zamkowy
> Nowogródzki ochraniasz z jego wiernym ludem!
> Jak mnie dziecko do zdrowia powróciłaś cudem
> (Gdy od płaczącej matki pod Twoją opiekę
> Ofiarowany, martwą podniosłem powiekę
> I zaraz mogłem pieszo do Twych świątyń progu
> Iść za wrócone życie podziękować Bogu),
> Tak nas powrócisz cudem na Ojczyzny łono.

[O Holy Virgin, who guards the Bright Mount of Częstochowa / and shines in the Pointed Gate of Wilno! You, who / shield the castle wall of Novogródek and its faithful folk! / Just as you miraculously returned me to health as a child / (When, surrendered to your care by my weeping mother, / I raised a dead eyelid / And could walk straightaway to the door of your temple / To give thanks to God for a life redeemed), / So by a miracle you will return us to the bosom of our homeland.][5]

Personally, I would add the magnificent words of a later poet, Leszek Serafinowicz, who took the pen name of Jan Lechoń (1859–1956), one of the founders of the Skamander Group:

> Matka Boska Częstochowska, ubrana perłami
> Cała w złocie i brylantach modli się za nami...
> O Ty, której obraz widać w kazdej polskiej chacie,
> I w kosciele, i w sklepiku, i w pysznej komnacie,
> W ręku tego co umiera, nad kołyszką dzieci,
> I przed ktorą dniem i nocą wciąż się światło świeci.
> Która perły masz od królów, złoto od rycerzy
> W którą wierzy nawet taki który w nic nie wierzy,
> Która widzisz z nas każdego cudnymi oczami,
> Matko Boska Częstochowska, zmiłuj się nad nami.

[Oh, Holy Mother of Częstochowa, dressed in pearls, / Covered in gold and diamonds, pray for us all... / You, whose image one sees in every Polish cottage, / In every church, in every humble shop, in every proud hall, / You are there in the hand of the dying and in the baby's cradle; / Night and day, the light burns constantly before you. / You have jewels from kings, and the golden gifts of noble knights. / Yet they believe in you, even those who believe in nothing. / You watch over each of us through miraculous eyes. / Oh Mother of God of Częstochowa, have mercy on our souls.][6]

---

5. Adam Mickiewicz, *Pan Tadeusz*, I, ll. 5–13, translated by Norman Davies.
6. Jan Lechoń, 'Matka Boska Częstochowska' in *Poezja Polska: Antologia w układzie S. Grochowiaka i J. Maciejewskiego*, Warsaw, 1973, vol. 2, p. 188.

I take the key line here to be: 'Yet they believe in you, even those who believe in nothing.' Lechoń could see, as many did not, that Poland's supremely mystical Catholic symbol can give strength to Christians and to non-Christians alike.

1768

Umań, or Human´, is a little town near the Dnieper, deep in Ukraine and close to the easternmost border of the old Polish Commonwealth. In 1768, it was the scene of a series of terrible massacres. A fearful peasant rising, the *Koliszczyzna*, had sent bands of serfs on the rampage; and in those parts, the peasants were Orthodox. In the mayhem, Catholics and Jews were butchered together in their thousands, or herded into their churches and synagogues and burned alive. A Russian army appeared to restore order by methods little different from those of the rebels.

It is in the setting of that Peasant Rising that one of the great prophetic figures of Polish (and Ukrainian) history and literature most usually makes his appearance. Little of certainty is known about the Cossack seer Mojsej Wernyhora. It is not even certain that he really existed, although one source suggests that he was born in Dymitrówka in left-bank Ukraine and that he fled to Poland after killing his brother. His prophecies first circulated by word of mouth, and were only later written down. In the nineteenth century, when the Commonwealth had already been destroyed, he became a symbol of hope and resurrection. He spoke of a 'Golden Age' before the age of disasters, when all the peoples of the former Commonwealth, especially Poles and Ukrainians, had lived in unity. And he foretold the day when honour, harmony and happiness would return. He was celebrated in many different poetic versions from Goszczyński to Wyspiański. The Romantics were specially susceptible to Wernyhora's spell, not least the sublime Słowacki:

> Czy znasz prorocką dumę Wernyhory?
> Czy wiesz, co będzie w jarze Janczarychy,
> Gdzie teraz gołab lub jelonek cichy,
> Ze łzą przeczystą w szafirowym oku,
> Gdzieś w księżycowym się przegląda stoku?
> Czy wiesz, że wszystkie te się sprawdzą śnicia
> W jednej godzinie rycerskiego życia?
> Ze zemścisz syna, ojca, matkę, brata,
> W tej błyskawicy, co na szabli lata?

[Do you know the prophetic tale of Wernyhora? / Do you know what there will be in the Canyon of Yancharykha / Where now the dove or the silent young stag, / Through crystal tear in sapphire eye, / Watches his reflection somewhere in the falling moon? / Do you know that all those dreams will all come true / In a single hour of this noble life? / That you will avenge father and son, mother and brother, / In the flash which flies from a swirl of the sabre?][7]

In the twentieth century, ideals similar to those of Wernyhora came to be associated with the Independence Movement of Józef Piłsudski, whose aspiration was to restore a modern version of the old multinational Commonwealth. In the work of historians, they were part and parcel of the so-called 'Jagiellonian Concept' — the idea that Poland's past should be shared by all the peoples who had once lived together in the *Rzeczpospolita*. They were abhorred — by Polish nationalists of the Dmowski persuasion who were looking to a 'Poland for the Poles'; by Ukrainian nationalists, who had a similar vision of 'Ukraine for the Ukrainians'; by the advocates of Russian and Soviet imperialism, who sought to divide and rule; and most bitterly by the post-war Communist regime. In a world of nationalisms and power politics, they may have been impractical; and they certainly lost out. But they were no less respectable for that. They had their moments — as during Piłsudski's ill-starred campaign in 1919–21 for a Federation of the Border Nations. In the spring of 1920, when Piłsudski and his Ukrainian allies liberated Kiev from the Bolsheviks in the name of an independent Ukraine, they seemed to be on the brink of realization. But a world misled by Bolshevik slogans shouted incongruously 'Hands Off Russia!', and the opportunity passed.[8] Yet their day may come again. After all, even today, a conscious policy of confraternity is the only barrier which stands between the sovereignty of the nations of Eastern Europe and the triumph of brute force.

1831

It is one of the ironies of Polish history that the national bard, Adam Mickiewicz, never saw Warsaw or Cracow. Born at Nowogródek in Lithuania, he spent most of his life in exile, first in Russia and later in France. In 1831, at the height of the Russo–Polish War that followed the November Rising, he was in Dresden, composing his mystical patriotic drama *Dziady* (Forefathers' Eve). Whilst his peers were fighting in vain for the survival of a constitutional Polish Kingdom, he was forging the allegories and metaphors which gave sense to their struggle. Most powerful of all for a Catholic nation was the idea first launched in the scene in Father Peter's Cell, where Mickiewicz

7.   Juliusz Słowacki, *Wacław*, ll. 28–36, quoted by W. Stabryła, *Wernyhora w Literaturze Polskiej* (1933), Cracow, 1996, p. 62.
8.   See Norman Davies, 'The Kiev Campaign' in *idem, White Eagle, Red Star: The Polish–Soviet War, 1919-20*, London and New York, 1972, pp. 105–29.

imagined Poland's suffering to be a necessary evil for the eventual salvation of all the world. Poland, it was clearly implied, was 'the Christ of Nations'. As had first been mooted during Kościuszko's National Rising forty years before, the Poles were fighting for 'Our Freedom and Yours': 'The Saviour Nation will arise, and united, will heal the whole of Europe.'

Mickiewicz's contemporary, Kazimierz Brodziński (1791–1835) put it most succinctly:

> Hail, O Christ, Thou Lord of Men,
> Poland in Thy footsteps treading,
> Suffers humbly at Thy bidding,
> Like Thee, too, shall rise again![9]

Elsewhere, in his *Books of the Polish Nation*, Mickiewicz repeated the formula in truly biblical tones:

But the Kings when they heard were frightened in their hearts, and said [...] 'Come let us slay this nation'. And they conspired together [...]. And they crucified the Polish Nation and laid it in its grave, and cried out 'We have slain and buried Freedom'. But they cried out foolishly [...].

For the Polish Nation did not die. Its body lieth in the grave; but its spirit has descended into the abyss, that is, into the private lives of people who suffer slavery in their own country [...]. But on the Third Day the soul shall return again to the body, and the Nation shall arise, and free all the peoples of Europe from slavery.[10]

Notwithstanding its great emotive power, the myth of the *Chrystus narodów* had several major drawbacks. In the first place, it borders on blasphemy. Whatever the injustices involved, no rigorous Catholic can accept that the political fate of a people may be compared even metaphorically to the crucifixion of Christ. There was, in fact, a profound conflict between the patriotism of Catholic Poles and their loyalty to the faith. Those who were more patriotic than Catholic felt that the Church had betrayed them. Those who were more Catholic than patriotic felt that the insurrectionaries had created an impossible dilemma. Even today, many Poles choose to forget that Mickiewicz was not a conventional believer, or that the Pope in Rome actively condemned the Rising which inspired Mickiewicz's near-blasphemous metaphor.[11]

In the second place, the Christ of Nations concept reinforced the divisions already opened up by the older idea of *Polak-Katolik*. By

9. K. Brodziński, 'Na dzień zmarchwystania polskiego w 1831r', *Poezje*, Wrocław, 1959, vol. 1, pp. 239–40; translated by Norman Davies.

10. A. Mickiewicz, *Księgi narodu polskiego i pielgrzymstwa polskiego*, ed. S. Pigoń, Cracow, 1927, pp. 55ff., quoted by Davies, *God's Playground*, vol. 2, p. 9.

11. See Norman Davies, 'The Religion of Patriotism' and 'The Divided Conscience' in *idem*, *Heart of Europe: A Short History of Poland*, Oxford, 1984, pp. 268–78.

strengthening Poland's mystical Catholicity, it weakened the bonds of a multinational society. It was more poetic than practical.

Lastly, there is the vexed question of altruism. 'Christ died for the sins of others.' Therefore, Poland fights for the freedom of all. What a wonderful political spin! Of course, there was a sense in which Poland, by opposing the three great empires of Eastern Europe, was *ipso facto* supporting the cause of other oppressed nations. There were many individual cases of generous exiled Poles who gave their lives in the service of far-flung causes. They belonged to an ancient and honourable tradition. The Republic of Haiti has never forgotten the Polish legionaries who helped throw off the rule of France in 1802–3. There is no Hungarian who has not heard of General Józef Bem, hero of the war of 1848–9. And there was Mickiewicz himself, who went to fight for the Roman Republic (that is, against the Pope) in 1849, and who died in Constantinople in 1855, whilst trying to organize auxiliaries to fight against Russia in the Crimean War.

Yet that is not the whole story. When it came to matters closer to home, the Poles were not always so generous. In the politics of the Austro-Hungarian Empire, there was little Polish sympathy for the cause of the Czechs or the Slovaks. In Russia, the task of the tsarist authorities in the western gubernias was greatly assisted by the growing animosities between Poles and Lithuanians, Poles and Jews, Poles and Ruthenians.

1892

The last decade of the nineteenth century saw the birth of Poland's modern political parties. The Polish Socialist Party (PPS) came into being, in exile in Paris, in 1892. The Polish Peasant Movement (PSL) held its first gathering at Rzeszow in Galicia in July of the same year. The National League, forerunner of Dmowski's National Democrats, emerged in Warsaw a year later. So too did the Polish Communist group, the SDKP, and its sister circle in Lithuania, the SDWKL. The Polish Christian Democracy or *Chadecja*, which was mainly based in the Prussian Partition, in Silesia, appeared a bit later, in 1902.

Of these, the two parties with the strongest mass support were undoubtedly the Peasants (known as the *ludowcy*) and the Nationalists, the *narodowcy*. The two groups appealed to very different social constituencies, but they both shared a belief in perhaps the most powerful ideological construct of early twentieth-century European politics — what political scientists sometimes call 'integral nationalism'. The central aspect of this construct, most eloquently expounded in this same period in France by the founders of *Action Française*, lay in the mystical union of the nation and the national territory. Germans invented the slogan 'Blut und Boden' (Blood and Soil). In the Polish case, similar ideas were rooted in the notion which came to be known as the *koncepcja piastowska*, 'The Piast Concept'. One of its early propagators was Bolesław Wysłouch (1855–1937), the founding father of the PSL. The other was Jan Popławski (1854–1908), a leading ideologist of the nationalists.

Reduced to its essentials, the Piast Concept rested on a simple and persuasive historical myth. A thousand years ago and more, the Polish nation had supposedly lived on its ancestral land in unity and harmony, ruled by the benevolent hand of its first legendary ruler, a peasant son called Piast. Over the centuries, however, the Poles lost their unity, and lost control of their native land. All manner of aliens and intruders — Germans, Jews, Ukrainians and Russians — abused Poland's natural hospitality and took large parts of Poland's towns and countryside for themselves. Foreign kings were seated on the Polish throne, to the point when the throne itself was abolished. Poland was robbed of her inheritance. So the message was clear. All patriotic Poles had a duty to unite and drive all foreigners from their native soil: 'Poland for the Poles!' The Piast Concept was the natural ally of the *Polak-Katolik*. It was diametrically opposed to the multinational Jagiellonian Concept which was preferred by the PPS and by Piłsudski's Independence Movement, and which gained the upper hand in the ruling circles of the inter-war period.[12]

One should perhaps recall that modern party politicians were by no means the only ones to have used the Piast legend for their own purposes. In the days of royal elections it had been used as an argument to oppose the rule of foreign kings. In the seventeenth and eighteenth centuries, it became the custom to give the name of 'Piast' to all Polish-born candidates for the throne. In the Romantic era, Piast was used as a symbol of Poland's distant pagan past, full of mystery, simplicity and bounty:

> Kmieć Piast, przed chatą, dobrego wieczora
> Używał, stary kmieć pełny dobroci;
> A wtem skrzypnęła domora zapora
> I weszli do wrót Aniołowie złoci.
> Wnet przed niemi stół, stągiew miodu spora,
> Pełno mięsiwa i mącznych łakoci,
> Pełno owoców rozsypano różnych.
> Duchów przyjęto jadłem — jak podróżnych
> [...]

[The peasant Piast stood in front of his hut, / A good natured old yokel enjoying the fine evening; / Then suddenly the balcony of his cottage creaked / And in through the gates came the golden angels. / Before them —

12. Davies, 'The Ethnic Core' in *ibid.*, pp. 323–7.

a table, laden with flagons of mead, / And groaning with meats and baked delights, / And covered with fruits of rich variety. / The spirits were treated to the food, as if they were travellers / ...][13]

It is perhaps futile for historians to discuss how much of the Piast Concept was true and how much was false. The point is that millions of Poles believed it, and many still do. What is more, many of the foreign statesmen and politicians, from Woodrow Wilson to Stalin, seemed to believe it. Although no one could actually agree where Poland's 'ethnographic territory' lay, and no one could easily define who exactly was a Pole and who was not, there was a widespread assumption that ethnographic Poland had somehow to be defined and that 'the Poles' were suffering an intolerable injustice until they were given it back. It was a ready-made recipe for blood-spilling. Every attempt to define and reorganize Poland along these lines, from the Paris Peace Conference to Potsdam, ran into immediate trouble. In a region of Europe where historical complexities and ethnic minorities abounded, the problem of Poland's frontiers could never be peaceably solved by the nationalist agenda. In the end, it was solved by brute force. In 1945, with Stalin's backing, the Polish Communists callously adopted the Piast Concept of their pre-war peasant and nationalist opponents, and imposed it by methods which would now be called 'ethnic cleansing'. Official maps were drawn up to show that Poland's frontiers under the first known Piast princes, c. AD 1000, coincided almost exactly with the frontiers of the Polish People's Republic as approved by the Allied governments at Yalta and Potsdam.[14] All that remained was to make the population fit the frontiers. All the millions of 'non-Poles', mainly Germans and Ukrainians, who lived on the wrong side of the new lines, had to be expelled from their homes; and millions of Poles, whose homes were now in territory 'recovered' by the Soviet Union, had to be expelled to the People's Republic. (All expellees were conveniently called 'repatriants'.) It was the biggest population exchange in European history. It was the natural consequence of nationalist myths about 'blood and soil' in which so many Europeans had believed since modern mass politics began in the 1890s.

13. Juliusz Słowacki, *Król Duch* (King-Spirit), I, ll. 9–16, translated by Norman Davies.
14. See endpapers, *Polska w Roku 1000* and *Polska Rzeczpospolita Ludowa, Słownik Historii Polski*, Warsaw, 1973.

1920

On 20 January 1920, at the little port of Puck, a ceremony took place
in which hundreds of Poles waded into the near-freezing waters of the
Baltic to celebrate Poland's mystical union with the sea. It was the day
on which the Treaty of Versailles was put into force and a stretch of
the Baltic shore was transferred from Germany to the newly
independent Republic of Poland. A similar ceremony was repeated a
quarter of a century later in January 1945, when, at the end of the
Second World War, Poland was to receive a much longer stretch of the
Baltic shore. The festivities were probably modelled on the annual
sposalizio del mar at Venice, the festival which celebrates the wedding
of St Mark's city with the Mediterranean Sea. In Polish, they are
known as the *Zaślubiny Polski z morzem*, the 'maritime nuptials'.

Far be it from a Cracowian like myself to suggest that Poland's
traditions lie much more with the plentiful plains and magnificent
mountains of the South than with the desolate dunes of the North. For
many, the notion of the Poles as a historic seafaring nation is, to say
the least, eccentric. Apart from the ancient cities of Danzig and Elbing,
both of which were heavily dominated by Germans, the historic
Kingdom of Poland had no important coastline from the fourteenth
century onwards.

Of course, in the very earliest years of Piast history, Poland had
controlled the coast of Pomerania from the Oder to the Vistula.
Western Pomerania, fiercely contested by Bolesław Krzywousty in the
twelfth century, fell into the hands of the local dynasty after
Krzywousty's death in 1138. Krzywousty's court chronicler, Gallus
Anonymus, immortalized the Pomeranian connection when he recorded
a popular Latin song of the day about the joys of life by the seaside:

> Pisces salsos et foetentes apportabant alii
> Palpitantes et recentes nunc apportant filii.
> Civitates invadebant patres nostri primitus
> Hii procellas non verentur neque maris sonitus.
> Agitabant patres nostri cervos, apros, capreas,
> Hii venantur monstra maris et opes aequoreas.

[Our fathers brought us reeking, salted fish. / But we, their sons, bring fish
that's fresh and wriggling. / In the olden times our fathers attacked and
captured cities. / But we fearlessly pit our strength against storms and
thundering waves. / Our fathers dealt with deer, and bees, and goats. / Their
sons hunt for the monsters and the treasures of the deep.][15]

In contrast, Eastern Pomerania, which was also known by its German
name of Pommerellen, remained part of the Polish Kingdom until

---

15.   'De expeditione in urbem Coloberg facta', *Galla Kronika Xięga*, II, 28, in
      Monumenta Poloniae Historica, Warsaw, 1968, vol. 1, p. 447.

conquered by the Teutonic Knights in 1308. From then on, until the incorporation of the League of Prussian Cities in 1454, Poland had no shoreline at all. But the memory survived. And when a reborn nation was handed back a stretch of the coast in 1920, it needed a suitable myth and pseudo-medieval ritual to justify it. The 'maritime nuptials' fitted the bill exactly.

22 July 1952

The Constitution of the Polish People's Republic was the most mythical document of contemporary Polish history, and may serve as a fitting conclusion.

As all competent commentators know, constitutions played only a marginal role in the workings of a Communist-type party-state. They were not, as in most true democracies, the supreme basis for the rule of law. On the contrary, they provided a set of regulations relating exclusively to the institutions of the state, behind and through which the institutions of the party could exercise an absolute, unaccountable, totalitarian dictatorship. In short, they listed all the official fictions which masked the reality of Communist power. It was no exaggeration to say that the only clause of a Soviet-style constitution which carried any real weight was the one giving the party 'the leading role' in the state. What this meant, in practice, was that the party comrades could manipulate, or ignore, all other aspects of the constitution with impunity. The odd thing is that the comrades who framed the Constitution of the PRL in 1952 were so complacent that they forgot to include the usual clause about the party's leading role. As a result, they were obliged, under Soviet pressure, to add the clause as an amendment to the Constitution in 1976, together with another clause about Poland's unshakeable alliance with the Soviet Union.

For whatever reason, many people in the West, including far too many political scientists, failed to understand these mechanisms. All too often, the Communist system was described as a 'one-party state', perhaps on the Latin American model, where small cliques of generals or politicians had eliminated their rivals and captured exclusive control of the government. This sort of description seriously underestimates the sophistication of the Communist dictatorship, ignoring the dual nature of the party-state and the fact that the party was itself the executive branch of government. Real power lay with the party's Secretary-General, the Politburo and the Central Committee

Secretariat, not with the 'President', the Council of Ministers, or the state bureaucracy.[16]

These elementary truths used to be all but inexplicable to Westerners unfamiliar with the conditions. If a personal reminiscence is permitted, I would recall a lengthy altercation with an American editor of the *Encyclopaedia Britannica* who consulted me in the mid-1980s about revising the entry on Poland. I had noticed that the existing entry began with a description of the Constitution of the PRL; and I told him that this gave a very misleading impression of how the country was really ruled. But the editor was unmovable. Several hours of pleas and explanations failed to shift him from the view that all country entries in his *Encyclopaedia* started with a description of the Constitution and that there was no reason why an exception should be made for Poland.

In retrospect, one of the most astonishing features of Communism lay in its addiction to myths, fictions, taboos and fetishes of all sorts. Although it claimed to be based on a rational and scientific ideology, it fostered the most irrational and unscientific practices imaginable. It was, in fact, a pseudo-religion, where black was routinely described as white and two plus two was officially proclaimed to make either three or five, as circumstances demanded. Prior to the amendments of 1976, the Constitution of the PRL revealed absolutely nothing about the ruling order. Yet is was published in millions of copies, studied in all schools, conscientiously expounded to all foreigners who were daft enough to listen, and regularly celebrated on the country's National Day (which, of course, was *not* the National Day). For people brought up in democracies, where constitutions set out the basic rules of public conduct, it is impossible to conceive of a so-called 'constitution' whose 'laws' were essentially irrelevant to a totally lawless polity.

All myths serve a purpose. As the purposes change, the myths change with them. The critical question in Poland today, therefore, is whether any of the traditional myths can be revived or modified to match the conditions of life in the 'Third', post-Communist, Republic. After only five or six years, it is difficult to say. Some of the myths are as dead as dodos; the constitution of the PRL is as *passé* as the Sarmatians. The myths of the *Polak-Katolik* or of 'Piast Poland' seem to have little point in a mono-ethnic country whose frontiers are no longer under threat. But the myth of the *antemurale* may rise again if Poland becomes the frontier zone of NATO or Russia renews its ambitions to dominate Central Europe. And the prophecies of

16. On the workings of the party-state, see 'Spiders' Webs and Galley-slaves' and 'Two Nations' in Davies, *Heart of Europe*, pp. 29–62; also in *idem*, *Europe: A History*, Oxford, 1996, pp. 1093–6, 1321.

Wernyhora are never out of date. There may never have been a truly 'Golden Age' on Poland's eastern borders. But the need for Poles to cultivate fraternal relations with their eastern neighbours has never been greater. We shall see. One thing is certain. If the old myths do not suffice, then new ones will be invented.

NATIONAL MYTHOLOGY IN THE HISTORY OF IDEAS IN LATVIA: A VIEW FROM RELIGIOUS STUDIES

Agita Misāne and Aija Priedīte

The topic of national mythologies has, until now, been addressed only as a political, and not a religious, issue by scholars. While social scientists have researched the myths shared by ethnic communities, scholars of religion, with very few exceptions, have remained silent on this subject. This silence persists, despite the immense potential comparative studies of religion, which have already been applied to the study of religious myth, have to offer in this area.

A closer look at both perspectives uncovers surprising and somewhat confusing results: the very notion of myth — and subsequently the use of the term — is fundamentally different in both. Generally, political scientists and historians describe myths as *beliefs* held by an ethnic community in order to establish, maintain or defend its identity. The repudiation of national myths is sometimes viewed as a sign of the political maturity of the nation, and the willingness to preserve them is considered to be destructive for the nation concerned, or threatening for other nations.[1]

This chapter approaches myth mainly as the sacred story of the nation. The understanding of myth as *sacred narrative* is almost unanimously shared by scholars of religion. This notion points to the specific quality and function of myth — the verbal revelation and justification of some sacred order, which myth performs along with sacred actions and sacred places. Discussing myth, we discuss the form (in the Aristotelian sense of the word), rather than the plot, of the narrative. Nobody expects the archaeological excavation of a temple site to confirm or deny the existence of gods who were worshipped there; equally, the study of myth narrative itself does not aim to discern the 'truth' or 'falsity' of a myth. The follies of attempting to do so were evidenced by Dorothea Wender's ironic analysis of the myth of

We are grateful to Professors Henning Sehmsdorf and Thomas DuBois at the University of Washington for inspirational discussions on national lore. Many thanks are also due to Dr Guntis Smidchens and Ms Jurate Avizienis for their comments on earlier drafts of this chapter.

1.   Eric Hobsbawm, 'Debunking Ethnic Myths' in *Open Society News*, (Winter) 1994, pp. 9–11.

George Washington, which 'proved' that this cultural hero of the American people had never lived as a real man.[2]

Wendy Doniger O'Flaherty defines myth as 'a story that is sacred to and shared by a group who find their most important meanings in it'.[3] Of all definitions of myth this seems to be most helpful here, as it makes clear exactly what we share when we share a national myth. First, we share knowledge of the story which we have learned over time from parents and/or through formal education, and which we recognize in everyday conversation as well as in literature, political discourse and even national kitsch. For insiders who know the myth, even fragmentary references are enough to recall the entire myth and its connotations. Two lines of the Latvian national anthem, 'Where Latvia's maidens bloom, where Latvia's sons sing', will connote little to the outsider. For the 'insider', however, who partakes in the myth, the national anthem evokes the image of *Latvia Felix*, which we will discuss later in this chapter.

Insiders in a culture share a wide range of feelings — pride, dignity, pain, shame, guilt — which are embodied in myth. Myths are often a means of dealing, more generally, with socio-cultural tension. They also serve as a psychological compensator, a vehicle through which we continually struggle to make our experiences intelligible and acceptable to ourselves. This is achieved by telling 'our story' — the one with which we identify psychologically — as one that happened to somebody else. Narrating a story is a way of recognizing a situation without needing immediately to act on it (by changing the law, driving the oppressor away, and so on), or to be responsible for it. As Lévi-Strauss said, myth allows us to state the problem, but is not, in itself, an answer to it.[4] Finally, meanings and values are shared through myth. Using a specific set of symbols and the language of simile, myth expresses complicated abstract concepts and allows one to possess or experience what may not be accessible by other means. Thus myth conveys notions of freedom, power, democracy, death, justice, evil, and so on. That there may be a discrepancy between the representation of these entities in myth, and people's everyday experience of them in life, is a fact of which those who sustain myths are fully cognizant.

Hence, myths need not be believed to retain their value and function successfully. In fact, the *differentia specifica* of myth as a form of narrative is that the veracity of a myth is not in question. Belief or disbelief, therefore, cannot seriously affect the validity of a myth, and

2.   D. Wender, 'The Myth of Washington' in *Arion*, 1976, 3, pp. 71–8.
3.   W. Doniger O'Flaherty, *Other People's Myths: The Cave of Echoes*, Chicago, 1988 (hereafter *Other People's Myths*), p. 27.
4.   C. Lévi-Strauss, *The Savage Mind*, Chicago, IL, 1966, p. 22.

those who share it may take different attitudes. When myths are being related, beliefs are held in a 'different directory', or, to use a phenomenological term, are 'bracketed'. Within religious experience, myths and beliefs refer to different modes or dimensions of religion. While myths are usually treated as a separate (mythological) dimension of religion, beliefs fall into the so-called intellectual mode of religion, which also includes doctrines and dogmatics. Beliefs are usually based on a proof of some kind — trust in the authority of scripture or of a religious leader, experience, rational reasoning or often simply evidence. Myths are authorized by traditions and by their specific relation to sacred time and space. Myths develop a sense of togetherness, they are the means by which human beings tie themselves to the world, feel at home there, and become the heirs of their ancestors. This explains why people who maintain myths may feel so vulnerable or even hostile to social scientists' comments on their sacred stories. Every single element in myth must be in its place and 'safe' — that is, untouched — 'for if they were taken out of their place even in thought, the entire order of the universe would be destroyed'.[5]

If 'the sacred' may seem a rather obscure and therefore loosely applied concept, this is probably due to the tradition, established by Rudolph Otto, to define it from the negative — as *das ganz Andere,* 'the complete otherness'. In practice, the closest synonym of 'sacredness' is 'power'. The sacred reveals the power distribution in the structured universe, a realm which could be best described with the help of several sets of oppositions. These are: (1) higher–lower, that is, the hierarchical opposition; (2) central–peripheral; and (3) here–there, which also differentiates 'us' and 'them'. An ethnic community needs a myth in order to find its place within the realm of holiness, sanctify its very existence and justify any claims it may have. 'The sacred' is often misunderstood as an entirely religious quality. There is much evidence in the modern world, however, of the sacred order revealed in secular entities. The nation or state may become a manifestation of the sacred and, therefore, an object of public or private devotion. One example is the icon of 'Mother Latvia', which has been concretized in the sculpture at the Brethren Cemetery in Riga and which has been evoked in countless speeches, especially during the Reawakening period of 1988–91.

Are social scientists and scholars of religion talking about the same thing, then, when they talk about national myths? If not, what is the difference between a national and any other kind of myth? Two scholars of religion have briefly commented on this question. Mircea Eliade first became interested in some aspects of what he called 'the

5.　*Ibid.,* p. 10.

modern myth' or 'the survivals and camouflage of myth' soon after the Second World War. Eliade's *The Myth of the Eternal Return: Cosmos and History* is known mainly for its discussion of mythological time; the fact that nearly half of the book is devoted to a passionate attack on Hegel's perception of history sometimes passes unnoticed. Eliade considers Hegel's efforts to confer value on the historical event, 'the event in itself and for itself', to have bequeathed a dangerous legacy to twentieth-century history and politics:

> In his study of the German constitution, Hegel wrote that if we recognize that things are necessary as they are, that is, that they are not arbitrary and not the result of chance, we shall at the same time recognize that they *must* be as they are. A century later, the concept of historical necessity will enjoy a more and more triumphant practical application: in fact, all the cruelties, aberrations, and tragedies of history have been, and still are, justified by the necessities of the 'historical moment'.[6]

For Eliade, the sacred history revealed in myth seemed more just than what he saw as the cynical expediency of academic history. He depicted the emergence of modern national myths as an unceasing process since, in the secularized era, they would assume the functions of religious myths.

More recently, Ninian Smart has described several areas in which the national idea is incarnate, and has stated that national histories — especially as taught in high schools — are purely versions of myth.[7] From the perspective of religious phenomenology, there is no basic difference between myth and history. Both are narratives and both tell how the present order came into being.

Terminological problems, however, do not end here. Folklorists would probably argue that many of the narratives branded as national myths are in fact historical legends, not myths. Once we distinguish between them, we begin to glimpse the complexity of the terminological issue. If the setting of the story is not in the remote past, and its principal agents are human beings, the story may be classified as historical legend.[8] Tales about revolutions, wars, migration, national resistance, liberation and key figures in these events, or about the origin of national regalia and holidays, are typical examples of this genre. In fact, legends (sacred or profane) are the core of any national lore simply by virtue of their number. They far outnumber other genres and 'represent the transitional field between

6. M. Eliade, *Myth of the Eternal Return: Cosmos and History*, London, 1954, pp. 147–8.
7. N. Smart, *Religion and the Western Mind*, New York, 1987, pp. 70–1.
8. W. Bascom, 'The Forms of Folklore' in A. Dundes (ed.), *Sacred Narrative*, Berkeley, Los Angeles and London, 1984, pp. 5–29.

everyday life and tale and myth'.[9] Usually, the national tradition houses a corpus of historical legends complemented by those incorporated into national myth and sacred history. 'National lore' is, perhaps, the most precise umbrella term to include national belief, national myth, sacred history and historical legend. Thematically, these could be the same stories: the story-tellers are not troubled by genres overlapping. The difference between myth and sacred history lies in the degree of fabulation; the difference between sacred history and legend lies in the historical scope, as well as in the relationship to the sacred. Moreover, legends are commonly less dependent on emotion as a component of the action, while sacred histories are intended to reveal a particular feeling which is commonly depicted as prevalent in the nation's historical consciousness. In the Latvian case, it is probably pain. History hurts us deeply. We carry it as a heavy load on our shoulders. Of course, such emotions are far from being exclusively Latvian. The Hungarian philosopher Mihály Vajda has written that:

The so-called 'small nations' of Central Europe have a specific world-view, deeply rooted in their mistrust of History. History — the goddess of Hegel and Marx, the embodiment of Reason and Spirit that directs and judges our conduct — is the history of champions. But the peoples of Central Europe have never been winners. Although closely bound to the history of Europe and unable to exist apart from it, they have always remained the inverse side of this history. This experience, fed on the feeling of frustration with history, houses the singularity of the culture of these small nations.[10]

Obviously, the issue here is not just about emotions. Vajda also elucidates the idea of the 'ownership' of history. According to the Baltic German scholar of the second half of the nineteenth century, Carl Schirren, history belonged to the Baltic German élite and the Latvians had no part in it. Instead of a discussion concerning peoples in the Baltic lands, Shirren found only a debate about winners and losers: 'the locals' lost, so history has 'sentenced' Latvia to be a colony and to remain so forever.[11] In the nineteenth century, on several occasions, the Baltic German clergy and nobility initiated laws and regulations in order to ban the teaching of history at parish schools. History became a mandatory course only after 1918.

It is not surprising, then, that historical consciousness sometimes seeks escape in a so-called 'flight from history'. In inter-war Latvia, Ernests Brastiņš, leader of Dievturi, the Pre-Christian revivalism

9. L. Honko, 'Methods in Folk Narrative Research' in R. Kvideland and H.K. Sehmsdorf (eds), *Nordic Folklore: Recent Studies*, Bloomington, IN, 1989, pp. 23–9 (28).
10. M. Vajda, 'Filosofija v Vengrii' in *Vengerskije meridiani*, 1991, 4, pp. 9–10.
11. C. Schirren, *Livlandische Antwort an Herrn J. Samarin*, Leipzig, 1869.

movement, was the author of the idea of 'Latvianized Latvia' as a fulfilment of the sacred mission of the Latvians. Brastiņš declared that:

The Balts do not create history, if we mean by history changes of certain phenomena. They preserve in their pristine state long-established material and spiritual traditions and stand guard over their land. Language, customs and religion have not been changed, but have been handed down and honoured. The Balts become part of history through no action of their own. But when that happens, they manifest themselves in a truly noble and heroic manner.[12]

This idea, and the false sense of freedom it offers, still retains some emotional attraction, although its attractiveness will wane as Latvia continues on the path towards modernization.

Facing history and using it as a weapon (or shield against the evil, destructive 'history of the others') has been far more effective. As Juris Dreifelds points out, 'in the struggle of Latvia's independence, history became a major vehicle for destabilizing communist rule'.[13] One should add that historical issues have been of paramount importance in all periods of Latvian awakening. The 'Singing Revolution' of 1988–91 in many ways followed the pattern set by the Young Latvian movement in the second half of the nineteenth century, the period notable for the historical orientation of humanistic inquiry in Europe. Inspired by Fichte's *Reden an die deutsche Nation,* Atis Kronvalds wrote his essay 'Tēvuzemes mīlestība' (Love for the Fatherland)[14] where he suggested that, for the purpose of developing patriotic feelings, national history is the most significant form of knowledge. Kronvalds stated that the only way for the Latvians to free their history from the clichés of the colonial mentality was to contextualize it themselves.

The Sacred Stories of Latvians

Saule Latvi sēdināja	Sun put Latvia
Tur, kur gali satiekas:	Where the ends meet:
Balta jūra, zaļa zeme –	White sea, green land,
Latvei vārtu atslēdziņa.	Latvia has the key to the gate.
Latvei vārtu atslēdziņa,	Latvia has the key to the gate,
Daugavina sargātāja.	Daugava stands on guard.
Sveši ļaudis vārtus lauza,	Foreign people broke the gate,
Jūrā krita atslēdziņa.	The key fell into the sea.

12. E. Brastiņš, *Mūsu dievestība tūkstošgadīga apkarošana,* Riga, 1936, p. 12.
13. J. Dreifelds, *Latvia in Transition,* Cambridge, 1996, p. 20.
14. A. Kronvalds, 'Tēvuzemes mīlestība' in *Rota,* 49, 1886, pp. 491–3.

Zilzibeņu Pērkons sper,
Velniem ņēma atslēdziņu,
Nāvi, dzīvi Latve slēgs:
Baltu jūru, zaļu zemi.

Blue-lightened Thunder struck,
Took the key from the demons,
Latvia tied together death and life:
White sea and green land.

Saule Latvi sēdināja
Baltas jūras maliņā,
Vēji smiltis putināja,
Ko lai dzēra latvju bērni?

Sun put Latvia
At the edge of the white sea,
The wind drifted the sand,
What could Latvia's children drink?

Saule lika Dieviņam
Lai tas raka Daugaviņu.
Zvēri raka, Dievinš lēja
No mākoņa dzīvūdeni.

Sun asked the God
To dig Daugava.
The animals dug, the God poured
Living water from the cloud.

Dzīves ūdens, nāves ūdens
Daugavā satecēja –
Es pamērcu pirksta galu,
Abus jūtu dvēselē.
Nāves ūdens, dzīves ūdens –
Abus jūtam dvēselē.

The water of life, the water of death
Poured into Daugava,
I touch it with my fingers,
I feel both in my soul.
The water of death, the water of life
I feel both in my soul.

Saule mūsu māte,
Daugav' sāpju aukle,
Pērkons velna spērējs,
Tas mūsu tēvs.

Sun is our mother,
Daugava soothes the pain,
Thunder, the slayer of the Devil,
He is our father.

The verses quoted above were written by the most celebrated Latvian poet, Rainis, in 1920. They were not widely known until 1989, however, when the composer Martins Brauns set them to music. The song 'Sun, Thunder, Daugava' became one of the anthems of the Latvian 'Singing Revolution' of 1988–91. The wide popularity of this song is not surprising, as it serves as an intensely poetic version of the Latvian national myth. The text is quoted in full here as it illustrates the principles of discriminating between myth and sacred history which were mentioned earlier in this chapter. The poem suggests that the divine election of Latvia — *Saule* (Sun), *Pērkons* (Thunder) and *Dievs* (God) being major deities of the pre-Christian pantheon — is also the cause of its tragedy. Suffering results from the desirability of Latvia, geographically, to 'foreign people', clearly marked as demons. It is worth remembering that Rainis wrote the poetic drama *Daugava* (including these verses) as a response to the events of the First World War and the declaration of Latvian independence in 1918. Hence, grim as it may seem, it is a poem about victory. In 1989, 'Sun, Thunder, Daugava' sounded more like a prayer, paradoxically addressed to the gods in whom nobody believed. More importantly, it consecrated the Reawakening movement by relating the opposing forces of that time to the motifs found in Latvian folk tradition and mythology (Thundergod's combat with the Devil, and legends of the origin of Daugava and Living and Dead Water).

Latvian sacred history, by contrast, has no supernatural agents. It tells of free and happy Latvian people living on the shores of Daugava. They cultivate their land, venerate their gods and are ruled by wise and just chieftains. The Latvian culture is, then, a peasant one, and it is a commonplace to say that there is a peasant hiding in every Latvian. As the Young Latvian poet Auseklis wrote in his poem 'Old Times', 'everything glitters and shines with wonderful light there'. This 'Golden Age' persists until the Teutonic Knights come to this land, and the so-called 'Seven Hundred Years' German Yoke' is established. For Latvians, the 'German Yoke' denotes the immediate loss of political freedom, and the establishment of poverty and serfdom. As for the German invaders, the story is little concerned with them. They have remained largely 'a mass without quality', as Latvians sometimes still tend to view the aliens. In a rock-opera, for example, based on the motifs of Andrejs Pumpurs's epic *Lāčplēsis*, the invaders are personified in the image of the Black Knight, whom the author of the libretto characterizes as deaf, blind and mute.[15] Indeed, for a long time, a similar approach was adopted in Latvian medieval studies, especially during Soviet times. Germans were present in the history books only as a political force or a social stratum, with barely a single word written about their culture.

The period of the Duchy of Courland (1561–1795), especially during the rule of Duke Jacob (1642–82), is often described as a second 'Golden Age' of Latvian history. In popular consciousness this period is often referred to as the age when 'Latvia had colonies'[16] and many Latvians are surprised when they hear that Jacob was, in fact, not an ethnic Latvian. The spread of these legends is most likely due to popular comics and other pulp fiction appearing in the 1920s and 1930s, describing the adventures of Latvian colonists in Tobago and Gambia. During the 'Seven Hundred Years of Slavery' Latvians are told to preserve their culture — particularly folklore — almost unchanged, retain the hope of freedom and resist the Germans, later the Russians, whenever possible. The Republic of Latvia of 1918–40 is consequently seen as the sacred legacy of distant ancestors.

A very interesting part of the story deals with the perception of the image of the Latvian Riflemen, also called the Red Riflemen from

15. M. Zālīte, 'Librets rokoperai pec Andreja Pumpura eposa "Lāčplēsis"' in *Avots*, 1988, 9, pp. 16–25 (25).
16. Duke Jacob bought the Island of Tobago and the tiny island of St Andrew's in the Gambia river.

1917, who were Latvian regiments in the Russian, and later the Red, Army. If Latvians ever had a legend or history of military valour, then this is the tale. The sacred aura attached to it is noticeable mainly in the language used, otherwise it would be deemed a profane historical legend. The Riflemen have an heroic epic of their own: Aleksandrs Čaks's lengthy poem *Mūžības skartie* (Touched by Eternity, 1937–9). The film director Juris Podnieks also made a documentary about the Riflemen, entitled *Strēlnieku zvaigznājs* (The Constellation of Riflemen, 1982). Interestingly enough, the changing political regime in Latvia has had little influence on the image of the Riflemen in popular historical consciousness. They are romantic heroes not through their actions, but because they were brave, even adventurous, and showed the Russians what real soldiers are like. If the Latvian Soviet historians saw the chief achievement of the Riflemen in the fulfilment of their international duties and ascribed their radicalization in 1917 to a highly developed class consciousness, Latvian historians in exile portrayed the Riflemen as nationalists fighting for the independence of Latvia as promised to them by Lenin in exchange for their services. Trusting Bolshevik promises, and ignoring the character of the regime they chose to support, was admitted as their chief mistake, or as a compromise — a sacrifice for the sake of Latvian independence. Ethical questions, namely those about the sometimes violent actions of the Latvian Red Riflemen, have been raised only recently, and almost entirely from the religious perspective. In 1988, Leons Taivans — then a historian at the Academy of Sciences in Moscow, now professor of theology at the University of Latvia — proposed the idea that the sufferings of the Latvian nation after 1940 could be understood as penance for the sins committed by the Riflemen in Russia and also for their role in the battle on Christmas Eve (23 December) 1916.[17] Only in clerical circles has this interpretation been widely accepted. Nowadays, however, more and more Latvians are concerned with the question of whether the Riflemen are a source of pride or shame for the Latvian nation. And shared shame is as strong a vehicle for unity and identity as any of the other feelings commonly married to national lore.

Formalization of Latvian National Lore: Past and Future

It is commonly agreed that the Young Latvians were the founding fathers of Latvian national mythology and sacred history. However, neither their approach nor the motifs they used were original. The tradition of writing the history of Livonia as *Volks-* and not

---

17. L. Taivans, 'Dievs Kungs ir mūsu stipra pils' in *Svētdienas Rīts*, 1988, 1.

Landesgeschichte was established by Baltic German historiography, which left the Latvians and Estonians almost out of consideration.[18] Hence, Atis Kronvalds argued for a different interpretation from the Latvian rather than the Baltic German viewpoint, but not for a different approach. From that time onwards, Latvian historians have focused on Latvian participation in, and experience of, events taking place in this territory. Depending on the dominant ideology of the period concerned, Latvians have been considered both happy and unhappy at various stages of their history.

The exercise of tracing how and when various segments of Latvian national myth and sacred history came into circulation seems to illustrate O'Flaherty's words that we 'find our myths rather than construct them'.[19] Her statement provides an answer to the frequently posed question: can myths be made *ex nihilo*? Together with O'Flaherty we would strongly argue in the negative — in the case of both myths and sacred national histories. However, one more reason to distinguish between these two genres of national lore is that they are formalized according to different patterns. Thus, national myths creatively address the symbol system of religious mythology and 'recycle it'. National mythology is a 'born-again' religious mythology; it does not incorporate alien symbols before they are accepted as a part of religious consciousness. What Latvian national mythology lacks is probably even more symptomatic than what it houses. It does not propose any claim to the supernatural origins of the Latvians. Some individuals might like to say that the Latvians are 'people of the Sun', but then they refer to the sun as a guardian (the sun is the mistress of the celestial household in Latvian pre-Christian mythology), not as a creator.

The above could be explained by the fact that motifs of the creation of the Cosmos in Latvian religious mythology are not well developed, so this useful pattern is missing. Similarly, there has never been a single Latvian saint. Sainthood for Latvians has no national connotation. Thus the idea of martyrdom, suffering for others — central in Polish or Russian culture — is alien to the Latvians' history of ideas.

In contrast,[20] various segments of Latvian sacred history have almost nothing to do with Latvian religious history. As one of the tasks of sacred history is to provide the nation with a dignified past,

18. W. Lenz, 'Alt-Livland in der Geschichtssreibung 1870–1910' in G. von Rauch (ed.), *Geschichte der deutschbalischen Geschichtssreibung*, Cologne and Vienna, 1986, p. 225.
19. O'Flaherty, *Other People's Myths*, p. 164.
20. Still, we must be aware that myths and sacred histories, originating in different circumstances, may be incorporated in the same extended narrative, as the biblical story of Exodus shows.

its history has to be shown according to equally dignified patterns borrowed from noble cultures. The idea of the Latvian 'Golden Age' belongs to the German *philosophé* Garlieb Merkel (1769–1850). The portrayal of the Latvians and their lifestyle was far from flattering in his works, although being a keen advocate of the abolition of serfdom in the Baltic provinces of Russia, Merkel described all the negative traits of the Latvian character as resulting from centuries of serfdom. In his *Die Vorzeit Livlands*[21] and *Die Letten*[22] (especially its first chapter) Merkel argued that, before the Germans appeared in the thirteenth century, the Latvians enjoyed a culture of the highest level, and that their real history is to be found in their folk-songs.

The proposition of a Latvian peasant identity goes back to the works of the so-called Livonian humanists, a group of authors living in sixteenth-century Riga and writing in Latin. They accepted the ideal of *nobilias literata*, that is, nobility achieved through classical education. They suggested that serfdom was natural for peasants as, in the light of the above ideal, they were only *plebs rustica*.[23]

The understanding of peasant (that is, folk) culture as a noble one came with the Enlightenment. But for Herder and his followers, including Garlieb Merkel, the peasants were still 'them', so there is no trace of identification with them. For the Young Latvians, peasants were 'us', and, consequently, this new segment was added to the story. The idea that serfdom (or slavery, as no particular difference was found between them) was introduced immediately in the thirteenth century also belongs to the Livonian humanists. Although educated society in the late sixteenth century knew that serfdom came to Livonia considerably later, humanists used this false statement to support the codification of serfdom. Ironically, the story of the 'Seven Hundred Years of Slavery' acquired a life of its own. It was incorporated in the speeches of the Young Latvians and still provides a basis for the common understanding of Latvian medieval and modern history.

Let us say something about the future now. Myths and sacred histories are cumulative entities and reflect certain trends in the political life of a society. Two of the current issues in Latvia that will most likely require not only political and/or economic steps, but also appropriate ideology, are the desired membership of the EU and the incorporation into the country of a vast number of people that do not identify ethnically with Latvia. The non-Latvian economic élite, in particular, may demand more extended political participation, as well

21. G. Merkel, *Die Vorzeit Livlands: Ein Denkmal des Praffen- und Rittergeistes*, 2 vols, Berlin, 1798–9.

22. *Idem, Die Letten, vozglich in Liefland, am Ende des philosophischen Jahrhunderts*, Leipzig, 1797.

23. R. Malvess, *Latviešu zemnieks humānistu darbos*, Riga, 1939.

as a share of the ideology pie. At the same time, the ethnic Latvian population, particularly while frustration with the present economic and political situation prevails, is not prepared to give up its notion of history as unjust. Some consensus could be gained by reviving the legend of Riga as a great multicultural centre, the formerly rich and proud Hanseatic *Freistadt*, the place where Kant's principal works were first published and where famous European figures like Herder and Richard Wagner have left their trace. The forthcoming millenary of Riga in 2001 will certainly drive the historical memory in that direction. This does not necessary imply a large-scale reading of Kant or listening to Wagner, but many of Riga's non-Latvian inhabitants (almost half of the population of Latvia live in the capital) may find the idea of living in 'the little Paris' (as Riga is sometimes called) attractive. The feelings of Latvians are rather ambiguous. It is often heard that Riga is not a Latvian city, as only one third of the inhabitants are ethnic Latvians. The Latvian culture still carries the Young Latvians' mistrust in the city: none of the principal figures of the movement was born in Riga or spent long periods of time there. In the epic *Lāčplēsis,* Andrejs Pumpurs described Riga as the matrix of all evils, a dark shelter of the occupants. And yet, Riga is the place where everything happens: the National Song festivals, the declaration and re-establishment of the independence of the Latvian Republic, as well as many other crucially important events in recent history. More than any other, Riga is *the city* of the Singing Revolution.

The function of the sacred history of Latvia is not exhausted by the recovery of the ethnic and cultural identity of Latvians. Neither should it nurture only those tendencies in the Latvian history of ideas that resist modernization and favour Euro-scepticism. Equally, it may support the notion of the Europeanness of Latvia, and Riga seems to be the most potent image for the celebration of it for all of the peoples living in Latvia.

THE MYTH OF ZION AMONG
EAST EUROPEAN JEWRY

John D. Klier

The Jews are always honoured guests at the table of any symposium presuming to discuss questions of national awareness and identity. They are the prime exhibit of an *ethnie*, to use Anthony Smith's term, which has survived through millennia despite being bereft of a national territory, a common language or even a common secular culture. Yet if the reality of Jewish survival appears a self-evident fact, less clear are the phenomena which have produced it. Smith himself has emphasized the importance of collective myths for fashioning both the self-awareness and staying power of ethnic groups.[1] In the case of Jews, numerous observers have specified three myths as instrumental in the maintenance of Jewish identity against all obstacles: the myth of divine election; the mythic tie to the land of Zion or *Erets Israel*; and the myth of the Messiah.

The objective of this chapter is to examine briefly the nature of the myth of Zion among the Jews of Eastern Europe, as well as the parallel myth of Messianic redemption. Revivified and linked together, it is claimed, they provided the raw material of the emergence and endurance of modern Jewish nationalism, especially in its Zionist forms. These myths, scholars have demonstrated, had heretofore been tamed and pacified. How then were they revivified, linked and given the power to generate action?

Most peoples envisage some special relationship with their gods — indeed, this is what makes these deities 'theirs'. The special strength of the Jews' sense of election lay in its ability to explain both the attainment and the apparent loss of divine favour. In a process which paralleled the national political disasters and the military defeats of ancient Israel, the realm of the Jewish God was decoupled from a particular time and place and achieved transcendence. The period of the prophets transformed the focus of the Jews' relationship with their God from a temple-based, collective sacrificial worship to a personal relationship, based on individual responsibility for a set of moral ethics. The prophets explained the loss of God's favour by attributing it to sin, individual and collective, while holding out the hope of divine forgiveness and redemption.

---

1. Anthony D. Smith, *The Ethnic Origins of Nations*, Oxford, 1986.

In an unintended way, this whole process proved to be practical training for survival in the *galut* (exile). The Jews refined survival techniques under the sceptre of generous conquerors. The exiled Jews of Babylon were able to maintain a collective and cultural existence. A community remained there even after 538 BCE when the Persian conqueror Cyrus the Great permitted the Jews to rebuild the temple in Jerusalem. The early diaspora situation prevented Judaism from becoming too isolated and territorial. Indeed, to some extent the existence of flourishing diaspora communities served to normalize exile. While the Romans ultimately expelled the rebellious Jews from their sacred land, no punitive measures fell on the Jews outside Palestine. Rather, the Romans recognized them as a *politeuma*, an ethnic community governed by its own traditions. The Jews maintained their pre-exilic right to refrain from the worship of the state cult.[2]

It took some time for Judaism's daughter faith, Christianity, to resolve its ambivalent attitudes to the Jews. The Church Fathers moved in two contradictory directions. The tendency associated with John Chrysostom, who railed against the 'synagogue of Satan', implied the expulsion and outlawing of Judaism.[3] Instead, a rival tradition, exemplified by Augustine of Hippo, but building upon the writings of Paul the Apostle, evolved a secure and necessary position for the Jews within Christian theology. Augustine provided an exegesis of the story of Cain and Abel (*Genesis* 4: 1–16). Just as the faith of Abel was preferred on high, and verified and exalted by Cain's treachery, so the survival of the Jews, coupled with their scepticism and fall from grace, reinforced the truth of Christianity. Jews, like Cain, were not to be killed, but to wander the earth as proof of their rejected status. Their continued, degraded existence was proof of the existence of a providential and just God. Augustine went further, and actually integrated the Jews into Christian eschatology. The return again in glory of Jesus Christ, the Son of God, would be accompanied by the conversion of the Jews. At a stroke, the power and graciousness of the Christian God would be demonstrated.[4]

The ambivalent religious toleration of Christian states was accompanied by a confirmation, albeit somewhat modified, of the legal status the Jews had enjoyed in Roman Law. Thus, the Theodosian

2. Menahem Stern, 'Antisemitism in Rome' in Shmuel Almog (ed.), *Antisemitism through the Ages*, New York, 1988, p. 15.
3. Steven T. Katz, *The Holocaust in Historical Context*, vol. 1, New York and Oxford, 1994, pp. 259–60. See also David Rokeah, 'The Church Fathers and the Jews in Writings Designed for Internal and External Use' in Almog, *Antisemitism through the Ages*, pp. 39–70.
4. Katz, *The Holocaust in Historical Context*, pp. 260–4.

Code of 438 CE retained the legal status of the Jews as citizens. Christian influence demanded that Jews be prevented from exercising any authority over Christians, but at the same time Canon Law forbade the forcible conversion of Jews.[5] The conditions were thus established for the survival of the Jews as a distinct entity in Christian Europe. This in turn forced the Jews to come to grips with their tolerated but subordinate and degraded status.

How could the Jews consider themselves a divinely elected people if their God was so insistently punishing them, and if their Christian masters, the self-styled 'New Israel', overtly laid claim to this same status? The Prophetic tradition, with its emphasis on sin and punishment, supplied one possible explanation: the Jews were being punished for their sins. But this was less credible alongside the behaviour of the apparently unpunished Christians, whose belief in the 'Son of God' bordered on idolatry. Explanations of Jewish exile assigned it a much greater role in the divine plan: the Jews had been chosen to atone for the sins of past generations or even the entire world (a curious echo of the role which Christianity assigned to Christ, as the redeemer of the world).[6] David Biale draws attention to a more imaginative response, developed in the Midrash (the explication of the text of the Hebrew Bible) and cabbalah (the mystical texts associated with Isaac Luria in the sixteenth century). According to this tradition, God exercised His power, not by meting out punishment, but actually by going into exile with His people, thus curtailing His ability to intervene in history.[7] The creativity apparent in the very diversity of responses to the problem of exile, rather than any one specific solution, demonstrates the contribution of the concept of divine election to the continued survival of the Jews.

What of the tie to Zion? The best-known expression of this sentiment is undoubtedly the toast, 'Next year in Jerusalem!', which concludes the Passover Seder. But there are numerous other examples which can be cited: the tri-daily prayer for return; the lamentation for the destruction of the temple in Jerusalem which occurs on the feast of Tish'ah be Av; and practices tied specifically to the land of Israel, such as prayers for rain (hardly a major concern for the Jews of Eastern Europe!), harvest festivals keyed to a Middle Eastern agricultural

---

5.   *Ibid.*, p. 266.
6.   David Biale, *Power and Powerlessness in Jewish History*, New York, 1986, pp. 36–7.
7.   *Ibid.* The implication of this tradition, as Biale and others point out, is that there is greater scope for human activity, an attitude which resulted in the strengthening of the power of communal religious leaders, the rabbis, who must act in lieu of divine intervention.

calendar, or the concern of the Talmudists over matters of land ownership.[8]

The land of Israel came to constitute a mythic garden of Eden for East European Jews. David Aberbach points to passages in *Of Bygone Days*, the semi-autobiographical portrait of his youth in nineteenth-century Lithuania penned by the great Hebrew and Yiddish writer Mendele Mokher Sefarim (S.J. Abramowitz). The young hero, Shloyme, knows more of 'mandrakes, myrrh, onycha, galbanum, vines, dates, figs, pomegranates, olives, acacia-wood and gopher-wood' than of the native rye, buckwheat and potatoes. The animals of his childish imagination are the lion, the leopard, the hind and the wild-buffalo, and the mythical animals of the Haggadah, rather than the common creatures of village reality.[9] Mendele depicts the world of Shloyme with gentle irony, but in other works he suggests that this is not just the perspective of naive children. In his comic novel *The Travels of Benjamin the Third*, the eponymous hero sets out to find the lost 'Red Jews' who live across the river Sambatyen and beyond the dark mountains. Benjamin acts for all the world as though the Jewish *shtetl* of Eastern Europe were located on the banks of the river Jordan, casually inquiring of local peasants the quickest way to reach *Erets Israel*.[10] Some of the first, and most popular novels in modern Hebrew, by Abraham Mapu, had biblical times as their setting.[11]

Erets Israel was not just the subject of literary imagination and satire. The wooden synagogues of Eastern Europe were elaborately painted with the plants and animals of the Bible. A specialist of East European synagogue art, R. Wischnitzer-Bernstein, observes: 'It seems incredible that immigrants from Palestine should have preserved intact for centuries on end their memories of the Middle Eastern flora and fauna and continued to reproduce images of remote past in the midst of a different environment.'[12]

While the tie to Zion may have kept Judaism from becoming just a religious community by infusing it with ethnic and national elements, to what extent did it actually encourage resettlement in Palestine? There was certainly communication back and forth between Eastern

8. David Vital, *The Origins of Zionism*, Oxford, 1975, pp. 5–6; Shlomo Avineri, *The Making of Modern Zionism: The Intellectual Origins of the Jewish State*, London, 1981 (hereafter *The Making of Modern Zionism*), pp. 3–4.
9. David Aberbach, 'Aggadah and Childhood Imagination in the Works of Mendele, Bialik, and Agnon' in G. Abramson and T. Parfitt (eds), *Jewish Education and Learning*, London, 1993, p. 234.
10. Mendele Mokher Sefarim, *The Travels and Adventures of Benjamin the Third*, trans. Moshe Spiegel, New York, 1949.
11. David Patterson, *Abraham Mapu: The Creator of the Modern Hebrew Novel*, London, 1964.
12. Z. Yargina, *Wooden Synagogues*, Moscow, n.d., p. 19.

Europe and Palestine. Ambassadors from the *yishuv*, the impoverished native community, were frequent visitors in search of alms. There was a steady stream of pious visitors, but they were often the elderly, seeking to die within the sacred precincts, rather than settle and live. There were a few episodes of settlers under an eschatological influence, such as adherents to the Hasidic movement in the eighteenth century, but they arrived as would-be participants in the Messianic age, not as any sort of causal agents who might help to bring it about.[13] In short, the 'love of Zion' possessed a mythic quality for East European Jews, but was devoid of any practical implications. This is explicable only by reference to the way in which the Messianic influence in Judaism, which should have been a catalyst for projects focused on Palestine, was instead tamed and pacified.

The raw material of Messianism may be found in the period of the Second Temple and at the dawn of Christianity (which borrowed the concept). While there was much disagreement among Jewish thinkers about the nature of the Messiah and the Messianic age, its active expression was linked to the disastrous uprisings against Rome in 66–70 CE and 132–5 CE. The latter episode, the Bar Kochba rebellion, culminated in the final dispersal of the Jews from *Erets Israel*. Such an outcome served to discredit Messianism as a practical policy. Jewish thinkers rescued the concept of Messianism by elevating it from the realm of man to that of God. God alone would decide how and when the Messiah would appear, and 'let him be cursed who tries to calculate the days of the Messiah'. David Biale points to the Midrashic tradition of the 'three oaths', supposedly demanded by God, which perfectly encapsulates this approach. Jews would not force the coming of the Messiah, nor would they prematurely emigrate to Palestine (one of the signals of the Messianic age) and the Gentile nations, in turn, would not persecute the Jews 'too much'.[14] The course of Jewish history threw up continual warnings of the consequences of violating this interdiction on action. The episode of the 'mystical Messiah', Shabbatai Zevi, sent shock-waves through the Jewish (and non-Jewish) world in the seventeenth century. Shabbatai Zevi's eventual fate — his conversion to Islam — as well as the inter-communal feuding which followed in his wake, was a graphic warning of the dangers of

---

13. This latter premise is not universally accepted by scholars. See Jacob Barnai, 'The Historiography of the Hasidic Immigration to Erets Yisrael' in Ada Rapoport-Albert (ed.), *Hasidism Reappraised*, London, 1996, pp. 376–88. Discussing the visit to Palestine of Nachman of Bratslav, when he did not even make the short journey to Jerusalem from the coast, Vital observes that the visits of such mystics involved 'not resettlement [...] but one's own relationship with the Divine': Vital, *The Origins of Zionism*, pp. 6–7.

14. Biale, *Power and Powerlessness in Jewish History*, pp. 39–40.

'calculating the days of the Messiah'.[15] There is a lively historiographical debate concerning the impact of Shabbatai Zevi upon East European Jewry, whether expressed in the form of the movement of another pretender, Joseph Frank in Poland, or in the rise of Hasidism in the eighteenth century.[16] In either case, the implications of action in pursuit of Zion could be seen as negative. This, many specialists have argued, was a lesson learned. In the view of a leading contemporary expert on Zionism, Shlomo Avineri, 'as a symbol of belief, integration and group identity it [the tie to Zion] was a powerful component of the value system, but as an activating element of historical praxis and changing reality throughout history, it was almost wholly quietistic'.[17]

Many commentators have been unable to resist the temptation of characterizing modern political Zionism as 'secular or secularized Messianism', and to conflate it with the myth of Zion into a neat ideological package. This approach raises a host of questions. On the basis of the above discussion, it could be argued that quietism was an integral part of Jewish Messianism — how then was it activated into praxis? 'Secularization' by itself could not accomplish this. In France, for example, secularization of the myths of Zion and the Messiah served to make them less Jewish. Judaism's mission was transformed into that of a 'world' religion with a universalist message. Emancipated French Jews — or Frenchmen of the Mosaic Faith — equated this message with the universalistic principles of the French Revolution, investing it with a redemptive, Messianic aura.[18] Secularization was a process which normalized the position of the Jews, making them into a nation, like all other nations, devoid of election or Messianic role. Avineri, for one, rejects the superficial links with past tradition envisaged by the proponents of Zionism as secularized Messianism. Instead, he sees the emergence of modern political Zionism as unprecedented, revolutionary in character, and attributes it to the challenges posed to the modernizing Jewish community by the ascendant ideologies of liberalism and nationalism.[19]

At first glance, this perspective has much to recommend it. The two individuals most often cited as the first proto-Zionists, Rabbi Yehudah Alkalai (1798–1878) and Rabbi Zvi Hirsch Kalischer (1795–1874),

15. Gershom Scholem, *Sabbatai Sevi: The Mystical Messiah, 1626–1676*, revised edition, London, 1973.
16. Bernard D. Weinryb, *The Jews of Poland: A Social and Economic History of the Jewish Community in Poland from 1100 to 1800*, Philadelphia, PA, 1982, pp. 236–61.
17. Avineri, *The Making of Modern Zionism*, p. 4.
18. Michael Marrus, *The Politics of Assimilation*, New York, 1971, p. 120.
19. Avineri , *The Making of Modern Zionism*, p. 13.

were products of geographical or cultural borderlands, Sarajevo and Posen respectively, where questions of national identity were acquiring a sharper focus amidst the emergence of new nations and new state systems. Kalisher, in his writings, specifically pointed to the national movements of the Italians, the Poles and the Hungarians as justification for analogous activity from the side of Jews.

Yet, under closer inspection, and *contra* Avineri, the activity of Alkalai and Kalischer might better be seen as evidence of an evolutionary rather than revolutionary emergence of Zionism from out of the religious milieu. Both men were religiously Orthodox, and justified their proposals for settlement in Palestine by reference to the religious texts of Judaism. They sought to show that Zionist activities were not a presumptuous effort to force the hand of God, but a legitimate human preliminary of the divinely accomplished restoration to come. By leaving Messianic functions to God, in fact, Alkalai and Kalischer produced settlement plans that were undramatic, practical and down to earth, encompassing little more than organic work. Alkalai bombarded the notables of his day with proposals to buy Palestine, in whole or in part, in pursuit of a practical programme of Jewish agricultural settlement. Kalischer, in his turn, helped to set up a group which bought agricultural land in Palestine for Jewish settlers.[20] We might call this activity 'Zionism without Messianism'.

Ironically, it was acculturated Jews who developed 'Messianism without Zionism'. (There is one important figure who did combine the two: Moses Hess. Hess was a pioneer of European ethical socialism and an early collaborator of Marx, before taking an interest in the Jewish Question.)[21] The two men who, more than any others, may be called the founders of modern Zionism were Lev Pinsker and Theodor Herzl. Disenchanted with the promises of mundane liberalism, they both turned to radical solutions to the Jewish Question, the creation of a Jewish homeland (Pinsker) or state (Herzl). Although both men, and Herzl in particular, sought to emphasize the rationality and common-sense aspect of their plans, their ideas were in fact infused with a high degree of mysticism and Messianism. They sought a sweeping solution which would solve the dilemmas of diaspora Jewry at a stroke. Pinsker's *Autoemancipation*, with its dream of a 'free, active development of our national force or of our native genius', was redolent of the Romantic nationalism associated with the epigones of Johann Herder. Herzl hit on his master plan only after trying and rejecting Romantic fancies, such as the mass conversion of the Jews of

20. *Ibid.*, pp. 47–55. For excerpts from the writings of Alkalai and Kalischer, see Arthur Hertzberg (ed.), *The Zionist Idea*, New York, 1959, pp. 102–14.
21. See Shlomo Avineri, *Moses Hess: Prophet of Communism and Zionism*, New York and London, 1985.

the Austrian Empire in order to regularize their situation and secure full equality.[22] Their apparently simple and direct Zionist solutions were meant to cut the Gordian knot of the Jewish Question. The plans of the two men were developed in a sort of creative frenzy, under the pressure of contemporary crises (the rude force of the Russian pogroms of 1881–2, or the sophisticated formulations of European antisemites in the 1890s). Most striking of all, neither Pinsker nor Herzl was originally a Zionist. They made *Erets Israel* (a religious term which they seldom used) the setting for their homeland projects only after they had been convinced of its centrality by others.

The above survey suggests that the myths of Messianism and *Erets Israel* may have been twins, but twins separated at birth. How were they brought back together? The answer should be sought in the context of East European Jewry, the population centre which was to serve as the reservoir of cadres of Zionism right up until the foundation of the state of Israel. Let us explore more specifically the process through which Zionism and the Messianism described above became linked as the foundation myths of modern Zionism.

The year 1881, when hundreds of anti-Jewish riots, or pogroms, erupted in the south-western provinces of the Russian Empire, has rightly been seen by historians as a turning point in modern Jewish history. However, many aspects of this turning point, such as the assumption that the mass of politically aware Jews turned their back on the premise that gradual emancipation was the surest remedy for the Jewish Question in Russia, or that this moment marked a sudden turn of politically active Jews away from the general revolutionary movement and towards more specifically Jewish forms of socialism, have been oversimplified or exaggerated.[23] Rather, the events of 1881–2 strengthened a phenomenon which had been gaining force in Eastern Europe since a major pogrom had rocked Odessa in 1871. It was the 1871 event, and especially the responses of Russian society to it, which began the discrediting of the liberal solution to the Jewish Question.[24] Instead of integration, acculturation and/or assimilation, Jewish publicists, exemplified by the journalist and novelist Peretz Smolenskin, sought refuge in the concept of Jewish nationhood.

---

22. Pinsker is discussed below; for a good recent treatment of Herzl's motives and motivations, see Jacques Kornberg, *Theodor Herzl: From Assimilation to Zionism*, Bloomington, IN, 1993.
23. Jonathan Frankel, *Prophecy and Politics: Socialism, Nationalism, and the Russian Jews, 1862–1917*, Cambridge, 1981 (hereafter *Prophecy and Politics*), p. 50. Frankel notes the role of Y. Leshchinskii and E. Cherikover in pioneering this interpretation.
24. See John D. Klier, *Imperial Russia's Jewish Question, 1855–1881*, Cambridge, 1995, pp. 358–63; Alexander Orbach, *New Voices of Russian Jewry*, Leiden, 1980, pp. 182–95.

Smolenskin rejected the definition of a 'Jew' accepted by both Russian law and the Jewish Orthodox as determined by religion: 'no matter what his sins against religion, every Jew belongs to his people as long as he does not betray it'.[25] This decoupling of ethnicity and religion always remained problematic in Russia, given the state's *de facto* acceptance of the religious category and the consequent temptation to convert for openly pragmatic reasons (a phenomenon which equally alarmed the Christian and Jewish devout). Thus the Jewish Duma member and convert to Christianity, M.Ia. Gertsenshtein, characterized himself in his official biography as a 'Russian of the Mosaic Faith'. Contemporary Jewish thinkers, such as Simon Dubnov, argued that conversion was precisely that act of betrayal of the Jewish people against which Smolenskin protested.[26] The crisis of 1881–2, however, forced Lev Pinsker to add greater specificity to Smolenskin's vague definition. For Pinsker, the Jews must be seen as a 'nationality'. He appropriated the racialist categories of the time to characterize the 'common, unmixed descent' of the 'semitic Jew', while at the same time identifying them with other peoples, 'the dependent and oppressed nationalities' of Europe who were also engaged in the task of nation-building.[27]

The invigoration of a Jewish sense of national identity helped to reactivate the myth of *Erets Israel*. In part this was a response to practical necessity. The pogroms had prompted the flight of Jews from pogrom centres. A large camp of such refugees pitched up in Brody, the first major urban centre across the border of the Austrian Empire. The Jewish refugees of Brody became a target of worldwide attention, and of the relief efforts of Jewish organizations such as the Alliance Israélite Universelle. Rumours which circulated widely among Russian Jewry about the provision made for the refugees by the Alliance prompted unrest and further flight to perceived safe-havens. What was to be the fate of the hapless victims? Logic suggested that a return to their original homes would be the most effective expedient, and this was, in fact, the objective usually preferred by relief organizations. But in Russia proper, against the backdrop of events which were often seen in apocalyptic terms, a lively debate erupted regarding the possibilities of emigration to either Palestine or the United States.[28]

25. Vital, *The Origins of Zionism*, pp. 46–7, 56–64.
26. S.M. Dubnov, *Nationalism and History*, ed. Koppel Pinson, Philadelphia, PA, 1958, pp. 91–2.
27. Lev Pinsker, *Road to Freedom: Writings and Addresses*, ed. B. Netanyahu, New York, 1944, pp. 82, 90.
28. See John D. Klier, 'Emigration Mania in Late-Imperial Russia: Legend and Reality' in Aubrey Newman and Stephen W. Massil (eds), *Patterns of Migration, 1850–1914*, London, 1996, pp. 21–9.

Although the disputants masqueraded behind apparently pragmatic arguments involving ease of transport or emigration, availability of land and absorptive capacity, any examination of the debate reveals its unmistakable millenistic and Messianic features. Plans for settlement in the United States, for example, envisaged that Jewish agricultural colonization would be organized into socialistic agrarian communes. Such plans were not just efforts to help Jewish refugees, but offered radical economic and social solutions to the broader Jewish Question.[29]

The proponents of radical emigration programmes, whether to America or Palestine, were overwhelmingly young students, many of them active or passive participants in the so-called *narodnik* or Populist movement. Russian Populism was based on theories of agrarian socialism. Its non-peasant theoreticians engaged in continual debate as to the best method of exciting the masses to action.[30] The Jewish activists of 1881, nurtured in this ideological environment, were as much interested in action for its own sake as they were in the eventual destination of migrating Jews. As one young activist wrote to a friend — in a letter intercepted by the secret police in Chernigov province — 'we will be *narodniki* [populists] [...] and we will be *narodniki* to the grave. Our happiness is tied to the happiness of the masses. To think of education, enlightenment and self-improvement is sinful now, when it is not intellectual activity which is valuable, but bread.' The author demanded action in order to set an example to the masses. At the same time, he was completely indifferent as to what the final destination of Jewish emigrants might be. Let the majority decide, he advised.[31]

The Populist movement was characterized by a number of dramatic episodes in the 1870s known as the 'going to the people', in which young idealists left the cities in order to spread the message of socialism among peasant masses. In the wake of the first pogroms, almost every contemporary commentator commented on analogous activity among young Jewish students, very much in the sense of a 'coming home to the Jewish masses'. Student activists centred their efforts on the synagogue, attending and giving speeches at services, especially during the public fasts called by the religious leadership to pray for the aversion of further pogroms.[32] Students composed and circulated in the synagogues throughout the Pale a long poem in which they pledged to return to their people and to share their travails and

29. Frankel, *Prophecy and Politics*, pp. 68–107.
30. The classic treatment of the movement remains Franco Venturi's *Roots of Revolution*, London, 1952.
31. Gosudarstvennyi Arkhiv Rossiiskoi Federatsii (hereafter GARF), f. 102 (3-oe deloproizvodstvo), op. 1881, d. 1227, ll. 10–12.
32. GARF, f. 102 (2-oe deloproizvodstvo), op. 38, d. 681, chast' 4 (1881), l. 24.

tears.[33] What is striking about such declarations is their departure from generic populist rhetoric about the downtrodden 'people' to a specific identification with the Jews alone. Declarations and manifestos (produced by that prime weapon of the revolutionary movement, the hectograph) were more symbolic than practical, and perhaps for this very reason they consciously began to incorporate the image of *Erets Israel*.

This was the case even when the authors were not calling for emigration to Palestine. On 1 March 1882, a student group in St Petersburg, styling itself the 'Brotherhood of Zion', sent a Hebrew-language proclamation to state rabbis throughout the Pale. It called for 'Israel' to hold its head high, and to pursue 'the restoration of our ruins and natal hearths'. The objectives of the Brotherhood of Zion were not overtly Zionist: they entailed the creation of a committee to organize emigration to a central point, which was not specified, where there would be sufficient land for all. In a number of places in the manifesto the authors implied that the 'cancer' that was eating up the Jews in Russia was the absence of a 'plot of land for their own fields and gardens'.[34] (This was a reflection of contemporary initiatives within Russian Jewry to combat widespread Jewish poverty and backwardness by making the Jews more productive through the pursuit of agriculture and craftsmanship.)

In April of 1882 the Kiev police discovered in the rooms of the Kiev university student Zelman Rotmin materials to produce literature for a 'Russian Jewish Emigration Society'. Found among the literature was the group's manifesto, entitled 'The Eternal People', and composed in 'Jewish'.[35] It was accompanied by an invitation, in Russian, to all like-minded groups to send representatives to a meeting in Kiev. The announcement was clearly more concerned with the need for solidarity rather than any concrete plan. The closest the invitation came to a specific proposal was an assurance that emigration 'will achieve a radical turning point in the fate of the Jewish people through creation of an autonomous centre of gravity for all Jewry'. This was to be a truly popular undertaking involving all of Russian Jewry except the upper bourgeoisie (that is, the traditional leadership in the capital), who always placed their own interests above those of the people.[36] This latter dismissal of the traditional leadership in the capital demonstrates the generational divide which characterized almost all the subsequent debates about emigration and resettlement.

33. *Ibid.*, 1. 27.
34. GARF, f. 102, op. 39, d. 280, chast´ 7 (1882), ll. 8–10.
35. The police report uses this characterization. Usually this term meant Yiddish, but my supposition is that it was in Hebrew. *Ibid.*, d. 280 chast´ 8, ll. 5–9.
36. *Ibid.*

Scattered bands of students, known as the BILU movement, actually emigrated to Palestine to create agricultural communes.[37] A group of young activists 'captured' Lev Pinsker, establishing him as the head of a movement to promote resettlement in Palestine known as Hovevei Zion (The Lovers of Zion).[38] All such efforts faced insurmountable practical difficulties which were further complicated when the Russian government declared the instigation of emigration to be illegal at the end of 1882.[39]

While the activities of the student activists of Eastern Europe may never have achieved more than a symbolic significance, they were all the more powerful for their myth-making quality. The crises of 1871 and 1881–2 led Jewish intellectuals to ponder the position of the Jews in a society which had unexpectedly turned hostile to them. In the course of constructing a new sense of Jewish identity out of the then fashionable European theories of race and ethnicity, they rediscovered the efficacy of the myth of Zion as a symbol of Jewish unity. The myth of Zion gained special force when it was linked to a Messianic concept of return to the sacred land. It should not be overlooked that the Messianic element was as much — if not more — plagiarized from Russian Populism as from the Jewish Messianic tradition. The new pretender had no difficulty in putting on the clothes of the religious Messiah, however. Thus, when Theodor Herzl launched political Zionism, there were refurbished myths ready at hand which could easily be reactivated. This was especially the case in Eastern Europe, which was to prove a reservoir of support for Zionism, filled with people who were already psychologically prepared for the new tasks of practical state-building.

---

37. Vital, *The Origins of Zionism*, pp. 80–8.
38. *Ibid.*, pp. 135–86.
39. Hans Rogger, 'Government Policy on Jewish Emigration' in *idem, Jewish Policies and Right-Wing Politics in Imperial Russia*, London, 1986, p. 179.

MYTHS OF NATIONAL HISTORY IN
BELARUS AND UKRAINE

Andrew Wilson

Introduction

The term 'myth' needs to be used with considerable care in any
discussion of historiography. Its popular association with a wholly
imagined or chimerical past is one problem, but so is its use in critical
or discourse theory,[1] given the tendency of the latter to limit itself to
wholly autonomous self-referential worlds of meaning, divorced from
any grounding in broader reality.[2] My intention in this chapter
therefore is to argue that, although national and/or nationalist
historiographies can indeed be understood as mythic structures, as
'narratives' in the broader sense, they must also resonate in a plausible
past and find an appropriate place in the mainstream of popular
memory in order to take root.

In the words of Anthony Smith, although

it is history, and history alone, which can furnish the bases of ethnic
identity and the psychic reassurance of communal security that goes with it
[...] it is not the amount of such history, or even its dramatic value, that is
important; what nationalists require from their historical researches is the
definition of a particular ethnic atmosphere, unique to that community, and
the provision of moral qualities (and heroic embodiments) peculiar to the
group.[3]

In other words, when acting as ethnic entrepreneurs, nationalist
historians must sell a plausible product that is both effective and
affective. The trick with historical myths, or identity myths in general,
is that they must help constitute the collective identity of a social
subject (in this case a 'nation') without that subject being aware it is

---

1. Ernesto Laclau (ed.), *The Making of Political Identities*, London, 1994; Chantal
    Mouffe (ed.), *Dimensions of Radical Democracy*, London, 1992; Agnes Heller, *A
    Philosophy of History in Fragments*, Oxford, 1993.
2. Bryan D. Palmer, *Descent into Discourse: The Reification of Language and the
    Writing of Social Theory*, Philadelphia, PA, 1990.
3. Anthony D. Smith, 'The Formation of Nationalist Movements' in *idem* (ed.),
    Nationalist Movements, London, 1976, pp. 1–30 (8, 17). See also *idem, National
    Identity*, London, 1991, pp. 22, 25, 87; *The Ethnic Origins of Nations,* Oxford,
    1986, chapter 9; and 'Gastronomy or Geology? The Role of Nationalism in the
    Construction of Nations' in *Nations and Nationalism*, 1, 1995, 1, pp. 3–23.

being so constructed.[4] National myths cannot be *perceived* to be inventions. Although the predictable nature of their construction and combination may lead observers to emphasize the element of artifice, historical mythologies as popular systems of belief also need to be understood through the eyes of their adherents, for whom they need to be perceived as first-order truths. Therefore, although all states are engaged in the social construction of national identity through their influence on public historiographical narrative (especially in the school system and in the mass media), some have more success than others.[5] Some historical myths simply 'fit' popular traditions better than others.

The two East Slavonic states of Ukraine and Belarus provide an appropriate testing-ground for this hypothesis. Nationalist historians in both states have set themselves similar tasks: namely disentangling a national myth of descent from traditional Russophile historiography, celebrating a lost 'Golden Age' before forcible incorporation into the Russian sphere of influence, and demonstrating that, in contrast to autocratic and 'Asiatic' Russia, their nations are naturally democratic, demotic and 'European'. As with other ideal-type nationalist historiographies,[6] the definition of the contemporary nation as a community of fate that shares a collective destiny with past and future generations requires that it first be distinguished from its neighbours and enemies. History can then be presented as a morality play of national resistance and revival against the main national 'Other'.

The 'Other' for nationalists in both Ukraine and Belarus is Russia.[7] In both states, however, the representation of Russia as the 'Other' is a task fraught with difficulty. One half of the population of Ukraine is Russian-speaking; 21 per cent are ethnic Russians, but 33 per cent are Russian-speaking Ukrainians.[8] The latter, in particular, are subject to a

---

4.   Roxanne Lynn Doty, 'Sovereignty and the Nation: Constructing the Boundaries of National Identity' in Thomas J. Biersteker and Cynthia Weber (eds), *State Sovereignty as Social Construct*, Cambridge, 1996, pp. 121–47. The term 'myth' is therefore only used with this point in mind.

5.   See, for example, Alexander Grant and Keith J. Stringer (eds), *Uniting the Kingdom? The Making of British History*, London, 1995; Gail Hershatter, Emily Honig, Jonathan N. Lipman and Randall Stross, *Remapping China: Fissures in Historical Terrain*, Stanford, CA, 1996; and, on India, Partha Chaterjee, *The Nation and its Fragments*, Princeton, NJ, 1993.

6.   Yael Tamir, 'Reconstructing the Landscape of Imagination' in Simon Caney, David George and Peter Jones (eds), *National Rights, International Obligations*, Boulder, CO, 1996, pp. 85–101.

7.   Poland no longer occupies the prominent place in national demonology that it did a century ago. Jews and Lithuanians are also 'Others', but space is too short to discuss how they are represented.

8.   Valeri Khmelko and Andrew Wilson, 'The Political Orientation of Different Regions and Ethno-Linguistic Groups in Ukraine Since Independence', paper

variety of cross-cutting cultural pressures; neither group traditionally sees Russia as alien, let alone hostile. Belarus is more homogeneous ethnically and linguistically (and regionally), but many, probably most, Belarusians have no idea of nationhood outside of a common cultural sphere with Russia.

This chapter compares nationalist historiography in Ukraine and Belarus by examining seven key myths that play a crucial role in nationalists' efforts to establish or solidify a national identity that is sufficiently distinguished from that of Russia/the USSR. It is argued that, although Belarus has had a particular problem with the physical dissemination of 'national' historiography, since the election of Russophile president Aliaksandr Lukashenka in 1994,[9] there were already more serious problems in Belarus than in Ukraine in terms of the popular 'receptivity' of the key nationalist myths. Belarusian nationalists have had to work with much less promising material, and their 'national idea' has been correspondingly weaker. In Ukraine, on the other hand, nationalist historiographical mythology has a powerful appeal for the Ukrainian-speaking half of the country and in key respects meets the requirements of *raison d'état*. Although more coherent, it remains, however, controversial. Its anti-Russian emphasis hampers its receptivity amongst the Russian-speaking half of the population of Ukraine, and is a potential factor inhibiting the development of their loyalty to the new state.

1. Myths of Origin

Myths of origin are one of the most important features of any national historiography, in so far as the questions 'Who are we?' and 'Where did we come from?' are vital first steps in establishing myths of national character. Significantly, Ukrainian and Belarusian nationalists have broadly similar myths of origin.[10] In contrast to traditional Russophile historiography, which imagined a relatively united East Slavonic community emerging in the second half of the first millennium AD (the so-called 'ancient Rus´ nation' — in Russian *drevnii russkii narod* or *tri-edinaia russkaia natsiia*), they argue that, firstly, the Eastern Slavs were then little more than a loose collection of warring tribes, and that, secondly, by mixing with other local elements, different

presented at the conference on 'Soviet to Independent Ukraine: A Troubled Transformation', University of Birmingham, 13–14 June 1996.

9.   Valentin Zhdanko, 'Perepisyvaem uchebniki, peredelyvaem istoriiu', *Belorusskaia delovaia gazeta*, 31 August 1995; *Pravda*, 25 August 1995.

10. Viktor Shnirel´man, 'Natsionalisticheskii mif: osnovnye kharakteristiki (na primere etnogeneticheskikh versii vostochnoslavianskykh narodov)', *Slavianovedenie*, 1995, 6, pp. 3–13, also deals with rival theories of 'ethnogenesis'.

geographic groups of these tribes created three very different ethnic 'substrata' for the Ukrainian, Belarusian and Russian nations. Thus, for the Ukrainians, their ancestors were south-western tribes such as the *poliany* and *siveriany*, mixed with Iranian and Ural-Altai (mainly Turkic) elements; for the Belarusians, the north-western *kryvichy* and *dryhavichy*, mixed with local Balts. In a similar fashion, more northerly tribes, such as the *viatychi* and *sloviany*, supposedly mixed with the Ugro-Finns to create the basis of the Russian ethnic group.[11]

The myth of East Slavonic unity is therefore challenged at its very beginnings. In telling this particular story, however, the Ukrainians have a substantial advantage. The main task of Russophile archaeology in the tsarist and Soviet eras was to develop a theory of Slavonic pre-history in the lands around the Dnieper, rebutting rival (mainly German) theories of Gothic pre-eminence in the region.[12] The Ukrainians can, to a large extent, simply adapt such theories wholesale, arguing that the whole line of development through the Trypillians (3,500 to 2,700 BC), Cimmerians (1,500 to 700 BC), Scythians (750 to 250 BC) and Antes (sixth and seventh centuries AD) ended in a local (proto-) Ukrainian culture rather than a general East Slavonic one.[13] As the story told by tsarist and Soviet historians mainly unfolded on what is now Ukrainian territory, it is easily rewritten. In the words of the leading Ukrainian historian Iaroslav Isaievych, head of the International Association of Ukrainian Studies, 'it is perfectly natural that the ideologues of the Ukrainian national movement have sought [to uncover] the deep historical roots of the Ukrainian people',[14] and the Ukrainians have been blessed with ready-made source material with which to assert their antiquity.

Belarusian nationalists, on the other hand, despite some archaeological evidence (mainly burial sites) for their claim that local

11. For the Ukrainians, see (especially) V.P. Petrov, *Pokhodzhennia ukraïns'koho narodu*, Kiev, 1992; Leonid Zalizniak, *Narysy starodavn'oï istoriï Ukraïny*, Kiev, 1994; and Iu.V. Pavlenko, *Peredistoriia davnikh rusiv u svitovomu konteksti*, Kiev, 1994. For the Belarusians, Liudmila Duchyts, 'Bal'ty i slaviane na terytoryi Belarusi ŭ pachatku II tysiachahodz'dzia', *Belaruski histarychny ahliad*, 2, 1995, 1, pp. 15–30.
12. Viktor Shnirelman, 'From Internationalism to Nationalism: Forgotten Pages of Soviet Archaeology in the 1930s and 1940s' in Phillip L. Kohl and Clare Fawcett (eds), *Nationalism, Politics and the Practice of Archaeology*, Cambridge, 1995, pp. 120–38.
13. Volodymyr Kyrychuk, 'Istorychni koreni ukraïns'koho narodu: do pytannia etnohenezu ukraïntsiv', *Heneza*, 1994, 1, pp. 142–9.
14. Iaroslav Isaievych, 'Problema pokhodzhennia ukraïns'koho narodu: istoriohrafichnyi i politychnyi aspekt', in his *Ukraïna: davna i nova*, Lviv, 1996, pp. 22–43 (22).

Slavonic and Baltic elements had a long pre-history of intermingling,[15] have to rely more on the testimony of local toponyms and hydronyms.[16] Moreover, there is no real evidence of pre-Slavonic civilization to establish the antiquity of Belarus *before* the period of contact with proto-Russian tribes. The best the Belarusians can do is to claim that the Slavs originated on or close to Belarusian territory, 'between the Orda and Dnieper rivers, in the river basins of the Visla and Prypiat'.[17]

2. Foundation Myths

All nations need a formal starting-point to their history, normally the moment when the process of 'ethnogenesis' is deemed to have culminated in the beginnings of formal statehood. Once again, for the Ukrainians this is relatively easy, as they can simply invert the history of Kievan Rus'. Given the Ukrainian nationalist argument that the Slavonic tribes who inhabited the Dnieper area from the seventh century AD were already 'proto-Ukrainians', then the state they established in the ninth century, Kievan Rus', can be claimed as 'the first Ukrainian state'. Furthermore, it is argued that Rus', although Byzantine in culture, drew on the proto-Ukrainian (pagan) traditions that had developed amongst the Trypillians, Sarmathians, Antes and others. The religion, art, architecture and language (see below) of Rus' were therefore all 'early Ukrainian'.[18] More northerly, proto-Russian, tribes played only a marginal or downright hostile role in the life of Rus', which was, after all, based in Kiev (the sack of Kiev by the northern armies of Andrei Bogoliubskii in 1169 occupies a prominent part in Ukrainian nationalist mythology).[19]

Belarusian nationalists, on the other hand, cannot claim the whole state of Rus' as their own; they have to make do with the assertion that its north-western marches were relatively autonomous. The principality of Polatskaia-Rus' (and later that of Novaharadok), founded by the *kryvichy* just as Kiev was founded by the *poliany*, is therefore described as 'the first state on the territory of Belarus', which was only briefly under the authority of rival centres of power such as Kiev and

15. Heorhi Shtykhaŭ, *Kryvichy: Pa materyialakh raskopak kurhanoŭ u Paŭnochnaŭ Belarusi*, Minsk, 1992.
16. Author's interview with Anatol' and Valentin Hrytskevich, 2 September 1995.
17. V.F. Holubeŭ, U.P. Kruk and P.A. Loika, *Tsi vedaetse vy historyiu svaëi krainy?*, second edition, Minsk, 1995, p. 6.
18. See for example, Raïsa Ivanchenko, *Kyïvs'ka Rus': pochatky Ukraïns'koï derzhavy. Posibnyk z istoriï*, Kiev, 1995, and Iaroslav Dashkevych, 'Natsiia i utvorennia Kyïvs'koï Rusi', *Ratusha*, 9 September 1993.
19. *Istoriia Ukraïny dlia ditei shkil'noho viku*, Kiev, 1992, p. 38.

Novgorod (Kiev and Polatsk were at war between 1127 and 1129).[20] 'Like ninth century "Britain" [therefore], "Rus'" was in fact a collection of rival kingdoms, with Kiev, Polatsk and Novgorod like Wessex and Mercia.'[21] However, semi-autonomous quasi-statehood provides nowhere near as resonant a beginning as the Ukrainian case.

In both cases the exclusion of (proto-) Russian elements from the history of Rus', as the first step in the trend towards the radical 'othering' of Russia, is potentially dangerous.[22] Too sharp a leap from the myth of East Slavonic unity to a one-dimensional portrayal of Russia as always and everywhere solely hostile can only strain the loyalties of Russophiles to the new Ukrainian and Belarusian states.

3. Myths of Descent and Myths of Statehood

Nationalist historiography likes to narrate a more or less continuous myth of national descent in order to refute the stereotypes of rival mythologies in which their nation plays only a temporary and/or marginal role. This is particularly important in the Ukrainian and Belarusian cases: in tsarist and Soviet historiography, treatment of the two nations was often perfunctory, save for the standard narrative of their teleological path towards eventual 'reunion' with Russia. *Myths of (past) statehood* are the most decisive way of counteracting such stereotypes; Ukrainians therefore claim a 'thousand years of state-building', Belarusians a 'centuries-long tradition of the development of statehood'.[23] However, in addition to its relatively weak beginning, the history of 'Belarusian statehood' has more natural gaps and discontinuities than in the Ukrainian case,[24] and rival Polish,

20. Heorhi Shtykhaŭ and Uladzimir Pliashevich, *Historyia Belarusi: Starazhytnyia chasy i siaredniavechcha*, Minsk, 1993, text approved by Ministry of Education for fifth to sixth classes, pp. 105–34. See also Mikola Ermalovich, *Starazhytnaia Belarus': Polatski i novaharodski peryiady*, Minsk, 1990.

21. Author's interview with Valentin Hrytskevich, 2 September 1995.

22. The Ukrainian historian Petro Tolochko continues to argue that Rus' was the cradle of all three East Slavonic nations; see his *Kyïvs'ka Rus'*, Kiev, 1996. See also M.F. Kotliar, 'Kyïvs'ka Rus'' in V.A. Smolii (ed.), *Istoriia Ukraïny: nove bachennia*, vol. 1, Kiev, 1995, pp. 40–94, especially pp. 73 and 89–90.

23. From the 1991 declaration of Ukrainian independence, *Holos Ukraïny*, 29 November 1991; from the 1994 constitution of Belarus, *Kanstytutsyia respubliki Belarus'*, Minsk, 1994, p. 66.

24. Iaroslav Malyk, Borys Vol and Vasyl' Chupryna, *Istoriia ukraïns'koï derzhavnosti*, Lviv, 1995; Alena Abetsedarskaia, Pëtr Bryhadzin, Leanid Zhylunovich *et al.*, *Dapamozhnik pa historyi Belarusi dlia pastupaiuchykh u vysheishyia navuchal'nyia ŭstanovy*, Minsk, 1995; and Mikhas' Bich, 'Dziarzhaŭnasts' Belarusi: stanaŭlenne, strata, barats'ba za adnaŭlenne (IX st.– 1918 hod)', *Belaruskaia minuŭshchyna*, 1993, 5–6, pp. 3–7 and 21.

Lithuanian and Russian myths of statehood are more difficult to displace.

After the collapse of Rus´ in the early thirteenth century, the Ukrainians can claim that its traditions passed to the kingdom of Galicia-Volhynia, which supposedly controlled nearly all the southern territories of Rus´ until the 1340s.[25] Thereafter, there is admittedly a fallow period when Ukrainian lands fell (mainly) under Polish or Lithuanian rule, although Ukrainian historians nevertheless claim that the lands around Kiev under nominal Lithuanian control in fact remained virtually autonomous until the Union of Lublin in 1569.[26] From the mid-seventeenth century onwards, however, the Ukrainians have the all-important Cossack era to celebrate.[27] Not only are the Cossacks lauded for their democratic traditions and defence of the (Orthodox) faith, but it is argued that they revived many of the traditions of Rus´ and that the polity they established after Bohdan Khmel´nyts´kyi's rebellion in 1648 was a true Ukrainian *state* rather than just an anarchic refuge for runaway serfs.[28] As the history of the Cossack 'Hetmanate' can be stretched up until the end of the eighteenth century, there is therefore a relatively short gap before 'national revival' begins early in the nineteenth century, culminating in the establishment of the Ukrainian People's Republic (UNR) in 1917–20 (see below).

The Belarusians, on the other hand, have no obvious polity to celebrate before the twentieth century. Despite claims that some Belarusians travelled south to participate in the Ukrainian Cossack movement, its influence on Belarusian society could only be indirect. To establish a tradition of statehood in the medieval period, therefore, the Belarusians have to displace Lithuanian historiography, claiming that the state established by Mendaŭh (Mindaugas) in the late fourteenth century was in fact a Belarusian, not a Lithuanian, state, founded on the remnants of Polatskaia-Rus´ and Novaharadok.[29] Subsequent confusion derived from the fact that 'the politonym [of the Lithuanian state] became used as an ethnonym [*litoŭtsy*], even though

25. Iaroslav Isaievych, 'Halyts´ko-Volyns´ka derzhava' in Iurii Zaitsev *et al.*, *Istoriia Ukraïny*, Lviv, 1996, as approved by the Ministry of Education, pp. 75–84.

26. O.V. Rusyna, 'Ukraïns´ki zemli u skladi Lytvy ta Pol´shchi' in Smolii (ed.), *Istoriia Ukraïny: nove bachennia*, vol. 1, pp. 113–51.

27. In fact, until the historian Mykhailo Hrushevs´kyi's pioneering reinterpretation of Rus´ at the turn of the twentieth century, the Cossack era was much the more important Ukrainian myth, so long as the Russophile version of the history of Rus´ held sway.

28. Valerii Shevchuk, *Kozats´ka derzhava*, Kiev, 1995; Valerii Smolii and Valerii Stepankov, *Bohdan Khmel´nyts´kyi (Sotsial´no-politychnyi portret)*, second edition, Kiev, 1995.

29. Mikola Ermalovich, *Starazhytnaia Belarus´: Vilenski peryiad*, Minsk, 1994.

80 to 90 per cent of the population was Belarusian'.[30] In fact, 'Lithuanian' (*litviny*) then meant Belarusian.[31] Belarusian law was the basis of the Lithuanian Statutes of 1529, 1566 and 1588, all of which were supposedly written in medieval Belarusian, which was only replaced by Polish as the official local language in 1696.[32] Elements of Belarusian statehood therefore survived even the political union between Lithuania–Belarus and Poland in 1569 (the Union of Lublin).[33]

However, the claim, even to a 'hyphenated' form of statehood in the Lithuanian–Belarusian era, is difficult to promote to modern-day Belarusians, who are accustomed to thinking of the late medieval and early modern periods in terms of religious conflict between Catholics and Orthodox. Traditionally, Roman Catholicism was associated with the Poles and Lithuanians and Orthodoxy with Russia, leaving little space for a separate Belarusian identity between the two. A narrative of separate Belarusian development therefore needs to be underpinned by some more positive attributes of national identity.

4. Myths of National Character: Religion, Democracy and 'Europe'

In the period in question, when religious adherence remained all-important, Ukraine at least was beginning to develop identity markers in terms of both an Autocephalous and a Uniate Catholic tradition. Ukrainian nationalists would claim that the original Church of 'Kiev, Halych [Galicia] and all Rus′' embodied a unique local style of Orthodoxy, that Kiev therefore contested Moscow's ecclesiastical authority after the latter unilaterally formed its own Metropolitanate in 1448 in supposed succession to the Church of Rus′, and that Kiev established a rival Church that flourished between 1620 and 1686,[34] subsequently revived on no less than three separate occasions this century, in 1921–30, 1941–3 and 1990. Although the Moscow Church

30. Author's interview with Uladzimir Arloŭ, 5 September 1995.
31. Uladzimir Arloŭ, 'Kali my byli litoŭtsami' in his *Taiamnitsy polatskai historyi*, Minsk, 1994, pp. 136–73; Vitaŭt Charopka, 'Litviny — slavianski narod', *Belaruskaia minuŭshchyna*, 1993, 3–4, pp. 12–14; Paŭla Urban, *Da pytan′nia etnichnai prynalezhnas′tsi starazhytnykh lits′vynoŭ*, Minsk, 1994.
32. Uladzimir Sviazhynski, 'Iakaia mova byla dziarzhaŭnai u Vialikim Kniastve Litoŭskim?' in Z′mitser San′ko (ed.), *100 pytanniaŭ i adkazaŭ z historyi Belarusi*, Minsk, 1993, pp. 12–13.
33. Vitaŭt Charopka, 'Liublinskaia uniia', *Belaruskaia minuŭshchyna*, 1995, 2, pp. 31–4.
34. Kost′ Panas, *Istoriia Ukraïns′koï tserkvy*, Lviv, 1992, pp. 15–89; Volodymyr Kisyk, 'Pro shliakhy rozvytku tserkvy v Ukraïni i Rosiï (XI-XVI ct.)' in *Ukraïns′kyi istorychnyi zhurnal*, 1993, 2–3, pp. 76–85.

has been dominant between times and the Ukrainian Orthodox have therefore tended to divide their loyalties between Moscow and Kiev, it is important that, in comparison to Belarus, a rival poll of attraction at least exists.

Ukraine also has a strong Uniate Catholic tradition.[35] Although the Union of Brest in 1596 that created the Uniate Church could originally be credited with provoking the Orthodox counter-reaction that produced the restoration of the Ukrainian Church in 1620, the redivision of Ukrainian lands in 1667 (the Treaty of Andrusovo) left the Uniate Church predominant in those western Ukrainian lands under Polish and later Habsburg rule, where it paradoxically became the main bulwark of Ukrainian national identity against the Roman Catholic Poles.

Belarus, on the other hand, had no real Autocephalous tradition before 1795 (or before 1596) to distinguish the Orthodox faithful in Belarus from their Russian counterparts. In order to make a claim of religious distinction, therefore, Belarusian nationalist historians rely on the claim that most of the population became Uniate Catholics after the Union of Brest in 1596. Furthermore, Belarusians supposedly accepted the Union more enthusiastically than the Ukrainians and the new Church was able to spread throughout Belarus, whereas in Ukraine it remained confined to the West.[36] It is therefore claimed that '80 per cent of the rural population' of Belarus was still Uniate Catholic when it was absorbed by Russia in 1795, and only 6–7 per cent were Orthodox.[37]

The Uniate Church was completely suppressed, however, by Nicholas I in 1839, and, unlike the Church in the Habsburgs' Ukrainian territories (Galicia and Transcarpathia), was unable to survive abroad, as virtually all Belarusian territory was now under Romanov rule. Therefore, even if nationalist claims about popular religious loyalties in 1795 are accepted (and more Russophile Belarusian historians continue to assert that the majority religion in

35.   I.F. Kuras *et al.* (eds), *Tserkva i natsional'ne vidrodzhennia*, Kiev, 1993; N. Tsisyk (ed.), *Ukraïns'ke vidrodzhennia i natsional'na tserkva*, Kiev, 1990. On the 1596 Union, compare V.V. Haiuk, Ia.R. Dashkevych *et al.*, *Istoriia relihii v Ukraïni*, Lviv, 1994, with the more scholarly Borys Gudziak and Oleh Tyhii (eds), *Istorychnyi kontekst ukladennia Beresteis'koï uniï i pershe pouniine pokolinnia*, Lviv, 1995.

36.   The 'West' included the Right (western) Bank of the Dnieper until the area was joined to the Russian empire in 1793–5. As in Belarus, Uniatism was eradicated on the Right Bank in 1839.

37.   Anatol' Hrytskevich, 'Relihiinae pytanne i zneshniaia palitika tsaryzmu perad padzelami Rechy Paspalitai' in *Vestsi AN BSSR*, 1973, 6, pp. 62–71 (63); and author's interviews with Hrytskevich, 2 and 5 September 1995.

Belarus was always Orthodox),[38] Belarusians and Russians have both been part of *Slavia Orthodoxa* for at least two centuries, which has left the Belarusians particularly vulnerable to retrospective myth-making concerning Russia's role in 'saving the Orthodox' from the Catholicizing threat of the Polish–Lithuanian Commonwealth or *Rzeczpospolita*.[39] (Belarusian nationalists, on the other hand, insist that Moscow's 'wars of liberation' in 1512–22, 1558–83 and 1654–67 were in fact wars of aggression against the Belarusian people.)[40] Significantly, it has proved extremely difficult to revive the Uniate Church in Belarus in the 1990s.

Outside the sphere of religion, both Ukrainian and Belarusian nationalists claim that their cultures are more naturally democratic and 'European' than Russia's (it is often argued that 'until the mid-seventeenth century links between Ukrainians and Belarusians remained so close that in many respects their cultures were inseparable').[41] Neither nation experienced Russia's 240 years under the 'Tartar yoke' or the consequent tendencies towards 'Asiatic despotism' (which Belarus supposedly escaped completely).[42] Moreover, even before the Renaissance and Reformation, Ukraine and Belarus had been organic parts of European culture, while 'the Muscovite state's ideological policy called for cultural isolation'.[43] Peter the Great's belated and only partially successful attempts to 'Europeanize' Russia only emphasized the breadth of the previous divide.

In further contrast to autocratic Muscovy/Russia, it is asserted that traditions of popular assembly (*viche*) and the urban autonomy provided by Magdeburg law survived in both Ukraine and Belarus until the end of the eighteenth century.[44] Both Ukraine and Belarus had early written constitutions, and Ukraine also had the democratic example of

38. For an attempt to steer between both points of view, see H.Ia. Halenchanka and L.S. Ivanova, 'Tsarkva na Belarusi' in M.P. Kastsiuk *et al.* (eds), *Narysy historyi Belarusi*, Minsk, 1994, vol. 1, pp. 166–78, especially p. 178.

39. See the three essays by V.V. Grigor´eva and E.N. Filatova on Russophile versions of religious history in *Nash Radavod*, vol. 3, 1994, pp. 642–68.

40. In the latter 'Commonwealth' war alone, 53 per cent of the local population supposedly perished at Moscow's hands; Henadz´ Sahanovich, *Neviadomaia vaina: 1654–1667*, Minsk, 1995, p. 130.

41. Iaroslav Isaievych, 'Cultural Relations between Belarusians, Russians and Ukrainians (Late Sixteenth through Early Eighteenth Centuries)' in his *Ukraïna: davna i nova*, Lviv, 1996, pp. 198–213 (201).

42. Henadz´ Sahanovich, 'Tsi byla na Belarusi manhola-tatarskaia niavolia?' in San´ko (ed.), *100 pytanniaŭ i adkazaŭ z historyi Belarusi*, pp. 8–9.

43. Isaievych, 'Cultural Relations between Belarusians, Russians and Ukrainians', p. 204; Leonid Zalizniak, 'Ukraïna i Rosiia: rizni istorychni doli' in *Starozhytnosti*, 1991, 19; Anatol´ Hrytskevich, 'Historyia heapalityky Belarusi' in *Spadchyna*, 1994, nos. 1, 3 and 4, pp. 85–93, 39–51 and 48–61.

44. Iazep Iukho, 'Shto takoe mahdeburgskae prava?' in San´ko (ed.), *100 pytanniaŭ i adkazaŭ z historyi Belarusi*, pp. 20–1.

the Cossacks to follow.[45] In the Belarusian case, however, 'democratic' and 'European' traditions form relatively weak boundary markers, in so far as they fail to overlap with other lines of distinction. In the Ukrainian case, they at least help to reinforce a sense of religious exceptionalism among Uniate West Ukrainians and the central Ukrainian intelligentsia, who are largely Autocephalous Orthodox, although, once again, too simplistic a portrayal of Russia risks alienating those who remain loyal to the Ukrainian Orthodox Church (Moscow Patriarchy), which is still the largest Church in Ukraine.

5. Myths of a 'Golden Age'

Belarusian nationalist historiography also suffers from the lack of a particularly obvious 'Golden Age'. Most Belarusians would date it to the Lithuanian period, between the Unions of Krevo (1385) and Lublin (1569).[46] The 'Lithuanian–Belarusian' state was then the largest in Europe,[47] whose armies won famous victories at Grunwald (1410) against the Teutonic Order, and at Arsha/Orsha (1514) and Ulla (1564) against Muscovy (the anniversary of Arsha was the occasion for a large anti-Russian demonstration in Minsk in September 1996).[48] Frantsishak (Francis) Skaryna (1490–1552?) translated the Bible into Belarusian and helped Renaissance and Reformation ideas percolate into Belarusian culture.[49]

45. Iryna Kresina and Oleksii Kresin, *Het'man Pylyp Orlyk i ioho konstytutsiia*, Kiev, 1993; Iazep Iukho, 'Kali byla stvorana pershaia belaruskaia kanstytutsyia?' in San'ko (ed.), *100 pytanniaŭ i adkazaŭ z historyi Belarusi*, pp. 25–6; Olena Apanovych, 'Demokratyzm derzhavnoho ustroiu i zhyttia Zaporoz'koï Sichi' in V.F. Huzhva (ed.), *Demokratiia v Ukraïni: mynule i maibutnie*, Kiev, 1993, pp. 93–102.
46. Aleh Loika, 'Tsi byŭ "zalaty vek" u historyi Belaruskai dziarzhavy?' in San'ko (ed.), *100 pytanniaŭ i adkazaŭ z historyi Belarusi*, pp. 41–2.
47. See, for example, the maps in Vitaŭt Charopka, 'Liublinskaia uniia' in *Belaruskaia minuŭshchyna*, 1995, 2, pp. 31–4; and Ivan Saverchanka, 'Shto takoe Vialikae Kniastva Litoŭskae?' in San'ko (ed.), *100 pytanniaŭ i adkazaŭ z historyi Belarusi*, pp. 26–9 (28), showing the Kingdom during the reign of Vitaŭt/Vytautas (1392–1430).
48. Anatol' Hrytskevich, 'Barats'ba Vialikaha kniastva Litoŭskaha i Ruskaha (Belaruska–Litoŭskai dziarzhavy) z Teŭtonskim ordenam u kantsy XIV–pershai palove XV st.' in *idem* (ed.), *Adradzhenne: Histarychny al'manakh*, Minsk, 1995, vol. 1, pp. 36–61; Iaŭhen Filipovich, 'Khto zh peramoh u Arshanshai bitve?', *Nasha slova*, 1995, 18. See also Henadz' Sahanovich, *Voiska Vialikaha Kniastva Litoŭskaha ŭ XVI–XVII stst.*, Minsk, 1994.
49. Adam Mal'dis (ed.), *Spadchyna Skaryny: zbornik materyialaŭ pershykh skarynaŭskikh chytannaŭ (1986)*, Minsk, 1989; Evgenii Nemirovskii, *Frantsisk Skarina: zhizn' i deiatel'nost' belorusskogo prosvetitelia*, Minsk, 1990; V.A. Chamiarytski *et al.*, *Skaryna i iaho epokha*, Minsk, 1990.

The difficulties of reinterpreting the Lithuanian–Belarusian period have already been detailed. The Belarusian 'Golden Age' failed to set Belarus off on a path that diverged from the Russian cultural tradition in the long term. Moreover, it is not an obvious model for contemporary Belarus. The Ukrainians, on the other hand, have at least two possible 'Golden Ages'. The first, Kievan Rus´ at its zenith in the tenth and eleventh centuries, would also be classed as a 'Golden Age' by Russian historians. Only its patrimony is disputed. Ukrainians, however, would also class the period of Cossack-Orthodox revival in the sixteenth and seventeenth centuries as a second 'Golden Age'. Kiev was once again the centre of learning for the whole of Eastern *Slavia Orthodoxa* and its main window on the Western world. A uniquely national style of architecture and religious art flourished to a greater extent than in neighbouring Belarus, and Church traditions were modernized and 'Europeanized' (see above).[50] In fact, many Ukrainians would argue that Kiev was then more 'advanced' than Moscow, and that without the strong southern influence the later Petrine revolution would have been impossible (although Belarusians, interestingly, make similar claims).[51]

6. Language Myths

The one obvious difference between the three East Slavonic nations is language. Nevertheless, rival mythologies concern the three languages' origin and development. Russophiles claim that the Ukrainian and Belarusian languages were invented by nineteenth-century philologists, as a corruption of Russian through the artificial import of Polish and other words (according to one Russian author, 51 per cent of the words in a typical Ukrainian dictionary were Polish in source, and 38 per cent 'Polish–Russian').[52] Ukrainian and Belarusian nationalists, on the other hand, claim that their languages are in fact older than Russian.[53] Just as there was no 'old Rus´ nation', there was therefore no 'old Rus´ language' shared between Ukrainians, Belarusians and Russians.

---

50. Oleksa Myshanych (ed.), *Ukraïns´ke barokko*, Kiev, 1993; Isaievych, 'Cultural Relations between Belarusians, Russians and Ukrainians' (see note 41 above).

51. Bohdan Korchmaryk, *Dukhovi vplyvy Kyieva na Moskovshchynu v dobu het'mans'koï Ukraïny*, Lviv, 1993; Ivan Saverchanka, 'Khto zasnavaŭ knihadrukavanne ŭ Maskve?', and Aleh Trusaŭ, 'Shto rabili belarusy ŭ Maskve ŭ XVII stahoddzi?' in San´ko (ed.), *100 pytanniaŭ i adkazaŭ z historyi Belarusi*, pp. 36–7 and 45–6; author's interview with Anatol´ and Valentin Hrytskevich, 2 September 1995.

52. I. Belich, *Otkuda vzialsia ukraiinskii iazyk?*, Munich, 1977.

53. Hryhorii Pivtorak, *Ukraïntsi: zvidky my i nasha mova*, Kiev, 1994; Ivan Laskoŭ, 'Adkul´ paishla belaruskaia mova' in *Z historyiai na "Vy"*, second edition, Minsk, 1994, pp. 298–312.

Moreover, both Ukrainian and Belarusian supposedly have strong West Slavonic influences, the latter-day adoption of Russicisms being the result of artificial state-directed 'Russification'.[54] Russian is in fact the corruption, with French and other influences predominant.

Ukrainians claim that the 'proto-Ukrainian (southern Rus´) group of dialects' were already well-developed even before Cyril and Methodius codified their alphabet in 863 AD,[55] functioning alongside and then gradually penetrating Church Slavonic to create early medieval Ukrainian–Belarusian (Ukrainians tend to argue that true linguistic differentiation between Ukrainian and Belarusian only took place after the Union of Lublin). Belarusian nationalists also argue that their language is older than Russian, but claim that Belarusian was already distinct from Ukrainian by 1569 (as the sixteenth-century 'Lithuanian' Statutes were supposedly written in Belarusian — see above).[56]

In the Belarusian case, however, language alone is likely to remain a relatively weak prop for national identity, for as long as so many Belarusians continue to regard their own language as lacking in prestige and, as a 'peasant tongue', incapable of serving as a means of access to the modern world. In Ukraine, the use of Ukrainian is on the increase, but outside of Kiev, and below the élite level, change has been slow since 1991. As only just over half of all ethnic Ukrainians are Ukrainian-speaking, language cannot be the only marker of national identity.

7. Myths of National Resistance and Revival

Ukrainian and Belarusian nationalists commonly characterize the 'Russian' period in their history as one of 'forcible occupation', 'imperial rule' and 'colonial status'.[57] There is no space here to discuss this particular myth, but the counter-myth of national resistance to occupation is of great importance to legitimizing independence in the modern period.

In the Belarusian case, however, national revival (*adradzhenne´*) only really began in the period after 1906 and was unable to make much of

---

54. Stanislaŭ Stankevich, *Rusifikatsyia belaruskae movy ŭ BSSR i supratsiŭ rusifikatsyinamu pratsesu*, Minsk, 1994; Oleksandr Serbezhs´koï (ed.), *Anty-surzhyk*, Lviv, 1994.

55. Isaievych, 'Cultural Relations between Belarusians, Russians and Ukrainians', p. 34.

56. Laskoŭ, 'Adkul´ paishla belaruskaia mova' in *Z historyiai na "Vy"*, pp. 299, 311.

57. See for example 'Khronolohii dukhovnoho ta fizychnoho nyshchennia ukraïns´koï natsiï', *Rozbudova derzhavy*, 1995, 1, pp. 10–15; Mikhas´ Bich, 'Ab natsyianal´nai kantseptsyi historyi i histarychnai adukatsyi ŭ respublitsy Belarus´', *Belaruski histarychny chasopis*, 1993, 1, pp. 15–24 (20–24).

the opportunities provided in the period after the 1917 Revolution.[58] Although a Belarusian National Republic (BNR) was briefly established in 1918,[59] it only survived for a few months and has nothing like the same mythic resonance of the Ukrainian National Republic (UNR) of 1917–20, let alone the period of inter-war independence for the Baltic states. The 1920 Slutsk rebellion against Soviet rule occupies a prominent place in nationalist historiography,[60] but Russophiles downgrade it to an event of minimal importance or even deny that it happened.[61] It is therefore extremely difficult to displace the 1917 Revolution as the central event in popular historical consciousness of the period.[62] (Significantly, Belarusian president Lukashenka originally proposed 7 November 1996 as the date for his controversial referendum on expanding his constitutional powers.) Similarly, efforts to portray the 1863 Polish rebellion under the tsars as in fact a Belarusian struggle for 'national liberation' suffer from years of popular association of the event with the uprising of the hated Polish landlords.[63]

Moreover, Belarus has no great liberation myth to rival the official Soviet version of the Second World War. The only serious rival to the Soviet partisans operating on Belarusian territory was the Polish Home Army;[64] the attempt by nationalists to set up a Belarusian Central Council and Belarusian Home Defence in 1944 is dismissed by Russophiles as the act of a handful of Nazi collaborators, whose main effect was simply to channel conscripted *Ostarbeiter* back to Germany.[65] Victory in the Second World War is still celebrated in traditional Soviet style.[66]

Ukraine, on the other hand, has more plausible myths of resistance and revival. Cossack resistance to the Russian state's gradual elimination of their rights and privileges continued up till the

58. Ryshard Radzik, 'Prychyny slabas´tsi natsyiatvorchaha pratsesu belarusaŭ u XIX-XX st.' in *Belaruski histarychny ahliad*, 2, 1995, 2, pp. 195–227; and Steven L. Guthier, 'The Belorussians: National Identification and Assimilation, 1897–1970' in *Soviet Studies*, 26, 1977, 1 and 2, pp. 37–61 and 270–83.
59. V.A. Krutalevich, *Na putiakh natsional´nogo samoopredeleniia (BNR–BSSR–RB)*, Minsk, 1995.
60. Anatol´ Hrytskevich, 'Slutskae paŭstanne 1920 — zbroiny chyn u barats´be za nezalezhnasts´ Belarusi' in *Spadchyna*, 1993, 2, pp. 2–13.
61. M.P. Kastsiuk *et al.*, *Narysy historyi Belarusi*, Minsk, 1995, vol. 2, pp. 71–2.
62. Significantly, the Kastsiuk volume refers to the Belarussian SSR rather than the BNR as the period when the Belarusian people established 'self-rule': see the section 'Samavyznachenne belaruskaha naroda' in *ibid.*, pp. 65–76.
63. Holubeŭ, Kruk and Loika, *Tsi vedaetse vy historyiu svaëi krainy?*, p. 96.
64. Iaŭhen Siamashka, *Armiia Kraëva na Belarusi*, Minsk, 1994.
65. A.M. Litvin and Ia.S. Paŭlaŭ, 'Belarus´ u hady Vialikai Aichynnai vainy' in Kastsiuk *et al.*, *Narysy historyi Belarusi*, vol. 2, pp. 265–323 (306–7).
66. *Ibid.*, pp. 309–15.

destruction of their headquarters, the *Sich* fortress, in 1775.[67] Although the national revival of the nineteenth century was nowhere near as strong as similar movements in Poland, Estonia or the Czech Lands,[68] it was certainly stronger than in Belarus. Moreover, many Ukrainian nationalists have attempted to elevate the Ukrainian National Republic (UNR) of 1917–20 to the status of a legitimate *status quo ante* the imposition of Soviet power, as with the three inter-war Baltic states.[69] The new Ukrainian flag, hymn, state emblem and (since September 1996) currency all date from this period.

Ukraine also has the powerful, albeit extremely divisive, myth of the Ukrainian Insurgent Army (UPA) and its long and bloody struggle against the Germans, Poles and Soviets from 1943 until the mid-1950s.[70] Claims as to the number of combatants mobilized by the UPA have recently risen as high as 400,000.[71] However, although the UPA is still revered as a historical symbol in west Ukraine, to which territories its support was largely confined,[72] it is reviled to an equal extent in eastern and southern Ukraine, where Soviet-era myths depicting the UPA as Nazi collaborators and the Red Army as the true liberators of Ukraine still hold sway. Ukraine can also point to a national dissident movement that, during its heyday in the 1960s, encompassed hundreds of activists, whereas Belarusian nationalist dissidents could be numbered on the fingers of one hand.[73] Many surviving dissidents are prominent political activists and have sought

---

67. I. Svarnyk, 'Natsional'no-vyzvol'ni rukhy u XVIII st.' in Zaitsev *et al.*, *Istoriia Ukraïny*, pp. 141–51; Larysa Bondarenko (ed.), *Ivan Mazepa i Moskva*, Kiev, 1994.

68. Cf. V.H. Sarbei, 'Stanovlennia i konsolidatsiia natsiï ta pidnesennia natsional'noho rukhu na Ukraïni v druhii polovyni XIX st.', *Ukraïns'kyi istorychnyi zhurnal*, 1991, 5, pp. 3–16.

69. Mykola Lytvyn, 'Vyzvol'ni zmahannia 1914–1920 rr.' in Zaitsev *et al.*, *Istoriia Ukraïny*, pp. 213–51; Stanislav Kul'chyts'kyi, 'Tsentral'na Rada. Utvorennia UNR' in *Ukraïns'kyi istorychnyi zhurnal*, 1992, 5 and 6, pp. 71–88 and 73–94; V.F. Verstiuk, 'Ukraïns'ka revoliutsiia: doba Tsentral'noï Rady' in *ibid.*, 1995, 2, 5 and 6, pp. 65–78, 79–88 and 66–78; Mykola Lytvyn and Kim Naumenko, *Istoriia ZUNR*, Lviv, 1995.

70. As the literature on the UPA is voluminous, the following are only paradigmatic examples; M.V. Koval', 'OUN-UPA: mizh "tretim reikhom" i stalins'kym totalitaryzmom' in *Ukraïns'kyi istorychnyi zhurnal*, 1994, 2–3, pp. 94–102; Oleh Bahan, *Natsionalizm i natsionalistychnyi rukh: istoriia ta ideï*, Drohobych, 1994. See also Bohdan Iakymovych, *Zbroini syly Ukraïny: narys istoriï*, Lviv, 1996, pp. 175–99.

71. The total includes members of other underground groups: Koval', 'OUN-UPA: mizh "tretim reikhom" i stalins'kym totalitaryzmom', p. 101.

72. Cf. Volodymyr Serhiichuk, 'V UPA — vsia Ukraïna' in *Viis'ko Ukraïny*, 1993, 6, pp. 74–84.

73. On Ukraine, see Heorhiii Kas'ianov, *Nezhodni: ukraïns'ka inteligentsiia v rusi oporu 1960–80-kh rokiv*, Kiev, 1995. On dissent in Belarus, see Jan Zaprudnik, *Belarus: At a Crossroads in History*, Boulder, CO, 1993, pp. 109–10.

to play up their role in preparing the ground for the changes of the late 1980s.[74]

In comparison to Belarus, Ukraine therefore has more useful legitimation resources when claiming that independence in 1991 marked the culmination of centuries of struggle, albeit not the all-powerful 'national liberation myth' enjoyed by states with powerful pre-independence movements such as the FLN in Algeria or Vietcong in Vietnam.

Conclusions

Neither Ukraine nor Belarus yet has a historical mythology capable of fulfilling all the functions which were cited at the beginning of this chapter. The problem for Belarusian nationalists is that it has proved extremely difficult to displace older pan-Slavonic and Soviet myths, without a powerful rival myth of anterior statehood or religious exceptionalism. In Ukraine, on the other hand, a relatively coherent narrative of origin and descent has powerful appeal to the nationally-conscious minority. However, because it excludes or caricatures genuinely complex aspects of the Ukrainian–Russian historical relationship, it runs the risk of alienating the Russian-speaking half of the population of Ukraine.[75] The new president, Leonid Kuchma, has therefore preferred to emphasize relatively safe topics, the Cossack movement in particular,[76] rather than the more divisive issues raised by his predecessor Leonid Kravchuk, such as the Great Famine of 1932–3, the UPA, or a history of Rus´ without the Russians. Thus, in both states, the use and abuse of national history is likely to remain a politically sensitive issue for a long time to come.

74. See, for example, the eulogy by Anatolii Rusnachenko, 'Iak Ukraïna zdobuvala nezalezhnist´ i shcho z toho vykhodyt´', *Suchasnist'*, 1996, 3-4, pp. 58–64; and the retrospectives in *Samostiina Ukraïna* (the organ of the former Ukrainian Helsinki Group), September 1993, no. 27, and April 1994, no. 13.
75. See also my *Ukrainian Nationalism in the 1990s: A Minority Faith*, Cambridge, 1997, especially pp. 157–61. For some attacks on nationalist historiogaphy, see the article by Petro Symonenko, leader of the revived Communist Party of Ukraine from 1993, '"Natsional´na ideia": mify i real´nist´' in *Holos Ukraïny*, 21 March 1996; and V.V. Kulesha, 'Simvolika dolzhna otrazhat´ istoriiu i traditsii strany' in *Komunist*, April 1996, no. 15.
76. *Holos Ukraïny*, 28 August 1995. Leonid Kravchuk was also more cautious before 1991, but thereafter increasingly associated himself with nationalist mythology. A prime example was Kravchuk presiding at the commemoration of the fiftieth anniversary of the Great Famine in Autumn 1993, which many participants characterized as attempted 'genocide' against Ukraine: *Literaturna Ukraïna*, 16 September 1993.

THE RUSSIAN NATIONAL MYTH REPUDIATED

Geoffrey Hosking*

Most students of Russian national consciousness in the nineteenth century would agree that it was formed in opposition to something called 'the West', to whose influence Russia was abruptly exposed by Peter the Great in the early eighteenth century. Thus Leah Greenfeld, for example, in her study of the evolution of nationalism, hypothesized that *ressentiment* — 'a psychological state resulting from suppressed feelings of envy and hatred' when confronted with apparently superior foreign models — provided the impetus for the distinctive forms taken by Russian nationalism. *Ressentiment* towards the West generated among Russians the paradoxical but very human reaction first wittily formulated by the late eighteenth-century dramatist Denis Fonvizin: 'How can we remedy two contradictory and most harmful prejudices: the first, that everything with us is awful, while in foreign lands everything is good; the second, that in foreign lands everything is awful, while with us everything is good?'[1]

Fonvizin's *bon mot* sums up the two wings into which Russian thinking polarized during the first half of the nineteenth century. The Westernizers adopted his first position, the Slavophiles his second. The two parties had much in common in terms of upbringing, education and social background, they were both preoccupied with the question 'What is Russia?', and they both regarded their country's future optimistically. Where they differed was in their assessment of her past: whether Russia had gained or lost from lack of contact with the more advanced West, and therefore whether Russia would progress by preserving her distinctive virtues or, on the contrary, by borrowing as fast as possible from the West, using the advantages of relative cultural immaturity and inexperience to make up lost time.

In either case their answer to the question 'What is Russia?' depended on their view of the West. In this sense, as Greenfeld has remarked, 'the West was an integral, indelible part of the Russian *national*

---

* I am grateful to Lindsey Hughes and Faith Wigzell for reading and commenting on a draft of this paper.

1. Leah Greenfeld, *Nationalism: Five Roads to Modernity*, Cambridge, MA, 1992, pp. 15, 222–3.

consciousness', and both 'Westernism and Slavophilism were steeped in *ressentiment*'.[2]

What is not often recognized is that the rift between Slavophiles and Westernizers was superimposed on another, even deeper rift with more ancient origins and in some ways even more damaging to Russians' confidence about their own national identity. This was the *raskol*, the mid-seventeenth-century split in the Russian Church, which generated a violent surge of *ressentiment* directed, not against the West, but rather against the East — that is, against other Orthodox churches — and against the Russian prelates and statesmen who accepted their influence. I want to suggest here that the reforms of Patriarch Nikon, which gave rise to the *raskol*, involved a symbolic disavowal of what many Russians believed about their national identity.

The collective consciousness of Rus´ took shape gradually, over many centuries. In so far as the chronicles and other written sources enable us to judge its evolving content, it focused, at least up to the sixteenth century, on the three concepts of the Russian Land, the Riurik dynasty (later the Muscovite Grand Prince or Tsar) and Orthodox Christianity. An early illustration is offered by the popular tale of Daniel the Pilgrim who, when he came to Jerusalem from Rus´, is said to have declared to Balduin, Prince of Jerusalem, that 'for the sake of God and the Princes of Rus´', he wanted 'to place an icon-lamp on the Lord's grave from all the Land of Rus´'.[3]

In his *Sermon on Law and Grace,* dating probably from the 1040s, Metropolitan Ilarion (the first non-Greek head of the Kievan church) celebrated the conversion of Rus´ to Byzantine Christianity as a movement from the realm of spiritual bondage to that of spiritual freedom, from the progeny of Abraham's handmaiden Hagar to that of his wife Sarah. 'The Grace of faith has spread over all the earth, and it has reached our nation of Rus´ [...]. For behold how we too, with all Christians, glorify the Holy Trinity, while Judea is silent.'[4]

In Ilarion's words there is no trace of a claim to an exclusive mission: the tone of his sermon is one of gratitude that Rus´ has been deemed worthy of inclusion among the Christian peoples. However, that inclusion implies the marking of boundaries against infidels and heretics: Muslims, Jews and, later on, Catholics as well.

2. *Ibid.*, pp. 254, 265; the contrast between Slavophile and Westernizer positions is well summed up in A. Walicki, *The Slavophile Controversy*, Oxford, 1975, pp. 445–55.
3. V.O. Kliuchevskii, *Sochineniia*, Moscow, 1956, vol. 1, pp. 204–5; L.A. Dmitriev and D.S. Likhachev (eds), *Pamiatniki literatury drevnei Rusi: XII vek*, Moscow, 1980, p. 106.
4. *Sermons and Rhetoric of Kievan Rus´*, ed. and trans. Simon Franklin, Cambridge, 1991, p. 14.

The motifs of land, prince and faith thus defined the essence and the boundaries of Rus´ from early times. It is important to note that the notion of the 'Russian people' was absent, perhaps because of the tribal and ethnic diversity of Rus´: as we shall see, it only became a component part of the Russian consciousness from the late seventeenth century at the earliest.

The notion of the Land of Rus´ is the master image which the princes and their chroniclers used throughout the eleventh to fifteenth centuries to conjure up the idea of what they were fighting to unite and to defend. It is the supreme value for which Igor's regiments are ready to lay down their lives in *Slovo o polku Igoreve* (The Lay of Igor´'s Host).[5] The *Slovo o pogibeli russkoi zemli* (Tale of the Devastation of the Russian Land) celebrates the 'brightly bright and beautifully beautiful Russian Land', with its lakes, rivers, fields and forests, its princes, boyars and great men: 'with all this thou art filled, O Russian Land, and Orthodox Christian Faith'. This very beauty makes its devastation by the invading Mongol hordes the more poignant. No doubt its vulnerability to surrounding enemies, enumerated in the *Slovo*, gave the Land the supreme value which it assumed in the records of that epoch.[6]

At a time of triumph, in the *Zadonshchina* (The Tale of Events beyond the Don), which recounted the victory of Rus´ over a Mongol army at the Battle of Kulikovo (1380), the same trinity returns. The Muscovite Grand Prince, Dmitrii Donskoi, is presented as fighting for 'the land of Rus´ and the Christian faith'. He calls upon 'Princes, boyars and all men of courage! Let us leave our homes, our wealth, our women and our children, our cattle, that we may receive glory and honour in this world. Let us lay down our lives for the Russian land and the Christian faith.'[7]

During the fourteenth and fifteenth centuries the focus of both 'land' and 'faith' was increasingly Moscow, seat of the Metropolitanate and of the Grand Prince who both kept order at home and defeated the foreign enemy. With the repudiation of the Mongol overlordship towards the end of the fifteenth century and the assumption of untrammelled sovereignty, the confidence of the princes of Rus´ grew, especially of those under Muscovite rule. The fall of Byzantium in 1453 both threatened and yet also paradoxically intensified this confidence. Threatened it, since Orthodoxy generally was threatened.

5. Dmitriev and Likhachev (eds), *Pamiatniki literatury drevnei Rusi: XII vek*, p. 372.
6. L.A. Dmitriev and D.S. Likhachev (eds), *Pamiatniki literatury drevnei Rusi: XIII vek*, Moscow, 1981, p. 130.
7. Serge A. Zenkovsky (ed.), *Medieval Russia's Epics, Chronicles and Tales*, New York, 1974 (hereafter *Medieval Russia's Epics*), pp. 212–13.

Intensified it, since Muscovy was the one remaining sovereign Orthodox realm: she now had the task of carrying the banner of Christ alone against the forces of infidelity and heresy. An awesome responsibility, yet also a mark of God's special favour! And it should be noted that this understanding of Rus´ implicitly excluded Lithuania, also a potential heir of the Kievan tradition, since its rulers had by this time converted to Roman Catholicism.

In its extreme form, Rus´'s divine mission was formulated in the idea of Moscow as the Third Rome. As monk Filofei wrote to Ivan III around 1500, 'This present church of the third, new Rome, of thy Sovereign Empire: the Holy Catholic [*sobornaia*] Apostolic Church [...] shines in the whole universe more resplendent than the sun. And let it be known to Thy Lordship, O pious Tsar, that all the empires of the Orthodox Christian faith have converged into thine one Empire. For two Romes have fallen, the Third stands, and there shall be no fourth.'[8] This challenging declaration could be read in two ways, either as a celebration of Moscow's greatness as secular and spiritual power, or as a warning that, if the Tsar did not live a life worthy of his solemn calling, then the Day of Judgement might be at hand.[9] Messianic greatness and apocalyptic doom were both potentially present in Muscovy's self-understanding by the early sixteenth century.

In many ways, however, this formulation of Moscow's role remained exceptional. It was seldom evoked by Grand Princes or tsars in their dealings with other rulers, perhaps because it could be interpreted as entailing the supremacy of the spiritual over the secular power, or perhaps because they did not wish to imply a military threat to the Second Rome, currently the capital city of the Ottoman Empire.

A widely circulated popular story which fully developed the idea of Rus´ as the true home of Orthodox Christianity was the *Povest´ o belom klobuke* (Tale of the White Cowl), which was apparently composed by Archbishop Gennadii of Novgorod towards the end of the fifteenth century. According to the narrative, the White Cowl, symbol of the Resurrection and of Orthodox Christianity, was originally presented by the Emperor Constantine to Pope Sylvester in the fourth century, as a token of his acceptance of the Pope's secular power in Rome. It remained in Rome as long as the Pope observed the original tenets of Christianity, but, when he fell victim to the 'Latin heresy'

---

8. V. Malinin, *Starets Eleazarova monastyria Filofei i ego poslaniia*, Kiev, 1901, pp. 533–4; for the dating and purpose of Filofei's epistle, see N. Andreyev, 'Filofei and his Epistle to Ivan Vasilievich' in *Slavonic and East European Review*, 38, 1959–60, pp. 1–31.

9. Paul Bushkovich, 'The Formation of a National Consciousness in Early Modern Russia' in *Harvard Ukrainian Studies*, 10, December 1986, 3–4, pp. 355–76, especially p. 358.

and broke with the Eastern Church, then the Patriarch of Constantinople reclaimed it. When, in turn, at the Council of Florence (1439), the Byzantine Church compromised with the 'Latin heresy', God punished it by allowing the infidels to overrun their capital city, and commanded the White Cowl to be handed on to Rus´, to the Church of Novgorod:

The ancient city of Rome has broken away from the glory and faith of Christ because of its pride and ambition. In the new Rome, which has been the city of Constantinople, the Christian faith will also perish through the violence of the sons of Hagar. In the third Rome, which will be the land of Rus´, the Grace of the Holy Spirit will shine forth. Know then [...] that all Christians will finally unite into one Russian realm because of its Orthodoxy. For in ancient times, by the will of Constantine, Emperor of the Earth, the imperial crown was given from the imperial city to the Russian Tsar. But the White Cowl, by the will of the King of Heaven, Jesus Christ, will be given to the Archbishop of Novgorod the Great. And this White Cowl is more honorable than the crown of the Tsar, for it is an imperial crown of the archangelic spiritual order.[10]

The image of the Third Rome was thus an ambivalent one, an expression not just of the earthly glory of the Muscovite state, but also a reminder of the spiritual majesty of the Church, even perhaps its superiority to the state, and also an evocation of Novgorod as an alternative centre of the piety of Rus´. Rather than an authoritative state doctrine, then, it remained an evocative religious and cultural undertone, with potentially subversive implications, an extreme embodiment of a more widely accepted idea, that Rus´ had a special mission among the peoples, to lead them all to the true Christian faith, both through strong political leadership and by offering an exemplar of that faith in the pious life of her people.

There was a secular version of the Third Rome, possibly more acceptable to the rulers of Muscovy. This was the *Skazanie o kniaz'iakh vladimirskikh* (The Tale of the Princes of Vladimir), composed in the first quarter of the sixteenth century. It maintained that the Princes of Rus´ were descended from the Roman Emperor Augustus through his brother, Prus, and that the eleventh century Kievan Prince, Vladimir Monomakh, had received regalia from the Byzantine Emperor Constantine in explicit recognition of his status as tsar.[11]

Ivan IV's churchmen made a systematic attempt to assemble all these strands into a coherent mythical edifice. In the early years of his

---

10. Zenkovsky (ed.), *Medieval Russia's Epics*, p. 328; G. Kushelev-Bezborodko (ed.), *Pamiatniki starinnoi russkoi literatury*, St Petersburg, 1860 , vol. 1, p. 296.
11. Michael Cherniavsky, *Tsar and People: Studies in Russian Myths*, New Haven, CT and London, 1961, pp. 41–2.

reign, his principal prelate, Metropolitan Makarii, collated the various narratives of origin in such a manner as to combine the themes of land, church and dynasty and tie them to the imperial heritage of Byzantium and Rome. He compiled two great books of readings, in some ways, though on a more modest scale, like the collections of legitimizing documents put together by the Chinese Emperors. They were the *Velikie chet´i-minei* (Great Reading Menaea) and the *Stepennaia kniga tsarskogo rodosloviia* (Book of Degrees of the Imperial Genealogy). The first included lives of the saints, resolutions of church councils, sermons, epistles (among them those of Filofei) and historical documents, edited and presented so that they could be read out in church on each day of the year. They were selected and arranged in order to demonstrate that, from the creation onwards, God had intended to found a truly Christian empire on earth, and that Rus´ was now called upon to fulfil this purpose.[12]

Two church councils, those of 1547 and 1549, confirmed these texts and set about canonizing a large number of princes and clergymen from the past, to attest to the divinely ordained mission of Rus´. A third, the Stoglav Council of 1551, attempted to make the contemporary church worthy of this mission by reforming it and laying down a code of discipline for clergy and laity. It also explicitly reaffirmed the rectitude of the existing Muscovite scriptures and liturgy in the face of a challenge to adopt newer practices currently in use in other Orthodox churches.[13]

The conquest of Kazan´ in 1552 consolidated the new identity. Ivan's propaganda represented the Khanate of Kazan´ as being part of the 'ancient Russian land', now ruled over by an infidel monarch who had broken his oath of fealty to the Muscovite Tsar, and who had thus offended against land, faith and dynasty.[14]

Even Ivan IV's leading ideological opponent, Prince Andrei Kurbskii, shared his fundamental view of monarchical authority and of the special mission of Rus´. He regarded Ivan as a tyrant who violated both his own laws and those of God, but he did not contest the monarch's right to exercise his undivided sovereignty in the name of land, faith and dynasty. In the correspondence which Ivan and Kurbskii conducted, each side repeatedly used the term 'holy land of Rus´' and accused the other of having 'defiled' it, Ivan by his overbearing and

12. David B. Miller, 'The Velikie Minei-chetii and the Stepennaia kniga of Metropolitan Makarii and the Origins of Russian National Consciousness' in *Forschungen zur osteuropäischen Geschichte*, 26, 1979, pp. 263–382.
13. A.V. Kartashev, *Ocherki istorii russkoi tserkvi*, Moscow, 1993, vol. 1, pp. 430–9.
14. Jaroslav Pelenski, *Russia and Kazan: Conquest and Imperial Ideology (1438–1560s)*, The Hague and Paris, 1974.

vicious behaviour, Kurbskii by apostasy and going over to the enemy.[15]

The concept of church, ruler and land bound together by a common assignment to fulfil Christ's task on earth had the potentiality to become widely popular, and, since it was embodied in everyday ecclesiastical ritual, we may assume that it had a resonance among ordinary believers. Probably its inspiration helped Rus´ to overcome the Time of Troubles in the early seventeenth century, when it was without a clearly legitimate ruler and was threatened by boyar feuds, foreign invasion and social rebellion. Certainly the election of Mikhail Romanov as tsar cemented the identification of the various strata of Muscovite society with the dynasty.

By the seventeenth century, however, it was becoming increasingly difficult to hold together the sacred and secular aspects of Moscow's mission. As Moscow expanded, not just to the Volga river and the Urals, but right across Siberia and, in the west, into Polish, Lithuanian and Baltic territory inhabited by non-Orthodox Christians, it became harder to arouse loyalty by the proclamation of Orthodoxy. Even among Orthodox Christians there was much disagreement about the outward forms of liturgy and scripture, an inconvenience which threatened to impede Moscow's absorption of Ukraine and its ambitions to penetrate further into the Balkans.

In reaction to this situation, in the mid-seventeenth century, Tsar Aleksei and Patriarch Nikon embarked upon a thorough reform of the Muscovite sacred texts and liturgical practice to bring them into line with those acknowledged elsewhere in the Orthodox world. The changes introduced were of form rather than substance — making the sign of the cross with three fingers rather than two, bowing to the waist rather than to the ground — but they were numerous, and above all they were initially imposed by Nikon without consultation even among the clergy, let alone at a church council, as canon law required.

Although Aleksei and Nikon shared the aim of reforming ritual and scriptures, their common attempt also dramatized the potential for conflict between the sacred and secular aspects of Russia's mission, and therefore between church and state. Aleksei wanted to strengthen the church as the principal bulwark of his holy monarchy, especially now that it was engaged in westward expansion into Europe. He wanted to make sure that his Orthodoxy was of an ecumenical kind acceptable in the newly conquered territories. Nikon wanted the same, but he also aimed to exploit Aleksei's needs in order to increase the power and standing of the church relative to the state. His motive for reforming

---

15. A.S. Lur´e, 'Perepiska Ivana Groznogo s Kurbskim v obshchestvennoi mysli drevnei Rusi' in A.S. Lur´e and Iu.D. Rykov (eds), *Perepiska Ivana Groznogo s Andreem Kurbskim*, Moscow, 1993, pp. 214–9.

the church was in part to fortify its claim to secular authority. In short, one might say, he was the Pope Gregory VII of the Orthodox Church, purifying its morals and correcting its liturgy in order to prepare it for earthly supremacy.

Eventually Aleksei became wary of his aspiring prelate, and provoked a conflict which led to Nikon's resignation. He then delayed arranging the election of a new Patriarch. He continued to support Nikon's reforms, but, realizing that they were controversial, he did not want to create a new figurehead who might lead the opposition to them. He also knew that most bishops, though they disliked Nikon personally, approved of his efforts to raise the status of the church relative to the state.

To help him find a way forward through the thickets of ecclesiastical intrigue and create a consensus for reform, Aleksei convened a church council and invited to it the Eastern Patriarchs, that is, the principal prelates of the Orthodox Church living under Ottoman rule. This was a double-edged move. The Patriarchs enjoyed immense moral authority, thanks to the venerable and imposing positions they occupied, but, at the same time, their subordinate secular position weakened them and made them envious of the Muscovite Church and only too ready to influence, even if possible to dominate its politics. They were also ignorant of its internal condition and liable to be swayed by any tendentious interpretation of events in Russia which might be put before them.

On their own, without outside interference, Russian clergymen were inclined to seek compromise, and had decided in an internal council of 1666 to confirm the new liturgy and service books, but had refrained from condemning those who held to the old ones, unless they explicitly denounced the reforms. The council of 1667, however, with the active participation of the Eastern Patriarchs, not only condemned the pre-reform practices, but actually pronounced an anathema on those who remained faithful to them. It decreed that those found guilty of this heresy should be delivered over to the state for condign punishment.

The 1667 council also condemned the Legend of the White Cowl, and repudiated some of the resolutions of the Stoglav Council, those which had explicitly upheld the existing Muscovite texts and liturgical practices in the face of Greek questioning. Now the resolutions of 1551 were declared to be motivated by 'unreason, naivety and ignorance'. This denigration of the most mythogenic of all Muscovite church councils was meekly accepted by the Russian churchmen present, no doubt intimidated by the tsar's clearly expressed wishes.[16]

16. My account of the schism in the Russian Church rests primarily on Sergei Zen'kovskii, *Russkoe staroobriadchestvo: Dukhovnye dvizheniia 17-ogo veka*,

It was none the less a fateful step. The Stoglav Council had been at the centre of the myth-making of Ivan IV and Metropolitan Makarii. To disavow it and the liturgical practices connected with it was in effect to repudiate the Russian national myth itself, especially in a country which proclaimed a mission to save mankind, but where educational standards were low, and where there was no sharp distinction between ritual and doctrine.

A highly paradoxical situation thus arose, in which the Russian myth became the heritage of those who opposed the imperial state. Those who clung to the old ways, the Old Believers, pointed out, with impeccable logic, that all tsars and church hierarchs had hitherto expressed their faith in practices now deemed so heinous that they merited anathema. 'If we are schismatics', they argued, 'then the Holy Fathers, Tsars and Patriarchs were also schismatics.' Quoting from the Church's own *Book of Faith* of 1648, they charged Nikon and Aleksei with 'destroying the ancient native piety' and 'introducing the alien Roman abomination'.[17] 'To make the sign of the cross with three fingers', they protested, 'is a Latin tradition and the mark of the Antichrist.' Archpriest Avvakum, the most articulate and consistent opponent of the reforms, wrote from his prison cell to Aleksei: 'Say in good Russian "Lord have mercy upon me". Leave all those Kyrie Eleisons to the Greeks: that's their language, spit on them! You are Russian, Aleksei. Speak your mother tongue and be not ashamed of it, either in church or at home.'[18]

The anathema backed by the secular power blew up minor liturgical differences not just into major theological issues, but also into touchstones of a person's whole attitude to the Church and the imperial state. During the following century, the Old Belief became a banner under which discontents and rebels of all kinds could rally, whatever their original grievances. The combining of religious and secular motifs intensified an apocalyptic mood which was already widespread. For if the piety of the Third Rome had indeed been disavowed by both Church and state, then what could one conclude but that the reign of Antichrist had arrived, and that the end of the world was at hand? After all, according to prophecy, there was to be no Fourth Rome.

Among communities of believers determined not to be defiled before the Judgement Day by contact with the forces of Antichrist, mass

Munich, 1970, and on N.F. Kapterev, *Patriarkh Nikon i Tsar´ Aleksei Mikhailovich*, 2 volumes, Sergiev Posad, 1909–12; the quotation is from vol. 2, p. 395.

17. V.V. Andreev, *Raskol i ego znachenie v narodnoi russkoi istorii*, St Petersburg, 1870, p. 68; P.N. Miliukov, *Ocherki po istorii russkoi kul´tury*, Paris, 1931, vol. 2, part 1, p. 48.

18. Pierre Pascal, *Avvakum et les débuts du Raskol: La Crise religieuse du XVIIème siècle en Russie*, Paris, 1938, pp. 407–8, 411, 511.

suicides began. At the approach of government agents or troops, they would barricade themselves inside their wooden churches and set fire to them. The first rebellions broke out in 1668 in the island monastery of Solovki in the estuary of the White Sea. Its monks refused to accept the new service books and stopped praying for the tsar, telling Aleksei 'We wish to die in the old faith, which sustained your lordship's father, the true-believing lord, Tsar and Grand Prince Mikhail Fedorovich of all Russia to the end of his days.'[19]

Many Old Believers fled south, especially to the region of the Don, which was in upheaval in the early 1670s, thanks to the rising of the Don Cossack leader, Stepan Razin. Over the following century the symbiosis of Old Belief and Cossackdom proved attractive to potential rebels. The one proclaimed the 'ancient piety', the other a spirit of *volia* (freedom from restraint) which seemed at first sight to fit ill with it. But their apparent mismatch in no way impeded their capacity to unite and inspire the discontented. Enserfed peasants and factory hands, Tartars and Bashkirs, however incongruously mixed, all flocked to banners inscribed with the symbols of the old faith.

Emel´ian Pugachev, pretender to the throne of Catherine II and leader of the greatest of all popular risings, adopted the Old Belief to augment his appeal to the peasants, and in his manifesto of July 1774 accused Catherine's regime of 'violating and abusing the ancient tradition of Christian law, and having with pernicious intent introduced an alien law taken from German tradition, and the impious practice of shaving and other blasphemies contrary to the Christian faith'. He promised his followers that, when (as the wrongfully deposed Peter III) he returned to the throne, his subjects would be rewarded 'with the ancient cross and prayer, with bearded heads, with liberty and freedom and to be for ever Cossacks'.[20]

Other Old Believers found refuge among the forests, lakes and trackless wastes of the far north, where fishing, logging and gathering provided the necessities of life and sometimes a wherewithal for commerce. The most settled and successful of these communities was one set up in the early eighteenth century on the River Vyg by the brothers Andrei and Semen Denisov. Their relative success encouraged them to abandon the fixation with impending doom, to reach minimal compromises with the imperial regime and to look into some kind of future. Semen, who eventually succeeded his brother as abbot, wrote a treatise, *Vinograd rossiiskii* (The Russian Vineyard), in which he argued that the Old Believer martyrs were the true successors of the

19. Richard Crummey, *The Old Believers and the World of Antichrist: The Vyg Community and the Russian State, 1694–1855*, Madison, WI, 1970, p. 13.
20. *Pugachevshchina*, Moscow and Leningrad, 1926, vol. 1 (*Iz arkhiva Pugacheva*), pp. 40–2.

great saints of Rus´ in earlier centuries, and he set forth his view of the Holy Rus´ they had all lost. According to him, Rus´ had been the model of a people ruled by the divine will, the one truly Christian realm in a world beset by Satan in the forms of Catholicism, Protestantism and Western rationalism. True, the Russians themselves had been tainted by these influences, first at the Council of Florence, then even more seriously in the impious reforms of Nikon, which touched the very heart of Russia's sacred mission.

Nevertheless, Denisov believed that something essential had been salvaged. This is where the common people first take their place as a constituent element in the Russian myth. Denisov was unable to follow Makarii in seeing the essence of Russian nationhood as residing in tsar and church, for both had deserted the true faith. Only the land remained, and it followed that, at least for the time being, the only possible bearer of ideal Russian nationhood was the common people. 'In Russia', Denisov wrote, 'there is not one single city which is not permeated with the radiance of faith, not one town which does not shine with piety, nor a village which does not abound with the true belief.' True, all this was overlaid by an apostate church and a state bearing the mark of the apocalyptic beast, but staunch cultivation of the faith and unyielding resistance to persecution would enable Russia one day to return to the true path. As Serge Zenkovsky has put it, 'Denisov transformed the old doctrine of an autocratic Christian state into a concept of a democratic Christian nation.' [21]

That was the real strength of the Old Believers. For all their narrow-mindedness and parochialism, they offered an alternative basis for conceiving of Russian nationhood, other than that offered by the imperial state. Their alienation deepened with the coming of Peter I, whose radical Europeanization of Russia affronted their convictions at least as harshly as Nikon had done.

Peter, it could be argued, had his own vision of the Third Rome, but it was a vision utterly incompatible with theirs. At the very least, his insistence that his courtiers shave their beards offended most Orthodox, who held that the beard was a symbol of male piety.

Peter's ideal was the pagan first Rome rather than the Christianized second. He had his formal title changed to the Latin 'Imperator' and persuaded the Senate to proclaim him, like the Emperor Augustus, as *otets otechestva* (*pater patriae*). In the pageantry which followed his military victories, he would enter through Roman-style triumphal arches, celebrated as Mars or Hercules. After Poltava (1709), he added Old Testament analogies (David slaying Goliath), and was greeted, as traditionally the Patriarch had been, with the anthem 'Blessed is He

21. Serge A. Zenkovsky, 'The Ideological World of the Denisov Brothers' in *Harvard Slavic Studies*, 3, 1957, pp. 49–66.

that cometh in the name of the Lord'. In this way he claimed spiritual as well as secular power — a preliminary to abolishing the Patriarchate — even though the secular power he evoked was a pre-Christian one.[22]

The Old Belief not only withstood two and a half centuries of discrimination and outright persecution: in numerical terms it flourished. By the early twentieth century, though the figures are uncertain, it claimed perhaps ten to twelve million believers, about a fifth of all adult Great Russians.[23]

An investigator of the Old Belief in the 1860s, V.I. Kel´siev, even asserted that it still represented the fundamental belief system of the peasants. 'The people continue to believe today that Moscow is the Third Rome and that there will be no fourth. So Russia is the New Israel, a chosen people, a prophetic land, in which shall be fulfilled all the prophecies of the Old and New Testaments, and in which even the Antichrist shall appear, as Christ appeared in the previous Holy Land.'[24] Even allowing for an element of romanticism in this statement, it is clear that the schism had long ceased to be about making the sign of the cross with two fingers. It marked the opening of a radical split in Russian consciousness, when large numbers of conservative believers became alienated from the imperial state and the official Church and took the decision to conduct their spiritual and even community life outside the framework they offered.

On the other hand, by the second half of the nineteenth century the rebellious impetus of the Old Belief had almost completely died out. Though still alienated by the official state and Church, few Old Believers could be roused to join movements dedicated to their overthrow. They had become set in their habits, embattled and conservative eccentrics, concerned to preserve their way of life, not to jeopardize it. Early Russian socialists who contacted them were sometimes inspired by them, but could not enrol them for any kind of subversive activity.[25]

Driven underground in the official Church and sublimated in the post-Petrine imperial state, the Messianic energy of the original Russian national myth eventually found an outlet in the distinctive Russian variant of socialism, from Bakunin to Lenin, with its passionate belief in the 'people', its expectation both of imminent destruction and of a subsequent perfect society. The idea of the God-

22. Richard S. Wortman, *Scenarios of Power: Myth and Ceremony in Russian Monarchy*, Princeton, NJ, 1995, vol. 1, pp. 42–51.
23. A.S. Prugavin, *Staroobriadchestvo vo vtoroi polovine XIX veka*, Moscow, 1904, pp. 7–23.
24. 'Ispoved´ V.I. Kel´sieva' in *Literaturnoe nasledstvo*, 41–2, 1941, p. 319.
25. James H. Billington, *Mikhailovsky and Russian Populism*, Oxford, 1958, pp. 121–8.

bearing people within a Christian state also re-emerged, pallidly, in the official doctrine of *narodnost'* expounded by Count Uvarov in the 1830s, and more full-bloodedly in the writings of Tiutchev, Dostoevsky and others. That is a well-known story. What I have presented in this chapter is, I think, the essential background to it. By the late nineteenth century a Russian Messianism focused on the people was ready to burst forth, the more powerful for bringing with it elements of a long suppressed national myth.

INDEX OF NAMES

211